The Riddle of Amish Culture

The Riddle of
Amish Culture

DONALD B. KRAYBILL

The Johns Hopkins University Press
BALTIMORE AND LONDON

For Gid, who taught me the secrets of the riddle

Second printing, hardcover and paperback, 1989
Third printing, paperback, 1989
Fourth printing, paperback, 1990

The Johns Hopkins University Press, 701 West 40th Street,
Baltimore, Maryland 21211
The Johns Hopkins Press Ltd., London

Photographs provided by the following photographers appear on the pages listed:
Carl F. Bowman: 58, 207; Richard Reinhold: 12, 19, 20, 28, 31, 35, 40, 51, 54, 66,
75, 87, 88, 101, 109, 127, 132, 139, 218, 225; Charles S. Rice: 53, 77, 121, 147, 221,
229, 230; Fred E. Sener: 42, 83, 174, 179; and Blair Seitz: ii, 4 (courtesy of the
Lancaster Mennonite Historical Society), 17, 62, 90, 97, 104, 128, 149, 156, 161,
164, 181, 187, 193, 198, and 204. Illustrations by Robert LeMin appear on pages
7, 9, 13, 15, 22, 26, 85, 135, 191, 195, and 196.

Library of Congress Cataloging-in-Publication Data

Kraybill, Donald B.
   The riddle of Amish culture/Donald B. Kraybill.
      p.   cm.
   Bibliography: p.
   Includes index.
   ISBN 0-8018-3681-6 (alk. paper). ISBN 0-8018-3682-4 (pbk.)
   1. Amish   I. Title.
E184.M45K73   1989
306'.088287—dc19   88-19868
                                                                      CIP

CONTENTS

Preface   *vii*

Acknowledgments   *xi*

1. The Amish Story   1

2. The Quilt Work of Amish Culture   24

3. Symbols of Integration and Separation   46

4. The Social Architecture of Amish Society   69

5. Rites of Redemption and Purification   94

6. Passing on the Faith   119

7. The Riddles of Technology   141

8. Harnessing the Power of Progress   165

9. The Transformation of Amish Work   188

10. Managing Public Relations   212

11. Regulating Social Change   235

12. The Dialogue with Modernity   250

Appendix A: Research Procedures   *261*

Appendix B: Old Order Amish Population Estimates, 1880–1990, Lancaster County Settlement   *263*

Appendix C: Old Order Amish Population Estimates by Settlement Areas in North America   *264*

Notes   *265*

Select Bibliography   *285*

Index   *301*

PREFACE

The year 1993 marks the three hundredth birthday of Amish society. Despite their rejection of modern ways, the Amish are thriving in the twentieth century. From a meager band of five thousand in 1900 they have blossomed to over one hundred thousand in North America today. How did they manage to flourish in the midst of industrialization? That enchanting riddle inspires this book. Apart from the big puzzle of Amish survival, smaller Amish riddles baffle the modern mind as well. Why, for example, do the Amish freely ride in cars, but refuse to own or drive them? And why are tractors used at their barns but not in their fields?

When the Amish look at contemporary society they are equally perplexed by the riddles of "progress." Why, they wonder, do governments build nuclear weapons that can scar the earth, if not destroy it outright? Even more astonishing to the Amish is why civilized people deposit their aging parents in retirement homes, where they are isolated from their grandchildren. And why do modern folks move around the country in pursuit of jobs, leaving family and neighbors behind?

This book initiates a conversation between the riddles on both sides of the cultural fence. Such a dialogue not only unravels the riddles of Amish culture but also encourages us to ponder the puzzles of our own culture. In this sense the following pages are a venture in cultural analysis, an attempt to understand the dynamics of Amish society. They are also an exercise in social criticism, a reflective critique of modern society. The conversations over the cultural fence help us to understand both the Amish and ourselves in new ways.

Social scientists seek to maintain an objective, neutral stance when they analyze human cultures. Yet social analysis always involves interpretation and judgment. It is in some ways like storytelling. Creating a narrative from interviews and historical documents involves selection, omission, interpretation, accent, emphasis, and embellishment. Stories have limits, and certain fragments must be snipped. Some episodes are enriched by the storyteller to underscore the theme. And stories, of course, have a slant. They are told from a perspective—a particular vantage point. As a social scientist, I have gathered the facts carefully and crafted them into a story that unravels the riddle of Amish culture.

The setting for this story is Lancaster County, Pennsylvania, home of the oldest surviving Amish settlement in the world. In addition to its age, the Lancaster Amish community holds several other distinctions. It is the world's most densely populated Amish settlement, with the largest group of Amish who share similar religious practices. Moreover, it rests on the fringe of the urban sprawl in the eastern United States—a region undergoing rapid suburbanization. These factors make Lancaster County an ideal setting for tracing the Amish struggle with modernization in the twentieth century. The details of Amish life vary from settlement to settlement across the United States, but the basic values described in this book are widely shared in other Amish communities as well.

I have chosen to tell the Amish story for several reasons. First, it is a fascinating tale. It was not easy for the Amish to successfully guide their traditional culture through the rapid changes of modern life. While not comprehensive, this book charts the intriguing journey of the Amish in the modern era and introduces the basic features of contemporary Amish culture.

Second, Amish culture is easily misunderstood. Despite inordinate publicity about the Amish, misconceptions about their life are afloat today. We applaud the Amish for caring for their elderly but are bewildered by their rejection of telephones in their homes. Many other Amish riddles also baffle modern logic. We shall learn that what seem to be perplexing puzzles are often reasonable solutions to the problems faced by a traditional group in the throes of industrialization. Untangling the Amish struggle with modernization helps us to solve the big riddle: How did they manage to thrive in the modern age?

Third, the Amish story clarifies the modern story—our story—in a new way. Venturing across the fence that separates our cultures allows us to glance back and view modern society from a different angle. In the same way that learning a foreign language teaches us the grammar of our native tongue, so an excursion into Amish society informs us about our own culture. Telling the Amish story enables us to understand our own story better.

We have much to learn from the Amish story. There is wisdom in their reservoir of experience. The Amish remind us that there are other ways of organizing social life. They have coped with progress in a radically different way than the rest of us. And in the process, they have distilled some insights that can enlighten those of us within the cultural mainstream.

The methods and data sources for the investigation are described in the appendixes. Although this book provides an introduction to Amish culture, it is not intended to be comprehensive. I have focused on those aspects of the Amish experience which are particularly relevant to their struggle with modernization. Therefore, topics such as weddings, funerals, foods, and crafts are treated lightly or not at all. The Select Bibliography will aid those who want to pursue such topics in depth.

Finally, a word on writing style. As much as possible, I have dispensed with technical jargon. In some instances, I have used German words that are basic to understanding Amish culture. Theoretical and technical issues are elaborated in the Notes. For stylistic purposes, I have used the term *Moderns* to refer to those of us living on the modern side of the cultural gap. The Amish typically refer to non-Amish people as *English;* except for direct quotations, I have chosen to use the term *non-Amish.*

ACKNOWLEDGMENTS

I am deeply indebted to dozens of Amish people whose kind and generous sharing of time and ideas made this book possible. A senior research fellowship from the National Endowment for the Humanities provided financial support for the archival research as well as face-to-face interviews and the gathering of survey data. I am also grateful to Elizabethtown College, the Lancaster Mennonite Historical Society, and anonymous individuals for financial assistance in all phases of the project.

The following people provided valuable counsel and reactions to earlier drafts of several chapters: Carl F. Bowman, Ivan Glick, James W. Hostetter, David J. Rempel Smucker, Mervin Smucker, and Diane Zimmerman Umble. John A. Hostetler, Gertrude Enders Huntington, David Luthy, and Stephen Scott offered detailed and thoughtful suggestions for improving the entire manuscript. Several anonymous Amish reviewers made valuable corrections to the manuscript. Helpful suggestions from dozens of students—my severest critics—who read an earlier draft enabled me to significantly improve the readability of the text. Personnel of the Library of the Lancaster Mennonite Historical Society, the Pequea Bruderschaft Library, the Amish Historical Library, Aylmer Ontario, and Zug Library of Elizabethtown College kindly assisted me in every way possible.

Noah G. Good translated many of the original source materials from German. Robert LeMin created the figures, and Blair Seitz provided professional advice in all aspects of the photography. Numerous professionals who work closely with the Amish graciously granted interviews that enriched the scope, accuracy, and depth of the story.

I am particularly grateful to Donna Berry, Maria Brodnick, Becky E. Hagenston, Elizabeth Kessler, Jeanette S. Martin, Y. H. Patt, and Kristen Shuman for their capable help in research and typing and for their editorial assistance. Alice Knouse diligently coordinated and performed most of the word processing.

I especially thank John A. Hostetler for his wise counsel and unwavering support throughout the project.

The Riddle of Amish Culture

The Amish Story

We wish especially that our descendants will not forget our
suffering.
—Anabaptist writer, 1645

Amish Riddles

The tale of modernization is a mixed one. From laser surgery to
satellite telecommunications, modernization has produced astonishing scientific advances. It is also a story of traditional cultures erod-
ing under the swift currents of progress. Some ethnic subcultures
have crumbled more readily than others. The Amish have demonstrated an amazing resistance to such cultural destruction. Their unusual dress and horse-drawn buggies set them apart as a people who
dare to snub progress. How have they managed to tame the powerful
forces of history?

Nostalgic from a distance, Amish culture is teeming with riddles
upon closer inspection. Many outsiders are baffled by the logic, or
lack of it, in Amish culture. Amish reasoning seems to defy common
sense. Contradictions and inconsistencies abound, confounding ad-
mirers and skeptics alike. Even some of their neighbors, understand-
ably, call them hypocrites for using the services of doctors, lawyers,
and accountants while forbidding their children to pursue such voca-
tions. Banning telephones from their homes but permitting them at
the end of a farm lane mocks common sense. By what rationale do the
Amish permit electronic calculators and prohibit computers? And by
what mystery does God smile on the use of electricity from batteries
but not from public utility companies? What system of logic makes it
plausible to purchase a modern hay baler but then pull it through
fields with horses? The puzzles of Amish culture are baffling not only
to outsiders, but sometimes to the Amish as well. When asked why
bicycles are off-limits, a young Amish farmer said: "I really can't give

you an answer to that." But before we criticize the Amish for not solving their own riddles, we should remember that Moderns would likely give the same answer if asked why men wear ties and women wear skirts.

Before the twentieth century and the arrival of cars, tractors, and electronic technology, the Amish blended more smoothly into the surrounding social environment than they do today. They were, of course, different even then, with hook-and-eye fasteners on their coats, wide-brimmed hats, distinctive dress, and austere buggies. Most of their riddles, however, have emerged in the past century as they have coped with the forces of industrialization. Is there an Amish logic beneath this cultural hodgepodge—a hidden web of meaning that explains the confusing riddles?

Clues

There are several clues to the riddles of Amish culture. First, many of the apparent inconsistencies become intelligible when viewed in historical perspective. Amish riddles did not suddenly appear out of the sky. Like the behavioral codes of other societies, Amish norms were socially constructed over time as the group grappled with material changes in its social environment. Placed in the light of history, many perplexing Amish practices begin to make sense. If tractors had been widely used before cars, it is possible that the Amish would be plowing their fields with tractors today. But the car came first, and its arrival shaped the Amish reception of tractors.

Second, the Amish advocate separation from the world but do not live in a social vacuum. In addition to Moderns, members of other plain churches also live side by side with the Amish in Lancaster County. Some of these churches branched off from the Amish. The more conservative of these religious groups draw fine lines to distinguish themselves from one another. Some Amish riddles have emerged from the historical interplay between the Amish and their plainly dressed cousins.

Third, other apparent quirks in Amish culture are actually bargains that the Amish have struck with progress. They have obstinately resisted some aspects of modernization, for they are reluctant to allow their identity to be swallowed up by the demands of modern life. But the common impression that the Amish do not change is false. In many ways they are up-to-date. Bombarded by technology, they have been forced to strike some deals in order to survive. While some of their cultural compromises appear odd, they are, in many cases, ingenious arrangements that permit the Amish to retain their distinctive identity and also to survive economically.

Fourth, other riddles (such as the taboo on jewelry) play important social functions in the Amish cultural system. The prohibition on photography, inexplicable to Moderns, enhances the larger goal of community solidarity. Refusing to use electricity from public utility companies also serves a useful role in the preservation of Amish values.

Our journey through Amish culture will not solve all of the riddles. But as we go backstage to unravel the riddles, we shall learn that Amish logic makes more sense behind the curtain than it does on front stage. Cultural practices that stupefy modern audiences are indeed sensible when interpreted in the dim light of Amish history. From behind the curtain, we shall discover that many of the puzzles are ingenious solutions to the practical dilemmas faced by a group struggling to retain its traditional identity amid rapid social change.

The Anabaptist Legacy

The Amish trace their religious heritage back to the Swiss Anabaptists of sixteenth-century Europe. Disgruntled with the faith and practice of the Catholic church in Europe, Martin Luther led a protest in 1517. His revolt inaugurated the Protestant Reformation, making Protestantism a permanent branch within Christendom. A few years later in Zurich, students of the Protestant pastor Ulrich Zwingli became impatient with the slow pace of the Protestant Reformation. These young upstarts criticized Pastor Zwingli and the Zurich City Council for continuing to baptize infants and conduct the Mass. After several heated consultations with the city council, the dissidents illegally rebaptized one another in a secret meeting on 21 January 1525. This simple service in a home initiated a new movement that soon became an offshoot of the Protestant Reformation.

The religious renegades believed that baptism should only be conferred on adults who were willing to live a life of radical obedience to the teachings of Jesus Christ. Adult baptism became the public symbol of the new movement, sometimes called the Radical Reformation, but the implicit issue was one of authority. Did the civil authorities have the right to interpret and prescribe Christian practice, or was the Bible the sole and final authority for the Christian church? The answer was clear in the minds of the rebaptizers. For them, Scripture was the ultimate authority. They felt compelled to obey the teachings of Christ even when such obedience jeopardized their own lives.[1]

The young reformers were nicknamed Anabaptists, meaning "rebaptizers," because they had already been baptized as infants in the Catholic church. The civil authorities, both Protestant and Catholic, were not about to be mocked by a small group of young radicals. Within five months of the first rebaptism, the first Anabaptist was

A drawing from the second Dutch edition of the *Martyrs Mirror* (1685) depicting an Anabaptist martyr, Jan Bosch, burning at the stake in Maastricht, 1559.

killed for sedition. The rebaptized heretics began to flee for their lives. Meetings were often held at night in caves. The Anabaptist movement soon spread northward into Germany and eventually into the Netherlands. Thousands of Anabaptists were executed by civil and religious authorities over the next two centuries. Anabaptist hunters were commissioned to torture, brand, burn, drown, imprison, dismember, and harass the religious heretics. Describing the persecution between 1635 and 1645, an eyewitness wrote: "It is awful to read and speak about it, how they treated pregnant mothers, women nursing infants, the old, the young, husbands, wives, virgins and children, and how they took their homes and houses, farms and goods. Yes, and much more, how they made widows and orphans, and without mercy drove them from their homes and scattered them among strangers . . . with some the father died in jail for lack of food and drink."[2]

In Switzerland the killing subsided by 1614. Other forms of persecution continued intermittently until the early eighteenth century. As the persecution waxed and waned, Anabaptists found refuge in Moravia, Alsace, the Palatinate, the Netherlands and eventually in

North America.[3] Even today, memories of the harsh persecution remain alive among the Amish. The *Martyrs Mirror,* a book of over a thousand pages found in many of their homes, chronicles the carnage. Stories of the persecution are also printed in the back of the Amish hymn book, the *Ausbund.*

The severe persecution, mobility, and a congregational form of government encouraged a variety of theological beliefs among the early Anabaptists. Some of the common convictions of the first leaders were articulated in a statement written in 1527.[4] The statement emphasizes, among other issues, the authority of the New Testament as a guide for everyday life and highlights the following religious beliefs:

> literal obedience to the teachings of Christ
>
> the church as a covenant community
>
> adult, or "believers," baptism
>
> social separation from the evil world
>
> the exclusion of errant members from communion
>
> the rejection of violence
>
> the refusal to swear oaths

One scholar has argued that the core of the Anabaptist vision contained three distinctive features: a radical obedience to the teachings and example of Christ which transforms the behavior of individual believers; a new concept of the church as a voluntary body of believers accountable to one another and separate from the larger world; and an ethic of love which rejects violence in all spheres of human life.[5] The bloody persecution engraved a sharp division between the church and the outside world into the Anabaptist belief system.

The harsh persecution and the missionary zeal of the Anabaptists scattered some of them into northern Europe. In the Netherlands, Menno Simons emerged as an influential proponent of Anabaptism. Ordained as a Catholic priest in 1524, Simons soon found himself caught between the authority of the Catholic church and the interpretation of the Scripture as taught by the Anabaptists. By 1531 he opted for the Anabaptist view of Scripture, but he did not formally leave the Catholic church until 1536. Simons became a powerful leader, writer, advocate, and preacher for the Anabaptist cause.[6] He became so influential that many Anabaptists were eventually called Mennonists, or Mennonites.[7]

The relentless persecution drove numerous Anabaptists, or Mennonites, to remote mountainous areas, where they could more easily hide from their tormentors.[8] Although persecution rose and fell with political fortunes, many Anabaptists turned to farming. Their initial religious fervor gradually chilled, and congregational life solidified into routine patterns over the generations. By the late 1600s a group of Swiss Anabaptists emigrated northward from Switzerland to the Alsace region, which lies in present-day France, between the Rhine River and the Vosges Mountains. A bitter controversy erupted between the Alsatian immigrants and those who remained in Switzerland. The quarrel came to a head in 1693 and gave birth to the Amish church.

Amish Birth Pangs

The Amish take their name from their founder Jacob Ammann, a young Anabaptist leader in Alsace. In the 1690s, Ammann began some innovative religious practices. He proposed holding communion twice a year rather than annually, as the Swiss Anabaptists typically observed it. He also argued that foot-washing should be practiced as a religious rite in the communion service. Unlike the Dutch Anabaptists, the Swiss Anabaptists did not wash one another's feet as part of their communion service. Ammann wanted foot-washing to be observed in obedience to Christ's command.

The decisive issue, however, that polarized the Swiss and Alsatian Anabaptists was the treatment of excommunicated members. Following the teaching of the Dutch Anabaptists, Ammann taught that expelled members should not only be banned from communion but also shunned in normal social relations. The more lenient position of the Swiss Anabaptists excluded wayward members from communion but did not ostracize them socially. Secondary issues, such as the excommunication of liars and the salvation of Anabaptist sympathizers, also hovered over the dispute. Cultural and regional factors, as well as personality conflicts, amplified the theological differences. However, the shunning of excommunicated members drove the final wedge between the Swiss and Alsatian Anabaptists in 1693.[9]

The charges and countercharges between Jacob Ammann and the senior Swiss bishop, Hans Reist, were harsh. Ammann's boldness was matched by Reist's stubbornness. The Swiss resisted Ammann's attempt to reform the church and maintain its purity, and Ammann surprised the Swiss ministers by excommunicating them for not accepting his strict interpretation of shunning. The Alsatian congregations supported Ammann's leadership and formed what eventually became the Amish church. Several years later, the Amish group apologized for excommunicating their Swiss elders, but it was too late to heal the wound. A series of conciliatory meetings continued until 1711 but failed to repair the breach.

Thus the Amish emerged out of a division among the Swiss Anabaptists, or Mennonites. Shunning was the decisive issue in the family

Figure 1-1 European Roots of the Amish

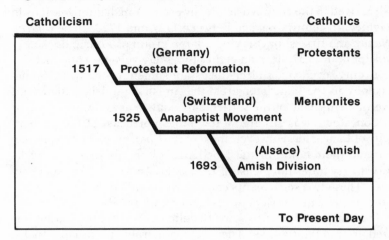

Catholicism   Catholics

1517   (Germany)   Protestants
     Protestant Reformation

1525   (Switzerland)   Mennonites
     Anabaptist Movement

1693   (Alsace)   Amish
     Amish Division

To Present Day

quarrel, but Ammann also taught against trimming beards, rebuked those with fashionable dress, and administered a strict discipline in his congregations. Although dress styles were not the catalyst for the schism, they gradually became distinctive among the Amish over the years. Eventually some Mennonites were nicknamed "button people" and the Amish were called "hook-and-eyers" because they rejected buttons as ostentatious. Ammann left no books and only a few letters for his followers. Today the Amish rely primarily on Anabaptist literature written before Ammann's time. Thus, the mainstream of Anabaptism that originated in Zurich in 1525 had a more conservative Amish branch after 1693. Although the Amish and Mennonite churches are parallel streams nourished by a common Anabaptist spring, they have remained organizationally separate to the present day.

The *Charming Nancy*

War, social upheaval, political turmoil, and intermittent persecution prompted the Amish and Mennonites to leave their homelands in the Palatinate and Alsace. A few Mennonites had arrived in the New World and established a settlement near Philadelphia in 1683, ten years before the Amish-Mennonite division. In 1710 Mennonite settlers purchased a tract of some ten thousand acres bordering the Pequea Creek, several miles south of the present-day city of Lancaster, Pennsylvania. Between 1717 and 1732, several contingents of Swiss Mennonites followed the early pioneers and settled in the Lancaster area.

It is possible that some early Amish immigrants accompanied

these Mennonite settlers, but historians are uncertain when the first Amish arrived in the New World. In any event, Amish immigrations in the eighteenth century peaked between 1727 and 1770.[10] The *Charming Nancy*, the first ship carrying a large group of Amish, docked in Philadelphia in 1737 after an eighty-three-day voyage. Thus in 1737, some twenty-seven years after the establishment of the first Mennonite colony in the Lancaster area, the Amish established their first two settlements. One of the settlements, known as Old Conestoga, or West Conestoga, was situated a few miles northeast of the present-day city of Lancaster. However, most of the *Charming Nancy*'s passengers made their home in the Northkill colony, in southern Berks County, thirty miles northeast of Lancaster. An Amish historian concludes: "These two settlements can rightly be called the mother colonies of our present districts in Lancaster County."[11]

The early settlements were fledgling communities loosely organized around family lines. They were vulnerable to Indian attacks, weather uncertainties, and crop failures. An Indian raid, an evangelizing raid by the Dunkards, and other factors such as soil depletion eventually dismantled the Northkill settlement.[12] The Old Conestoga colony also dwindled for unknown reasons, and the survivors of the two settlements were eventually dispersed to more friendly places, where they joined new Amish immigrants.

Several congregations took root in the Lancaster area in the Revolutionary War era, but they remained rather small until the end of the nineteenth century. The Conestoga congregation began about 1760, and the Pequea congregation began about 1790. The Lancaster Amish community consisted of these two congregations, with probably no more than 150 adult members, until 1843, when a third congregation was formed. A fourth group blossomed in 1852, and by 1880 there were six congregational clusters in the Lancaster region. Although the Mennonites settled the best land in Lancaster County before the Amish arrived, the Amish have had the last word, as they have steadily bought up the rich limestone farmland in the twentieth century.

The Lancaster Settlement

Over the years, Lancaster County has been a pleasant home for the Amish settlers, whose hard work helped to forge its distinguished agricultural reputation. Known locally as the world's Garden Spot, the county ranks first nationally in agricultural production among nonirrigated counties. Fertile soils, a moderate climate, ample rainfall, and the hard toil of farmers have transformed the 946-square-mile area into an agricultural paradise. With some five thousand farms and 69 percent of its acreage in farmland, the county leads

Pennsylvania in the commercial value of milk, eggs, poultry, meat, corn, hay, and tobacco.

Situated about 65 miles west of Philadelphia and 135 miles north of Washington, D.C., Lancaster rests on the western edge of the sprawling urban belt—also known as the megalopolis—stretching from Norfolk, Virginia, to Boston, Massachusetts. Lancaster City is surrounded by a quilt work of farms, small towns, and suburban developments. The county is the fastest-growing of Pennsylvania's thirteen metropolitan areas. Between 1980 and 1985, it grew at twice the rate of any other Pennsylvania urban area. Its present population of 400,000 will likely top 450,000 by the turn of the twenty-first century.

Figure 1-2 Amish Church Districts in the Lancaster Settlement

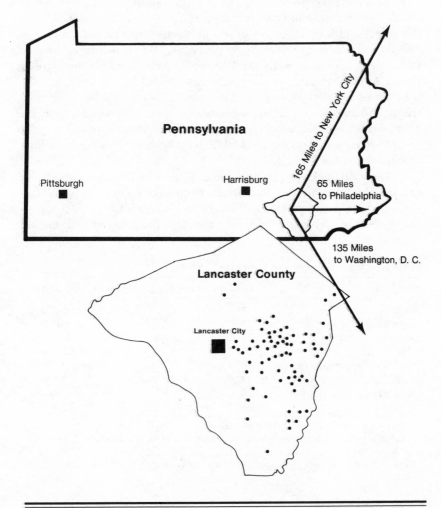

Agriculture continues to thrive in spite of urbanization. In 1986 the county lost eleven thousand acres of cropland, but added 3.3 million farm animals. Farmland preservation, manure pollution, traffic congestion, and intense development pressures dominate the county's public agenda.

Despite its robust agricultural output, not all Lancastrians are Amish or farmers. Today less than 5 percent of jobs in the county directly involve agriculture. Nearly eight hundred industrial establishments dot the Garden Spot, twenty of which have over five hundred employees. Twelve major shopping centers serve the county, with nearly six hundred separate stores. Each year, Lancaster Countians host some 5 million tourists, who spend over $400 million. Tourism, which has over six hundred facilities, creates more than eighty-six hundred jobs for local people, including some Amish.

This industrialized Garden Spot is the habitat of Lancaster's Old Order Amish community of fourteen thousand children and adults, the oldest and largest Amish group in North America with common beliefs and practices.[13] Nearly 86 percent of the Amish in Lancaster County are affiliated with the Old Order Amish, sometimes called House Amish because worship services are held in their homes. At least six varieties of more progressive Amish (some of whom use electricity and own automobiles) number nearly one thousand members. These groups splintered off in progressive directions over the past seventy-five years, leaving the Old Order Amish as the sole guardians of traditional Amish culture.

Their distinctive garb and use of horses visibly distinguish the Amish from their modern neighbors. Unlike the communitarian Hutterites, their Anabaptist cousins, the Amish do own private property.[14] Despite private ownership, a strong tradition of mutual aid

Table 1-1 Plain Churches in Lancaster County

Affiliation[a]	Groups	Congregations	Members[b]
Old Order Amish	1	82	6,300
Other Amish Groups	6	10	1,000
Lancaster Conference			
Mennonites	1	84	12,100
Other Mennonite Groups	20	57	9,000
Church of the Brethren	1	20	8,200
Other Brethren Groups	8	36	5,000
Total	37	289	41,600

Sources: Appendix B; Kraybill (1985:4–5); Kraybill and Fitzkee (1987:3).

  [a]Includes groups that presently wear plain clothing, as well as those groups that wore it earlier in the twentieth century.

  [b]Membership rounded to nearest hundred. Includes only baptized members, not children.

permeates their community. Barn raisings, work "frolics," economic aid, and personal assistance during emergencies are routine expressions of community life. Although they borrow money from banks, the Amish are reluctant to accept government subsidies in the way of farm supports, Social Security, and Medicare.

Cottage industries have sprung up recently within the Amish community, but farming and agricultural work remain their primary occupations. Dairying, the chief type of farming, is sometimes supplemented by tobacco, poultry, and hogs. Married Amishwomen work hard, but usually at home. Single women often work in restaurants and as domestics in motels and private non-Amish homes. Others are teachers, clerical workers, and clerks in vegetable markets.

Extended families spanning two or three generations often live in adjoining houses on a farmstead. Other Amish own single dwellings along country roads or in small towns. Children are usually born at home, and grandparents typically retire on the farm. Amish youth walk to one-room schools, where Amish teachers stress practical skills and teach English as well as German. The primary language of the Amish is a German dialect known as Pennsylvania German. The English they learn in school enables them to communicate fluently with English-speaking neighbors and business contacts. Amish social life centers almost exclusively around family, home, and church. Religious beliefs prohibit membership in "worldly" organizations, such as service clubs, professional organizations, and political parties.

Amish society is organized around three basic social units: *settlement*, *district*, and *affiliation*.[15] A *settlement* encompasses the cluster of Amish families living in a common geographical area. It may range in size from a dozen families to several thousand, such as the one in Lancaster County. The Lancaster settlement spans twenty-four of the county's forty-one townships. Amish and non-Amish homes are interspersed throughout the settlement. The density of the Amish population increases toward the settlement's center, where they may own the bulk of the farmland. In one Lancaster County township the Amish hold about 90 percent of the farmland. However, even in the hub of the community they are far outnumbered by non-Amish, who live beside them in small towns and along country roads.

The congregation, or church *district*, is the basic organizational unit above the family in Amish society. A church district typically includes some twenty-five to thirty-five families that live in the same immediate locale. Because church services are held in the home, houses need to be large enough to accommodate all district members. As the membership grows, districts divide. Two or three new districts are added each year in the Lancaster settlement.

A cluster of Amish congregations, in spiritual fellowship within a settlement, is called an *affiliation*. Congregations in an affiliation

Shown with a typical Amish homestead in the background, a family heads for a favorite sledding spot.

follow similar religious practices and exchange preachers. For instance, the nearly ninety Old Order Amish congregations near Lancaster constitute one affiliation. The smaller, progressive groups of New Order Amish and the Beachy Amish are outside the Old Order affiliation because of their more liberal practices.[16]

Today in North America, 660 Amish congregations are scattered throughout twenty states and the Canadian province of Ontario.[17] They total more than one hundred thousand adults and children.[18] Extinct in their European homeland, the Amish are prospering in the United States. Of the 175 settlements across the nation, 70 percent were founded after 1960. Settlements vary considerably in size. Ninety contain only one congregation, whereas the largest settlement in Ohio has over 110 congregations. Approximately 70 percent of the Amish live in three states: Indiana, Ohio, and Pennsylvania. Moreover, half of the Pennsylvania Amish live in the Lancaster community.

Plain Cousins

The Amish are not the only religious group in Lancaster County. In fact, they represent merely 3 percent of the county's adult popula-

Figure 1-3 Adult Religious Affiliation in Lancaster County

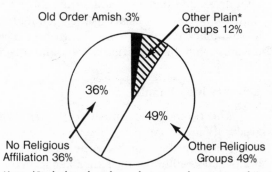

Old Order Amish 3% Other Plain* Groups 12%

36%

49%

No Religious Affiliation 36% Other Religious Groups 49%

Note: *Includes churches whose members wear plain garb today, as well as those with a heritage of plain dress. Estimates for all groups include baptized members, or youth over twelve years of age.

Sources: Kraybill (1985), Kraybill and Fitzkee (1987), Appendix B.

tion, as shown in figure 1-3. The complexity of religious expression in the Lancaster environs is matched by few other areas of the United States. The county, home of some seventy-six religious groups ranging from Buddhists to Unitarians, has over 700 churches.[19] At least thirty-seven of the county's seventy-six denominations are dubbed "plain" because of their traditional dress and austere lifestyle. Like their Amish cousins, they also trace their theological roots back to the Anabaptist movement of sixteenth-century Europe. The plain churches represent roughly 15 percent of the county's adult population. Some of these churches maintain strict standards of dress and behavior. Others, such as the Church of the Brethren and progressive Mennonite groups, have blended into the surrounding culture in recent years. Progressive Mennonites, who have largely assimilated into mainstream culture, number about sixteen thousand and are divided into ten different church affiliations. The Old Order Mennonites, the conservatives, also have some ten subdivisions, with a total of five thousand members.[20]

The colorful array of religious practices perplexes outsiders and insiders alike. Although many of the groups have similar theological and cultural origins, they have split into factions with spirited fervor over such issues as cars, tractors, Sunday schools, television, and shunning. Some permit central heating in their homes and others oppose it. Telephones and electricity, which are found in some conservative Mennonite homes, are condemned by other groups. One faction of Mennonites paints its car bumpers black to avoid an ostentatious appearance. A New Order Amish church permits tractors in the field and on the road, but forbids the use of cars. Each group specifies its own dress and behavior code, thus differentiating themselves from their plain cousins. Beneath the seemingly petty distinctions lies a fervent piety. For these unique cultural expressions, in the eyes of believers, symbolize spiritual loyalty and obedience to the will of God.

A Flourishing People

The floundering Amish settlements of the revolutionary era gradually took root in the nineteenth century, but the twentieth century has been the Amish century. Ironically, with the advent of the Industrial Revolution, the Lancaster settlement flourished.[21] Families in pre-industrial societies are typically large, and the Amish are no exception. Their long agricultural tradition has nurtured large families. When asked how many children they think are ideal for an Amish family, older women answer, "As many as come," but young women on the average want about 6 children.[22] These young women know their business well, for the completed Amish family includes 6.6 children, nearly triple the number in the average American family. About 15 percent of the Amish couples in the Lancaster community have 10 or more children.

Although the Amish live in the midst of a spreading urban region, rife with temptations of all sorts, their attrition rate is surprisingly low. The majority of Amish children join the church as adults. Church members recently reported that 88 percent of their children over twenty-five years of age had joined the church. This 12 percent attrition rate is likely a low estimate, because young adults between twenty-five and thirty-five years of age may still leave the Amish fold. An earlier study in Lancaster found attrition ranging from 18 to 24 percent over several decades.[23] Amish leaders estimate the fallout rate at 10 percent and think it has declined over the past thirty years. In any event, four out of five Amish children will likely remain Amish.

The combination of a high birth rate and a low dropout rate has produced vigorous growth. Lancaster's settlement expanded from merely six church districts in 1878 to nearly ninety today. The number of districts has doubled in the past twenty-two years. Today's Amish population of fourteen thousand, including children, is some thirteen times larger than it was at the turn of the century.[24] Due to the high birth rate, 53 percent of the population is under eighteen years of age. Because of the pressures of a high growth rate and shrinking farmland, the Amish have experienced a severe demographic squeeze. As a result, some families have moved to more remote sections of Lancaster County and others have migrated out of the county.

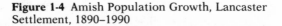

Figure 1-4 Amish Population Growth, Lancaster Settlement, 1890–1990

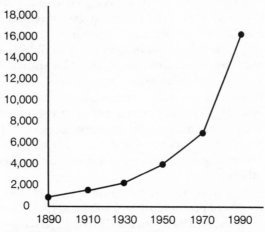

Note: The 1990 estimate is based on current trends. Population estimates include children and adults.

Source: Appendix B.

The Lancaster settlement has spawned at least twenty-three new congregations in other Pennsylvania counties since 1940. A group of families migrated south to St. Mary's County, Maryland, in 1940. A year later a second outpost opened in Lebanon County, bordering the northern edge of Lancaster County. The migrations halted for two decades, until the late sixties, when new settlements were founded in a half-dozen other Pennsylvania counties. Today some two dozen young church districts, representing nearly four thousand people, trace their roots back to the parent community in Lancaster.

Modern Traditionalists

The Amish are often described as traditionalists who have withdrawn from the modern world. This simplistic stereotype portrays them as a fossilized subculture—a relic of bygone days.[25] Folks who read by lantern light, ride in buggies, and shun high school in the late twentieth century are obviously not modern. Or are they? Walk into a booming Amish machine shop and you will see sophisticated manufacturing equipment powered by air and hydraulic pressure. Visit a successful Amish dairy farm and you will witness an efficient operation using the latest feed supplements, vitamins, fertilizers, insecticides, artificial insemination, and state-of-the-art veterinarian practices. (An Amishman recently received the "most improved" dairy farmer award in Lancaster County.) Wander through a new Amish home and you will discover up-to-date bathroom facilities and a modern kitchen with lovely wood cabinets, Formica countertops, vinyl floor coverings, and the latest gas stove and refrigerator. Despite our cherished stereotypes, the Amish are quite modern in many ways.[26]

The Amish do indeed cling to older customs in their worship services and attitudes toward education. Without electricity, their homes have no microwaves, toasters, doorbells, televisions, or blow dryers, but does this absence make these people diehard traditionalists? This unusual mixture of progress and tradition poses questions about the meaning of modernization.[27] What strategies have the Amish used to cope with the pressures of modern life? Why have they accepted progress in some aspects of their culture and resisted it in others?

Throughout the twentieth century, the Amish have tenaciously sought to preserve their traditional life. They have been tantalized by progress and have obviously benefited from the by-products of industrialization, but they have remained skeptical of the long-term consequences of technological advancement. The Amish are suspicious that beneath the glitter of modernity lurks a divisive force that, in time, might fragment and even obliterate their close-knit community. The fear that modernization might pull their community apart is not an idle one. Indeed, some analysts argue that social separation is a major by-product of industrialization.[28]

The technological age has brought electronic communication and high-speed travel, which multiply the number of possible ties an individual might have with others around the globe. But in other ways modernization is a process of separation which partitions whole systems—psychological, social, and organizational—into smaller parts in the name of efficiency. The social bonds of modern systems are typically abstract, complex, and separated from an individual's immediate context. The fragmentation of modern life is often experienced on the personal level as alienation, when ties with meaning, friends, work, and place rupture.

The hallmark of Amish society has been a highly integrated community, where the bits and pieces of social life are woven into a single fabric that stretches from cradle to grave. To avoid the fragmentation that accompanies modernity, the Amish have tried to separate themselves from the modern world. In order to stay whole, to preserve their snug community, they have separated themselves from the great separator—modernity.

Seen in this light, it is not surprising that a fundamental tenet of Amish religion is separation from the world, a belief that was shaped by their European persecution. This link between the fragmentation of modern life and the integration of Amish society unlocks many

A modern kitchen in a contemporary Amish home.

Amish riddles, for only by being a separate people have they been able to remain together, and only by shunning modernity have they been able to survive. Many of the odd Amish riddles that perplex outsiders are social devices that shield their subculture from the fragmentation of modernity.

Cultural minorities use a variety of social strategies to protect their cultural identity. When things get too bad, groups may *migrate* in search of a serene habitat. From the early days of European persecution, the Amish have migrated when faced with harsh conditions. The Lancaster Amish have started new communities in other areas, but they have never migrated en masse. In recent years, migrations from the Lancaster community have ended, suggesting that the Amish have chosen to *resist* and *negotiate* with modernity rather than run from it.[29] *Resistance* and *negotiation* are the primary social strategies that the Amish have used to preserve their identity in the face of modernization. The traditional side of Amish life, maintained by *resistance*, tilts backward to the past. However, their willingness to *negotiate* with modern life reflects an openness to change and progress.

Resisting Modernity

Groups (such as athletic teams, armies, corporations, and ethnic minorities) that face hostile opponents often use defensive tactics to resist being overwhelmed by their adversaries. A group under cultural attack will also develop an exclusive set of beliefs—an ideology—to justify its existence. Finding ways to rally individual members behind collective goals is a pressing problem of threatened groups. The aspirations, whims, and rights of individual members must be sacrificed to common goals if a group is to survive. Personal aspirations must give way to collective ones for successful military campaigns, sports teams, corporations, and marriages. Defensive groups must find ways to suppress individualism, or at least to persuade individuals to find fulfillment through collective objectives, rather than personal ones. Such organizations tend to emphasize obedience, surrender, sacrifice, commitment, and discipline in order to harness personal resources for group purposes.

Two cornerstones of Amish religious doctrine are *separation* from the world and the conviction that members must be *obedient* to the church's teachings and leaders. Only members who remain *separate* from the world and *obedient* to the church will receive God's blessing of peace and eternal life. These beliefs funnel the energy of individuals toward the shared goal of preserving a disciplined and distinctive community.

To resist being swallowed up by a cultural adversary, religious minorities must develop comprehensive programs of social control. Techniques of social control keep individuals in line with group objectives and serve as cultural barricades against outside encroachments. Groups, such as the Amish, that believe the surrounding culture threatens their survival will likely engage in at least five defensive tactics.[30]

1. Symbolization of core values. Cardinal values are symbolized by objects and rituals that call for group loyalty and accent ethnic identity. Uniforms, badges, flags, special jargon, rituals, and ceremonies are used to strengthen the cohesive ties that bond members to the group.

2. Centralized leadership. Threatened groups often welcome authoritarian leadership because it speeds decision-making and offers a sense of security. Centralized leadership marshals collective resources in a single direction. Democratic, shared authority cripples a group's ability to respond quickly to external threats.

3. Social sanctions. A system of social rewards and punishments is necessary to encourage conformity to group standards. Leaders establish the standards and administer the sanctions (both formal and informal) to keep members in line with group norms.

4. Comprehensive socialization. Like other defensive groups, the Amish must find ways to pass on their world view to their offspring, as well as to newcomers. Indoctrination in the group's "story,"

Uniform dress is one of the ways that the Amish symbolize their resistance to modern culture.

through formal and informal schooling, must start early in life and be repeated again and again in order to build group loyalty.

5. *Controlled interaction with outsiders.* The fewer the opportunities to mingle with outsiders, the less likely that members will leave the ethnic fold. When interaction with outsiders is necessary for economic survival, the time, place, and mode of interaction must be carefully regulated. A special language, taboos on public behavior, and social isolation are common ways the Amish limit social interaction. Such cultural fences make it difficult for group members to join the larger society.

The Amish have used these five defensive tactics to preserve and safeguard their distinctive cultural heritage. Defensive ploys are not distinctive Amish practices—they are generic social strategies used to some extent by virtually all groups. The use of defensive tactics intensifies in direct relation to the amount of perceived hostility in a cultural environment. Thus, sports teams facing aggressive opponents, corporations battling competition, and armies engaged in combat are all likely to amplify their defensive strategies. The Amish have merely

An Amishman developed this machine, which lays plastic on cantaloupe rows to prevent weeds and preserve moisture. Using horses and modern materials together is one of many compromises the Amish have negotiated with modernity.

applied to community and religious life the standard techniques of social control which are routinely used by other groups.

Negotiating with Modernity

In addition to resisting modernization, the Amish have also negotiated with it. They have changed, indeed modernized, in many ways over the twentieth century. Yet on some issues—education, for example—they have stubbornly refused to concede to modern ways. Minority groups that hope to strike a balance between resistance and wholesale accommodation may negotiate with the larger society. Concessions are traded back and forth in a social bargaining process until a compromise of sorts is reached. When the negotiable items are values, ideas, beliefs, and ways of thinking—cultural phenomena—we can call the process *cultural bargaining*. But when group structures and patterns of social organization are on the negotiating table, the exchange involves *structural bargaining*.

The negotiating metaphor implies a dynamic process of give and take. Indeed, this has been the case in the Amish encounter with modernity, for on some issues the Amish have acquiesced to the demands of modernity, whereas in other instances modern society has bent the rules or made special ones for the Amish. This way of viewing the Amish struggle with modernization identifies the negotiable issues as well as the nonnegotiable ones. The concept of negotiation captures the dynamic interaction between Amish society and the larger society and solves many of the baffling puzzles, which are often compromises hammered out at the bargaining table.[31] Over the years the bargaining sessions have produced compromises between tradition and modernization—cultural settlements that have both safeguarded Amish survival and spawned the perplexing riddles of Amish life.

The Ultimate Strategy

What happens when resistance and negotiation fail? The Old Order Amish experienced three internal divisions in Lancaster County in the modern era: 1877, 1910, and 1966. In one sense, the three schisms represent a failure in Amish policies. Amish resistance to social change and their refusal to bargain prompted liberal factions to leave the Amish family on all three occasions. However, the expulsion of the detractors is not a policy failure, but rather the ultimate strategy for the preservation of Amish culture. To permit the progressive activists to agitate for rapid change within the group would have surely accelerated the Amish drift toward modern culture.

The first major dissension erupted in 1877. Following Amish divisions in the Midwest, two progressive factions withdrew from the Lancaster community and formed independent congregations. Within five years each group built a meeting house for its worship services. Sometime after this division, the traditional Amish became known as the Old Order Amish or House Amish because they continued to worship in their homes. The splinter groups, labeled Amish-Mennonite or "Meeting House Amish," held their worship services in a church building. The progressive groups eventually became full-fledged Mennonites.

The second division occurred in 1910, as cars, telephones, electricity, and mechanized farm equipment were beginning to revolutionize the social landscape of rural America. Disturbed by a strict interpretation of shunning, a liberal faction formed an independent group, eventually known as the Peachey church.[32] Although very similar to the Old Order Amish in dress and outlook, the group embraced evangelical religious expressions (such as Sunday school) and tolerated technological innovations (such as telephones, electricity, tractors, and, eventually, cars). Today this group is affiliated with the Beachy Amish church.

The third division came in 1966 when a group of so-called New

Figure 1-5 Old Order Amish Divisions in Lancaster County

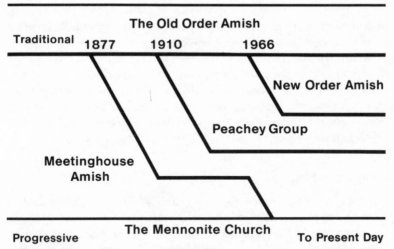

Note: The Peachey church has had several names at different stages of its history, as described in chapter 7, note 6. The New Order Amish church has had several divisions since 1966.

Order Amish left the Amish fold over differences related to the use of modern farm machinery. This faction subsequently splintered into several subgroups of New Order Amish, which vary in dress and in the use of cars, tractors, electricity, and church buildings. The various pockets of progressive Amish groups in the Lancaster area number less than one thousand members.

The three divisions—1877, 1910, and 1966—are crucial benchmarks in Amish history. Memories of the schisms, alive in the minds of leaders, function as turning points in Amish oral history. The residual effects of these schisms touch the decision-making process in the Amish community even today. The three divisions released progressive social steam in periods of rapid change as the Amish church grappled with technological innovations. Interestingly, there have been no conservative or reform divisions within the Old Order Amish community.

In retrospect, the expulsion of the dissidents served useful social functions over the years. The offshoots of 1877, 1910, and 1966 provide negative examples for the Old Order Amish—demonstrations of the corrosive effects of worldliness. Through their ownership of cars and use of electricity, the liberal groups have displayed the folly of worldliness to several generations of young Amish. By extracting the progressives, the Old Order Amish were able to tighten their grip on traditional practices—the ban on electricity, cars, and tractors—

because they no longer had to placate liberal agitators. Thus the divisions left the Old Order Amish as the guardians of tradition, a role they gladly assumed. Safeguarding their socioreligious traditions is an overarching goal that engenders wide support. The Amish view the larger culture as a direct threat to their religious identity. Expressions of modernity—or "worldliness," as the Amish would say—ranging from cars to television, are viewed as intrusions that, if not deflected, could eventually eradicate their religious faith and community. The Amish are social engineers who have masterminded an effective program of cultural survival without the benefits of higher education or the advice of professional consultants.

2

The Quilt Work of Amish Culture

I completely abandoned myself to the Lord.
—Anabaptist martyr, 1527

Sacred Patches

Amish women are noted for their lovely quilts. They symbolize
the complex patchwork of Amish culture—the beliefs, myths, and images that shape their world. Symbolic patches of soil, martyrdom,
obedience, family, humility, work, tradition, and community, stitched
together by history, form a cultural quilt that envelops the Amish.
These patches of meaning, quilted into a single fabric, fill daily routines with significance. Religious threads hold the quilt work together. Silent prayers before and after meals embroider each day
with reverence. Daily behavior, from dressing to eating, is transformed into religious ritual with eternal significance.

The Amish subscribe to basic Christian doctrines—the divinity
of Christ, heaven and hell, the inspiration of Scripture, and the church
as the body of Christ in the world today. Yet the practical expression
of Amish faith is quite different from that of mainline Christian
churches. Modern religion is often restricted to brief episodes of
life—an hour on Sunday morning, a wedding, a confirmation. Amish
faith has not been separated from the other spheres of life. It penetrates their entire culture. Amish beliefs, worship services, and ceremonial rituals remain virtually untouched by modern influences.
Basic Amish doctrines are outlined in an Anabaptist creed written in
1632, some sixty years before they separated from the Swiss Anabaptists.[1] Although the Amish have revised their practical definitions of
worldliness in response to social change, their fundamental religious
tenets have remained intact over the years. This chapter describes the

religious values of Amish culture—the patches of meaning that are stitched together in their quilt work.

Yielding the Right Way

The solution to the riddle of Amish culture is embedded in the German word *Gelassenheit* (Gay-las-en-hite). Roughly translated, *Gelassenheit* means "submission"—yielding to a higher authority. An abstract concept, it carries a variety of specific meanings—self-surrender, resignation to God's will, yielding to God and to others, self-denial, contentment, a calm spirit. Various words in the Amish vocabulary capture the practical dimensions of Gelassenheit: obedience, humility, submission, thrift, and simplicity.

Gelassenheit stands in sharp contrast to the bold, aggressive individualism of modern culture. The meek spirit of Gelassenheit unfolds as individuals yield to higher authorities: the will of God, church elders, parents, community, and tradition. Gelassenheit confirms that Amish culture is indeed a counterculture whose core value collides with the heartbeat of modernity, individual achievement. Modern culture produces individualists whose prime objective is personal fulfillment. By contrast, the goal of Gelassenheit is a subdued, humble person who discovers fulfillment in the community. Amish who give up their selves to the community receive, in return, a durable and visible ethnic identity.

The meaning of Gelassenheit penetrates many practical dimensions of Amish life—values, symbols, ritual, personality, and social organization. It is a way of thinking about one's relationship to God. The faithful Christian yields to divine providence without trying to change or influence history. Gelassenheit is also a way of thinking about one's relationship to others. It means serving and respecting others and obeying the consensus of the community. It entails a modest way of acting, talking, dressing, and walking. Finally, it is a way of structuring social life so that organizations remain small, compact, and simple. Like a social equation, Gelassenheit spells out the individual's subordinate relationship to the larger social order. It regulates the tie between the individual and the community by transforming the psychic energies of the individual into group capital.

The early Anabaptists used the term *Gelassenheit* to convey the idea of yielding absolutely to God's will with a dedicated heart—forsaking all selfishness.[2] They believed that Christ called them to abandon self-interest and follow his example of suffering, meekness, humility, and service. True Christians, according to the Anabaptists, should not take revenge on their enemies but should turn the other cheek if attacked. They should pray for their persecutors and love their enemies, as commanded by Christ. Self-will stands in the way of

Figure 2-1 The Dimensions of Gelassenheit

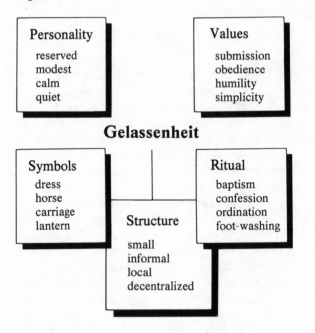

Personality
reserved
modest
calm
quiet

Values
submission
obedience
humility
simplicity

Gelassenheit

Symbols
dress
horse
carriage
lantern

Ritual
baptism
confession
ordination
foot-washing

Structure
small
informal
local
decentralized

obedience to God's will. Jesus' words "Not my will but thine be done" became their primary script of faith. Hence, giving up self and yielding to God's will was the crucial test of true faithfulness. Thousands of Anabaptist martyrs yielded to the sword as the ultimate test of their willingness to mortify self and submit to God's will. The blood of martyrs seared Gelassenheit into the sacred text of Amish history. It is not surprising that such a bloody history would leave the indelible print of Gelassenheit on the quilt work of Amish culture. What is surprising is that the imprint has not faded several centuries after the persecution.

Yielding the right way—God's way—is the stance of Gelassenheit. Although the Amish rarely use the term in everyday speech, Sandra L. Cronk contends that Gelassenheit orders their whole social system.[3] All things being equal, the higher the psychological price of joining a group, the more attractive it will appear to its members. In other words, groups that demand very little will not be valued very highly by their members. Amish values of simplicity, humility, and austerity call for personal sacrifices that build commitment to the community.

The nonresistant stance of Gelassenheit forbids the use of force in human relations. Thus the Amish avoid serving in the military, holding political offices, using courts, filing lawsuits, serving on juries, working as police officers, and engaging in ruthless competition. Legal and personal confrontation is avoided whenever possible. Silence and avoidance are often used to manage conflict. A lowly spirit denies luxuries, worldly pleasures, and costly entertainment. Purging selfish desires means yielding to the plain standards of Amish dress, transportation, farming practices, and home furnishings. The submissive posture of Gelassenheit discourages high school education, abstract thinking, competition, professional occupations, and scientific pursuits, which lead to conceit and arrogance.

An Amish petition to state legislators concerning a new school law depicts the lowly tone of Gelassenheit: "We your humble subjects . . . do not blame our men of authority for bringing all this over us. . . . We admit, we ourselves are the fault of it. We beg your pardon for bringing all this before you, and worrying you, and bringing you a serious problem."[4] The yielded person submits to the authority of God-ordained leaders, engages in mutual-aid activities, respects the wisdom of tradition, and washes the feet of others in a sacred rite of humility.

Amish attempts to harness selfishness, pride, and power are not based on the premise that the material world or pleasure itself is evil. Smoking, for example, is a common practice among men.[5] Good food abounds. Sexual relations within marriage are enjoyed. Recreation and play, in the proper time and place, are welcomed. Evil, the Amish believe, is found in human desires for self-exaltation rather than in the material world as such.

The Paradox of *Gelassenheit*

Talk of self-denial defies modern culture, which is saturated with dreams of self-fulfillment. Although Gelassenheit seems repressive to Moderns, it is a redemptive paradox for the Amish. They believe that the followers of Christ and the martyrs of old were called to lose their lives in order to save them. The death of Christ redeemed the world, and the sacrifice of the martyrs fertilized the growth of the true church. The Amish believe that individuals who deny self and submit to divine precepts bring honor and glory to God. Members who yield to their neighbors are ultimately revering God. The person who foregos personal advancement for the sake of family and community makes a redemptive sacrifice that transforms the church into a common body—the body of Christ. Gelassenheit is a social process that recycles the individual's energies for the community's purposes, a recycling empowered by the words of Jesus, the blood of the martyrs, and the blessing of Amish ancestors.

Etched into Amish consciousness, Gelassenheit regulates the entire spectrum of life from body language to social organization, from

The contented
smile of
Gelassenheit.

personal speech to symbolism. Submission to God's will, meekness, and small-scale organizations merge in Amish culture. Life takes on religious meaning as people place themselves on the altar of community, a sacrifice that brings homage to God. The Amish are urged to "patiently bear the cross of Christ without complaining."[6] Bearing the cross of Christ is not an abstraction, but in the words of one leader, "We wear an untrimmed beard and ear length hair because we are willing to bear the cross of Christ."[7] Dressing by church standards, raising a neighbor's barn, cooking for the family, pulling weeds in the garden, forgoing electrical appliances, and plowing with horses are ritual offerings whereby individuals give, serve, sacrifice, and yield to the community—an incarnation of God's will on earth.

The Yielded Self

The size and number of mirrors in a society indicate the cultural importance attached to the self. Thus it is not surprising that the mirrors in Amish homes are smaller and fewer than those found in modern ones. Whereas Moderns are preoccupied with "finding themselves," the Amish are engaged in "losing themselves."[8] The Amish work just as hard at losing themselves as Moderns work at finding themselves. Either way, it is hard work. Although uncomfortable to Moderns, who cherish the flowering of individuality, losing the self in Amish culture assumes a dignity because its ultimate redemption is the gift of community.

In daily life, Gelassenheit means "giving up" and "giving in." The child learns this at an early age. Parents teach their children that self-will must be given up if they want to become children of God.[9] The large size of Amish families teaches young children to wait their turn as they yield to other siblings. Large families prepare the child for an adult life of yieldedness. Mervin Smucker discovered that Amish children are less likely to use first-person-singular pronouns—I, me, mine, myself, and my—than non-Amish children.[10] Using a standardized personality test administered to Amish children in several settlements, John Hostetler found that Amish personality types differed significantly from non-Amish ones. Indeed, the Amish personality exemplified Gelassenheit: "Quiet, friendly, responsible, and conscientious. Works devotedly to meet his obligations and serve his friends and school . . . patient with detail and routine. Loyal, considerate, concerned with how other people feel even when they are in the wrong."[11]

The Amish believe that the quickest way to spoil children is to let them have their own way. Parents and teachers are encouraged to "work together so that bad habits . . . disobedience, disrespect, etc. can be nipped in the bud so to speak."[12] For young children, a spanking may help to nip disobedience in the bud. Children are taught to yield, to wait, to submit. An Amish leader noted: "By the time that the child reaches the age of three the mold has started to form and it is the parents' duty to form it in the way that the child should go. When the child is old enough to stiffen its back and throw back its head in temper it is old enough to gently start breaking that temper."[13]

The Amish think modern children are spoiled by being driven from club to club and lesson to lesson in hopes that they will find and express their true selves. In contrast, Amish children are washing dishes by hand, feeding cows, hauling manure, pulling weeds, and mowing lawns. They are learning to lose their selves, to yield to the larger purposes of family and community. JOY, a widely used school motto, reminds children that Jesus is first, you are last, and others are in between. The essence of Gelassenheit is tucked away in a favorite school verse:

> I must be a Christian child,
> Gentle, patient, meek, and mild;
> Must be honest, simple, true
> In my words and actions too.
> I must cheerfully obey,
> Giving up my will and way; . . .
>
> Must remember, God can view
> All I think, and all I do.
> Glad that I can know I try,
> Glad that children such as I,
> In our feeble ways and small,
> Can serve Him who loves us all.[14]

It would be wrong to conclude that losing one's self in Amish society is a demeaning or dehumanizing process. Bending to the call of community does not smother individual expression. The Amish neither wallow in self-contempt nor champion weak personalities. Within limits, there are many opportunities for self-expression, from quilting patterns to stickers on lunch pails, from gardening practices to hobbies, from farming methods to household furnishings. As in other societies, in Amish life there is a diversity of personality styles, value preferences, intelligence, and personal habits. The constraints of Amish culture would certainly suffocate the "free spirits" of the modern world. But Amish children, who are taught to respect the primacy of the community over that of the individual, do not feel as stifled by the constraints, as would Moderns, who cherish individualism.

The Amish reflect Gelassenheit in the way they interact with others. How one smiles, laughs, uses silence, shakes hands, takes off one's hat, and drives one's horse signals Gelassenheit or its absence. A boisterous laugh and a quick retort betray a cocky spirit. An aggressive handshake and a curt greeting disclose an assertive self. Such characteristics do not befit Gelassenheit. Rather, a gentle chuckle, a hesitation, and a refined smile embody the yielded and submissive spirit. A slow and thoughtful answer, a deference to the other's idea, and a reluctance to interrupt a conversation are signs of Gelassenheit. In a small community, individuals know one another well enough that there is no need to "sell" themselves. Thus the yielded self does not flaunt itself in everyday life. An Amish bishop ended his letter to one of his members with these words: "Remember us in your prayers, for we are likewise minded in weakness. Only me."

The goal of Amish life is a tame, gentle, and domesticated self,

Schoolchildren enjoy the pleasures of community over lunch.

yielded to the community's larger goals. But even in Amish society there is room for manipulation. A coy person with selfish goals may learn subtle ways of presenting a "yielded front" to others for personal gain. A yielded self is especially valued in formal church activities and in relations to elders and others in authority. Bold, untamed selves are more likely to flare up in business deals, at play, around the barn, and particularly among teen-agers.

Waiting on Divine Providence

Gelassenheit has important implications for the expression of religious experience. Religious doctrines are often packaged in theological formulas designed to hold the faithful and convince nonbelievers of the truth. Some formulas contend that one can "find the answers," be "sure of salvation," and have "no doubts" about one's faith. In this view, eternal salvation is attainable by those who believe and act properly. Such logic reveals a calculating religious attitude, one that separates the ends from the means; for example, "I have to be saved in order to achieve eternal life." This rational view assumes that one can decide, that one must decide, and that ultimately one has control over one's own eternal fate.

It is precisely at this point that Amish faith bewilders those of evangelical and fundamentalist persuasions. Amish faith is wholistic. The Amish resist separating means and ends—salvation and eternal life. They are reluctant to say that they are sure of salvation. They prefer being faithful while waiting on providence—hoping things will turn out well. Announcing that one is eternally saved reveals a haughty attitude, far from the modest spirit of Gelassenheit. Rather, one must yield to God's eternal will and hope that things turn out for the best. After all, it is God that makes these weighty decisions. Boldly declaring oneself "saved" is a pretentious self-assertion that borders on idolatry, for only God can make such claims.

The code words of the evangelical mind-set—personal salvation, personal evangelism, and personal devotions—focus on the individual rather than the community as the center of redemptive activity. In refusing this modern language, the Amish are indeed traditionalists, for they prefer to yield to divine fate. Whereas evangelical Christians want to know, control, plan, believe, and act properly so that they can guarantee their salvation, the Amish outlook is a more modest view of divine activity and perhaps a more honest one. It resists separating ends from means and the individual from the group. The Amish view the Bible as a trustworthy guide for living, but they do not quote it incessantly, as do some Christians. Amish who do so are accused of being "Scripture smart," for showing off their biblical knowledge. Personal interpretations of Scripture are downplayed. But the Bible, read in family and church settings, is the authoritative voice for Amish tradition and culture.

Some religious groups seek to transform or save the world by seeking converts and engaging in missionary programs. Evangelism is foreign to the Amish. Rather than trying to save the world, the Amish wait on divine providence. In this sense, they are surprisingly tolerant of other religious groups. They yield to the brotherhood, live faithfully in community, and hope that their offering of a yielded self will be acceptable to God. Being faithful does not guarantee eternal salvation, it is simply *the* way to yield to life.

The Habit of Obedience

Paired oppositions—obedience and disobedience, church and world, humility and pride, slow and fast, work and idleness—provide clues to the structure of meaning in Amish consciousness. Abundant throughout the culture, these code words of Gelassenheit are particularly stressed in the training of young children. Obedience tops the Amish value hierarchy as the most visible expression of Gelassenheit.

Yielded individuals are obedient. Obedience to the will of God is the cardinal religious virtue. Disobedience is dangerous. It signals self-will and, if not confessed, leads to eternal separation from God. The creed for baptismal instruction predicts that the unbelieving, disobedient, and headstrong will enter eternal damnation.[15]

Obedience to church regulations signals inner obedience to the will of God. Those who crush selfish desires are willing to comply with church standards. Belligerent, headstrong individuals, who challenge the order of the church, lack spiritual submission. Religious phrases and Bible verses are used to underscore the importance of obedience throughout Amish life.

Childhood training ingrains obedience into daily routines, so that it becomes a taken-for-granted habit. Learning obedience at an early age is a powerful means of social control. Children are taught from the Bible: "Obey your parents in the Lord for this is right."[16] An Amish booklet on child rearing speaks of the "habits of obedience." The Amish believe that parents should be "ready to punish disobedience," "insist on obedience," "allow no opposing replies," and should realize that "if orders are disobeyed once and no proper punishment given, disobedience is likely to come again." Parents are expected to make children "understand that they must obey you."[17] Retorts and challenges from children, often accepted as amusing forms of self-expression in middle-class culture, are not tolerated by Amish elders. The child obeys the teacher in the Amish school, for "the teacher's word is the final authority and is to be obeyed."[18] Yielding one's will at an early age is a crucial step in preparing for a life of obedience to authority.

Adult members are expected to obey church rules and customs. A husband and a wife discuss many issues together, but a wife is expected to obey her husband. Deacons and ministers are obedient servants of the bishop. The younger bishops defer to the senior bishops. Obedience to divine and human authority regulates social relationships from the youngest child to the oldest bishop, who in turn is called to obey the Lord.

These rites of surrender are offered as sacrifices to the larger goal of an ordered and unified community. While expectations for obedience are firm and final, loving concern permeates the social system. A father spanks his child out of love. The bishop expels and shuns a member in "hopes of winning him back." There are, of course, ruptures in the loving concern, but a tone of reverent obedience governs the social system.

The Virtue of Humility

Pride and humility frame Amish consciousness. Humility is encouraged with biblical sanctions. *Pride*, a religious term for the sinister face of individualism, has its own share of biblical condemnation. An Amish devotional guide says: "Read much in God's word and you will find many warnings against pride. No other sin was punished more severely. Pride changed angels to devils. A once powerful king, Nebuchadnezzar, was transformed into a brute beast to eat grass like an ox. And Jezebel, a dominant queen, was eaten of dogs as the result of her pride."[19]

A cancerous threat to group commitment, pride elevates individuals. Proud individuals display the spirit of arrogance, not Gelassenheit. The Amish view the proud person as "showing off," "making a name for himself," "taking care of herself," and in all of these ways hoisting himself above others. Proud people "call attention to themselves." They are "pushy," "bold," "forward," and "always jumping the fence." Pride, a persistent threat to community welfare and stability, must be rooted out promptly by church leaders, for, if left to sprout and grow, it will spread and debilitate the community. "It was pride," said one minister, "that brought down the world the first time at the flood."

Pride has many faces. The well-known Amish taboo against photography is legitimated by a biblical command: "You shall not make for yourself a graven image or a likeness of anything" (Exod. 20:4). In the latter part of the nineteenth century, as photography was becoming popular, the Amish applied the biblical injunction against "likenesses" to photographs. Their aversion to photography is a way of suppressing pride. If people see themselves displayed in a photograph, they might begin to take themselves too seriously. They might think "that they are somebody." Such people are obviously "out to make a name for themselves." With religious sanction, this taboo suppresses individualism and cultivates Gelassenheit.

The Amish believe that public recognition of personal achievement also erodes humility. Moderns committed to individual rights and self-advancement eagerly "take credit" for anything that will enhance their résumés. The legal apparatus of copyrights, credits, permissions, and acknowledgments is designed to assure that individuals get "proper credit" for their efforts. Just as Moderns work hard at getting credit, the Amish work hard at disavowing it. Amish who yield properly are careful not to make a name for themselves, for that would lead to pride. If credit comes, it must be modestly shared with others.

Amish writers often write anonymously to avoid attracting attention (pride) to themselves. An Amishman who started using his

Faced with prosecution for not sending their children to high school in 1953, Amish fathers show the resignation of Gelassenheit as they yield to the authority of the state.

name at the end of published articles said: "I got my wings clipped and so I just stopped using my name." The Amish believe that proud individuals tack their name on everything, draw attention to themselves, and take personal credit for everything. The humble individual, by contrast, freely gives time and effort to strengthen the community and, in the spirit of Gelassenheit, declines public recognition.

The Amish abhor publicity, that delight of modern organizations. They leave their public relations to the imagination of outsiders. In rare moments when Amish achievements appear in newsprint, as in the instance of the man who was designated the "most improved" dairy farmer of the year, names are conspicuously missing. Tagging names on accomplishments turns them into acts of idolatry designed to solicit human praise and applause. The Amish deplore public recognition, but in face-to-face conversation there are many warm moments of recognition and gentle praise for personal contributions. The Bible teaches that pride comes before a fall, and the Amish believe publicity leads to pride, which in time will harm the community.

The presentation of the self is particularly vulnerable to pride. Vocabulary, dress, and body language subtly indicate a proud or humble self. Modern society provides the individual with an enormous repertoire of props for making up and presenting a self for every occasion. Hair styles, clothing, jewelry, cosmetics, and suntans help individuals to "package" themselves in a variety of ways. These same tools of modernity ironically provide ways of conforming to the latest fashions. The Amish believe that feckless preening rituals, repeated morning after morning in suburban bathrooms, are infested with pride. Self-exaltation is diametrically opposed to the core values of Amish culture. Thus, cosmetic props are considered signs of pride, signals of pushy selves showing off "number one" and scorning the spirit of Gelassenheit. Moreover, the false mask of the "made up" face is seen by the Amish as a lie, of sorts, that covers up the real face.

In the close interaction of friends and family, the authentic Amish self becomes known and is accepted without cosmetic props. Thus jewelry (including wedding rings and wrist watches) is taboo, because it reveals a proud heart. Any form of make-up, hair styling, showy dress, manufactured clothing, flashy color, and bold fabric which calls undue attention to the self is off-limits in Amish culture. Make-up is proscribed, even in the casket. The rejection of outward adornment is rooted in biblical teaching.[20]

Pride, however, pops up in virtually all avenues of Amish life. Traces of pride are shown by professional landscaping around houses, fancy harnesses, and windshield wipers on carriages. One farmer described another as "horse proud"; that is, too concerned with the appearance of his horses. Unnecessary trappings are pretentious signs of individuals clamoring for self-attention, elevating themselves above others.

Humility is a barometer of Gelassenheit. The Amish are taught: "If other people praise you, humble yourself. But do not praise yourself or boast, for that is the way of fools who seek vain praise . . . in tribulation be patient and humble yourself under the mighty hand of God."[21] Once again, Jesus, the meek servant, is the model of true humility. The Amish ritualize the virtue of humility by washing one another's feet during their fall and spring communion service. According to the command of Christ (John 13:4–17), they teach that stooping to wash the feet of a brother or sister "is a sign of true humiliation."[22]

Separation from the World

Taking their cues from the Bible, the Amish divide the social world into two categories: the straight, narrow way to life and the broad, easy road to destruction. The Amish embody the straight and narrow way of self-denial. The larger social world represents the broad, easy path of vanity and vice. To the Amish, the term *world* refers not to the globe, but to the entire social system outside Amish society—its people, values, vices, practices, and institutions; in short, modernity itself. Sectarian groups typically oppose the dominant social order. The Amish contrast church versus world, Amish and non-Amish, and "our people" versus "outsiders." A leader put it simply: "If you're not Amish, you're English and part of the world." Even the five-year-old son of an Amish hat maker said: "We sell most of them to *our people*, but a few of them to *the English*." Such a simple division of the social terrain is common even in the modern mind, where democracy is pitted against communism, capitalism against socialism, and Americans against Soviets.

The world—savoring individualism, secularism, rationality, competition, relativism, fragmentation—threatens Gelassenheit. The social system of the larger world functions as a negative reference group with perverted values. Daily press reports of government scandal, drug abuse, violent crime, divorce, war, economic greed, homosexuality, and child abuse confirm again and again in the Amish mind that the world is teeming with evil abominations. Just as the fear of communism intensifies American patriotism, so the fear of an evil world strengthens Amish solidarity.

This sharp dualism between church and world crystallized in the sixteenth century, when many Anabaptists were tortured and executed. An early Anabaptist theological statement, written in 1527, underscored the deep chasm between the church and the world: "All of those who have fellowship with the dead works of darkness have no part in the light. Thus all who follow the devil and the world, have no part with those who are called out of the world into God."[23]

The split between church and world, imprinted in Amish consciousness by decades of persecution, is also legitimated by Scripture. Using biblical imagery, the Amish see the church as "a chosen generation, a royal priesthood, a holy nation, a peculiar people . . . who were called out of darkness" (1 Pet. 2:9). The Amish believe that in all ways they "are not to conform to the world" (Rom. 12:2) or to be "unequally yoked with the world" (2 Cor. 6:14).[24] Moreover, Scripture teaches that they should be "equipped with the whole armor of God to stand and prevail in this strife torn world." Children are taught "not to love the world nor the things of the world" (1 John 2:15). The church is called not to join or fraternize with the world but to "be a light unto it" (Matt. 5:14). One Amishman said: "Jesus through his direct plea has commanded us to come out from the world, and be separated, and touch not the unclean things. . . . In other words, we shall not be conformed to this world, but be transformed."[25]

To the Amish, worldliness denotes specific behaviors and life-styles. High school, cars, cameras, tape recorders, television, films, showy houses, certain farm machinery, and bicycles, all tagged *worldly*, are censured. But the term is a slippery one, for its meaning evolves over time. White enamel stoves and bathtubs, for instance, were obvious signs of worldliness in the forties. Today modern gas stoves and bathtubs are common in Amish homes. Many children and even some adults wear sneakers, which were once forbidden. Pliable over time, the term *worldly* is a convenient way of labeling changes, products, practices, and beliefs that appear threatening to the community. The stigma of this label stalls their acceptance and keeps them at arm's length. However, not all new things are dubbed *worldly*. For example, battery-operated calculators, synthetic materials, solid-state gasoline engines, hot dogs, and fiberglass have escaped the stamp of worldliness.

The Amish paranoia of worldliness is rooted in a spiritual concern to preserve the purity of the church. The drama between the church and the world is a battle between good and evil, between the forces of righteousness and those of the devil. It is the ultimate struggle, and to succumb to worldliness is to surrender the community to apostasy. This key unlocks many riddles in Amish society. The impulse to separate from the world infuses Amish consciousness, guides personal behavior, and shapes institutional structures. The sectarian suspicion of the world confounds Moderns, who are enchanted by tolerance, acceptance, diversity, and religious pluralism. If social separation is indeed a by-product of technological progress, the Amish believe they can only preserve their integrated community by remaining separate from the great separator, modernity itself.

The Joy of Work

In contrast to some Moderns who hate their jobs and love to shop, the Amish enjoy their work and despise conspicuous consumption. Although there is mischief, play, and leisure in Amish life, work predominates. Although often hard and dirty, it is good and meaningful work that, for the most part, reinforces community life. Amish work integrates. It binds the individual to the group, the family, and the church. It is not a personal career, but a calling from God, and, in this sense, as Cronk has noted, it becomes a redemptive ritual.[26]

Housework, yard work, barn work, and field work are offerings that contribute to the family's larger welfare. Family, community, and work are woven together in the fabric of Amish life. Work is not pitted against the other spheres of life, as is often the case in modernity. Work encompasses life. It is pursued for the sake of community, not just for individual profit and prestige. A great deal of work is done in small groups, where it also becomes a celebration of togetherness. The profits of Amish work support family and church, not exotic hobbies and expensive tours and cruises. Children are expected to "help out" soon after they can walk. It is not unusual for children under the age of ten to drive a team of horses or mules in the fields. The routine of daily chores is woven into the rhythm of Amish life. Labor-saving technology thus threatens the sacred ritual of work.

Because work is a meaningful rite that contributes to the community's greater welfare, idleness is deplored as the "devil's workshop." If there is any doubt that work is a sacred ritual, there can be no doubt that the Amish loath idleness. They are told to "detest idleness as a pillow of Satan and a cause of all sorts of wickedness, and be diligent in your appointed tasks that you not be found idle. Satan has great power over the idle, to lead them into many sins. King David was idle on the rooftop of his house when he fell into adultery."[27] Idle minds fill up with vulgar thoughts and become dangerous. A young Amish businessman worries that with more Amish working in shops there will be too much free time in the evenings and on weekends and that people will start going away to the mountains. The family farm has provided abundant home work in the context of family, neighborhood, and church.

Amish work is "hands-on," practical work. Plowing, milking, sawing, quilting, and washing do not involve the manipulation of abstract symbols, as does the work of an information society. A "useful" versus "impractical" opposition underlies Amish thinking. Amish work is useful, down to earth. The farmer or carpenter sees, touches, and shapes the final product and is held responsible for it. Manual work breeds a pragmatic mentality that values "practical" things and eschews abstract or "impractical" information derived from "book learning." A consistent theme in the Amish opposition to public high schools was the fear that academics would teach Amish youth to despise manual work.

Quoting a biblical verse (Col. 2:8), the Amish caution: "Beware lest any man spoil you through philosophy and vain deceit after the rudiments of the world and not after Christ."[28] Practical things are useful. "Children," according to one leader, "should grow up to be useful men and women, useful in the community and also useful

Using horses to pull a modern hay baler, a family works together to harvest a new crop of hay.

members of the church of Christ."[29] Decorative art work displayed on walls is disdained because it is not useful and is considered vain. Embroidered family registers, calendars, and genealogical charts hang on Amish walls. Some Amish write poetry, keep journals, and decorate crafts with pastoral scenes. Art that exalts the individual artist is unwelcome. An Amish artist complained: "It's okay to paint milk cans but not to display your work at art shows." Artistic impulses in their modern forms are viewed as worldly, impractical, and self-exalting, a waste of time and money.[30] Useful artistic expression is encouraged in quilting patterns, recipes, flower gardens, artistic lettering in Bibles, toys, dolls, crafts, and furniture designs. The Amish spend an enormous amount of creative energy making crafts for gifts and family needs, as well as to sell to neighbors and tourists. The goal of Amish schools is "to prepare for usefulness by preparing for eternity" rather than to spoil children with the abstractions of philosophy.[31]

The Practice of Thrift

When things become too practical and handy, they border on luxury. A hay baler is practical, but an automatic bale thrower to load the bales on a wagon is "too handy" and thus worldly. Automatic devices generally are considered too handy. The polarities of "luxury" and "thrift," "gaudy" and "simple," and "pleasure" and "sacrifice" underscore the tension between negative and positive values in Amish culture. Sacrifice is a sign of the yielded self, but luxury signals pride. No longer content to work and sacrifice for the common good, the pleasure-seeker is preoccupied with self-fulfillment. The Amish are urged to "suffer affliction with the people of God rather than to enjoy the pleasures of sin for a season."[32]

"Extravagance" and "self-denial," "ease" and "discipline," and "fancy" and "plain" are also symbolic oppositions that pinpoint the difference between Gelassenheit and self-enhancement. An Amish essay on thrift explains that "some people are extravagant. They spend too much time and money, or both, needlessly. They want fine-looking buildings or livestock and pay too much for looks. Others want everything handy and pay too much for machinery that they could do without. Others, like the rich man (Luke 16), want fine clothes and lots of rich food. Others, with self-denial and good management, can live quite comfortably with far less expense."[33]

The yielded self does not seek pleasure, buy luxuries, make things too handy, or pay for "looks." Rags are recycled into rugs. Clothing is worn out rather than tossed away after every passing fad. Older children pass toys down to younger ones. The Amish pursuit of thrift and austerity is not a masochistic drive to win divine favor or guarantee eternal life. It is an acceptance of the historical fact that their austere way of being—developed over the years—has produced a wholesome life. In short, it has worked and, to the Amish, is the way things are supposed to be, the way they work best.

The Value of Tradition

Amish culture balances delicately between tradition and social change. In the modern world, where new is best and change is equated with progress, the Amish offer a different view. They believe that tradition provides a healthy drag that "slows things down" and provides an anchor to a solid past. A young minister noted:

The Amish outlook on tradition is somewhat different than other churches. We consider tradition as being spiritually helpful. Tradition can blind you if you adhere only to tradition and not the meanings of the tradition, but we really maintain a tradition. I've heard

The Amish make crafts, an acceptable form of artistic expression, and sell them to tourists.

one of our members say that if you start changing some things, it won't stop at some things, it will keep on changing and there won't be an end to it. We have some traditions, that some people question and I sometimes myself question, that are being maintained just because they are a tradition. This can be adverse, but it can also be a benefit. Tradition always looks bad if you're comparing one month to the next or one year to the next, but when you are talking fifty years or more, tradition looks more favorable. Don't get me wrong, I don't feel that everybody who is traditional is okay. But there still is a lot of value in tradition and we realize that.

Another Amishman said: "Tradition to us is a sacred trust, and it is part of our religion to uphold and adhere to the ideals of our forefathers."[34]

The spirit of Gelassenheit calls for yielding to tradition. Economic pressure, expansion, curiosity, greed, and youthful innovation foster social change. But change, though suspect, is not necessarily all bad. New things are not rejected immediately by the Amish just because they are new. Innovations are cautiously evaluated to see where they might lead and how they might eventually affect the community. Traditional sentiments, however, regulate everything from clothing to education.

Modern societies face forward and plan their future. The Amish face their past and treasure their tradition as a resource for coping with the present. Tradition functions as a brake on the dangerous wheel of change. The Amish increasingly glance forward as young entrepreneurs plan, forecast, and strategize to expand markets for their products. Despite these forward glances, the Amish have not lost sight of their past and its precious legacy. Moderns are preoccupied with the present and the immediate future. The Amish take a longer view backward and forward. Echoes of previous generations and concerns for future ones merge and enlarge their sense of the present.

A Slower Pace

An Amishman described an Amishwoman who had her yard professionally landscaped as "a little on the fast side." The cadence of Amish life is sluggish compared to that of modernity. The spirit of Gelassenheit is reserved—slow to respond, slow to embrace change, slow to push ahead. Another Amishman said: "Our way of living differs greatly from others living in the fast pace of this world."[35] The Amish have separated themselves from the pace of modernity by adjusting their clocks in two ways. In the first part of the twentieth century, it was customary for Amish families to set their clocks a half-hour ahead of standard time. This "fast half" time was a symbolic reminder to both insider and outsider of the boundaries between Amish and modern culture. Some older families continue this practice. Second, the Amish did not join the popular switch to daylight saving time but have continued to follow standard time. Because of increased interaction with the outside world today, Amish families involved in business often change their clocks in the spring and fall to comply with daylight saving time. Other families still follow standard time as a symbolic practice of separation from the world. Church services, of course, always follow standard time.

Perceptions of time vary enormously from culture to culture. Time organizes human consciousness as well as everyday behavior.[36] Anyone stepping into Amish society suddenly feels time expand and relax. The battery-operated clocks on Amish walls seem to run slower. From body language to the speed of transportation, from singing to walking, the stride is slower. Traveling by buggy, plowing with horses, and going to church every other week creates a temporal order with a slower, more deliberate rhythm.

Fast tempos, quick moves, and rapid changes are suspect in Amish culture. The slow pace of Amish singing reflects an utterly different conception of time. Holding church services every other week stretches the temporal space of Amish life. The rhythm of the seasons, and the agricultural calendar of planting and harvesting, widens the temporal brackets and slows the pace of Amish life. The "wide" intervals of time contrast sharply with the abbreviated ones of modern time, dictated by half-hour segments of television programming sliced up even more by commercials.

The great irony here is that in Amish society, with fewer labor-saving devices and other technological shortcuts, there is less "rushing around." The perception of rushing seems to increase directly with the number of "time-saving" devices. Although much time is "saved" in modern life, for some reason there is less of it and rushing increases. The perception of rushing increases as the number, complexity, and mobility of social relations soar. Thus the simplicity, overlap, and closeness of Amish life slow the pace of things and eliminate the need for time-management seminars. Visiting, the Amish "sport," is often spontaneous. Drop-in visits without warning are welcomed. There are planned family gatherings, but spontaneity generally prevails in Amish socializing. There is some rushing. Children are sometimes told to hurry up, but the stride of life generally is slower.

There are, however, impending changes. Time clocks, appointment books, and telephones springing up around Amish shops reflect a livelier tempo. Appointments, unheard of in the past, are now commonplace among Amish businessmen, who must synchronize their work with that of the larger society. A "punch-in" time clock in one Amish shop is a sure sign of a new temporal order. Telephones near Amish work sites make it easier to arrange appointments. One person complained: "Now you even have to make an appointment to have your horse shod by an Amish blacksmith. In the past you could just take it there and wait." Patient waiting, a virtue of Gelassenheit, is threatened with extinction. Moderns, of course, also have moments of surrender, yielding, and waiting, but they are momentary. In Amish society, pausing at the yield sign *is* the way of life.

Upside-down Values

The quilt of Amish culture is upside-down in many ways. The basic values of this counterculture defy the taken-for-granted assumptions of modernity. It is a subculture in which:

The individual is not the supreme reality.

Communal goals transcend personal ones.

The past is as important as the future.

Tradition is valued equally with change.

Personal sacrifice is esteemed over pleasure.

Local involvement outweighs national acclaim.

Work is more satisfying than consumption.

Obeying, waiting, and yielding are embraced.

Newer, bigger, and faster are not better.

Preservation eclipses progress.

Staying together is the supreme value.

In all of these ways it is obvious that the Amish have not capitulated to modernity. Their core value system has withstood the torrents of progress. There is, of course, slippage from the ideal of Gelassenheit. Egocentrism, pride, envy, jealousy, and greed sometimes fracture community harmony. Retaliation in family and church spats at times splinters the otherwise peaceful social order. Even leaders sometimes balk when asked to yield to the authority of elders. Businessmen in a competitive world face serious clashes with the spirit of Gelassenheit. The emphasis on conformity to explicit rules sometimes cultivates an attitude of hollow ritualism among some. After all, these people are people.

Despite aberrations and episodes of self-enhancement, Gelassenheit is not only a religious ideal; it is the governing principle, the core value, that unlocks the riddle of Amish culture. Definitions of worldliness and pride have been cautiously updated to permit a slow drift forward. But submission, simplicity, obedience, and humility still prevail. They continue to structure the Amish world view—a sure sign that Gelassenheit has not faded from the quilt work of Amish culture.

3

Symbols of Integration and Separation

Telephones, electricity, cars, and tractors set us off from the
Mennonites, and then, of course, there is television and all the
other stuff.
—Amish farmer

The Flags of Ethnicity

The Amish share many cultural objects with other Americans.
They read newspapers, throw baseballs, and barbecue hamburgers
on gas grills. Other aspects of their material culture are unique: windmills, lanterns, harnesses, bonnets. Such artifacts serve both *symbolic* and *substantive* functions in Amish culture. They symbolize
Amish identity but also shape daily life and social interaction. For instance, lanterns hanging in homes and shops announce the ethnic affiliation of Amish homesteads to members and outsiders alike. The
lack of electricity also makes a substantive difference in daily living.
Without radios, televisions, air conditioners, sweepers, and other
electrical appliances, Amish homes are quieter. Manual housework
increases without electricity. Homes are also more immune from the
intrusion of outside media. Amish families are more likely than modern ones to be found together in a common room of their home, partially because they use space heaters and have fewer sources of light.
And they typically go to bed earlier—often by eight or nine in winter
evenings. In these and other ways, the absence of electricity changes
Amish behavior. This chapter focuses on four symbols—language,
dress, horse, and buggy—that shape Amish identity and make a difference in everyday life.[1]

Like other people, the Amish live in a symbolic world of their
own creation. The symbols of Gelassenheit articulate surrender, bond
the community, and mark off territorial boundaries with the larger
society. Symbols stir deep emotions. A nation's flag is not just another
piece of cloth to be burned or trampled on at will. In similar fashion,

the horse in Amish culture is not merely another animal. It evokes special memories and meanings. Amish symbols are not hollow; like flags, they are filled with emotions that embody the very essence of Amish identity. The Amish have refused to put these ethnic markers on the bargaining table. And, over the years, they have crystallized into durable symbols of Amish identity.

The Dialect of Separation

In many ways, people are captives of their own language. Vocabulary and grammatical structure impose images of reality in our consciousness. These definitions of reality, written in the mind of a child, are taken for granted as "the way things are." Because language defines the "way things are," it is the most subtle and powerful means of social control. Language also integrates and separates. It unites those who speak the common tongue and excludes outsiders.

The Amish speak English, German, and a local dialect known as Pennsylvania German or Pennsylvania Dutch. The dialect is the Amish native tongue and should not be confused with the Dutch language of the Netherlands. Originally a German dialect, Pennsylvania Dutch was spoken by Germanic settlers in southeastern Pennsylvania. The folk pronunciation of the word *German* (Deutsche) gradually became *Dutch* in English, and eventually the dialect became known as Pennsylvania Dutch.[2]

Except for the Amish and a few related plain groups, its use has declined in recent years. In Amish culture, the dialect is the language of work, family, friendship, play, and intimacy. Young children live in the world of the dialect until they learn English in the Amish school. Students learn to read, write, and speak English from their Amish teachers, who also learned it from Amish teachers. But the dialect prevails in friendly banter on the playground. The dialect functions primarily as an oral language. Idioms of the dialect are frequently mixed with German in Amish sacred writings.

By the end of the eighth grade, young Amish have developed basic competence in English, although it may be spoken with a slight accent. Adults are able to communicate in fluent English with their non-Amish neighbors. When talking among themselves, the Amish sometimes mix English words with the dialect, especially when discussing technical issues. Letters written between the Amish are often written in English, with salutations and occasional phrases in the dialect. Words such as *mandated* and *chaperone,* as well as abstract terms, are typically missing from their English vocabulary. A word such as *embalm* may be mispronounced *embam.* Competence in English varies directly with occupational roles and the frequency of interaction with English speakers. Amish businessmen, for example, develop an extensive English vocabulary. They talk about marketing strategies and use legal terminology with ease. But even they stumble when searching for English words to communicate religious ideas. Finally, with a tone of frustration, they say: "I could just say it much better in German." Such acknowledgment underscores the importance of the dialect in creating and perpetuating a different world view.

If English is a trade language and the dialect is the mother tongue, German is the language of the sacred. An Amish version of standard German is used for reading and writing religious documents. An editor of an Amish publication noted: "Our policy forbids the publishing of Amish church revered matter in English."[3] Scripture verses, church regulations, religious booklets, and sayings of respected leaders are usually printed in German. Although German is used to read the Bible, the *Martyrs Mirror*, and other inspirational materials, the ability to speak standard German varies considerably.[4] Church leaders speak and read German to the best of their ability. Preachers read from a German Bible or prayer book with the flavor of local idioms, but most sermons are in the dialect. A few English words may even slip in. One preacher, reciting the biblical story of the execution of John the Baptist, referred to Herod's "birthday party" in his sermon. Amish schools have been crucial in preserving the dialect and expanding the use of German. Thus, though all members of the community speak the dialect fluently, the use of written English and German varies considerably by training, occupation, intelligence, and personal motivation. A weekly Amish newspaper, *Die Botschaft* (The Message), and a monthly periodical, the *Diary*, are both published in English. Many Amish receive a daily newspaper and subscribe to the *Reader's Digest*.

The dialect preserves Amish identity in several ways. It provides a direct link to their religious roots. The Amish faith was forged in a Germanic context. Thus the Amish believe that the use of German and the dialect engenders sacred communion with God. The Bible, the *Martyrs Mirror*, and other religious materials can be read in the "original," sacred tongue. English is the language of the world, the verbal currency of an evil society. To offer prayers in English or conduct religious services in English is considered worldly. The dialect also functions as an oral depository for folklore, an essential vehicle for transporting Amish traditions. A shift to English as the primary tongue would erode oral traditions. Moreover, the dialect integrates the present with the European past.

The dialect also separates. Although most Amish can speak English, they are never quite at home with it. There are moments of hesitation when the Amish grope for an English translation or stumble on the vocabulary of an English speaker. It is difficult to tease, joke, dream, and communicate intimate emotions before mastering the nuances of a language. Retaining the dialect has been a prudent way of keeping the world at bay. It controls interaction with outsiders and stifles intimate social relationships with non-Amish neighbors. It also shields the Amish from written mass media, whose vocabulary is often beyond their grasp. Progressive Amish leaders and businessmen subscribe to magazines such as *Newsweek, U.S. News and World Report,* and *Farm Journal,* but the sophisticated vocabulary of such media keeps it out of the reach of many others. The dialect in all these ways obstructs the discourse with modernity.

Historically, English was viewed by the Amish as a symbol of high culture and worldly society, a sophisticated language at odds with the lowly spirit of Gelassenheit. The Amish note that liberal groups that leave their church eventually drop the German language and embrace English as their mother tongue. These progressive groups inevitably drift toward the social mainstream. Knowing that the dialect is essential for preserving their ethnic identity, the Amish have refused to concede it to modernity.

The Garb of Humility

The dress of the Amish, more than any other symbol, sets them apart. Unique dress styles have provided a constant source of symbolic separation for the Amish since their origin. By the late 1800s, observers identified plain dress and strict religious discipline as the key indicators of Amish identity.[5] As late as 1924, a scholar described Amish dress in great detail and then noted, in passing, that the use of automobiles, electric lights, and telephones was considered worldly.[6] As manufactured clothing became popular in the twentieth century, dress became the distinctive badge of Amish identity. Traditional clothing became a defensive tactic to sharpen their cultural separation. Other symbolic forms that set them apart today—such as horses, buggies, lanterns, and windmills—crystallized as the Amish responded to the mushrooming technology of the twentieth century.

Both Amish and Moderns dress for success, but the standards of success differ radically in the two cultures. In modern society, dress symbolizes individualism, social class, and wealth. It highlights the body, conveys messages of status, reflects one's niche in the larger culture, and garners social acceptance. In Amish society, dress signals Gelassenheit, submission to the collective order. Modern dress accentuates individual expression, whereas Amish dress enhances group solidarity.

As a symbolic language, dress communicates information about the self, the occasion, and group ties. In modern life, outfits are frequently changed to fit social settings, to project "fronts," to announce group membership, and to signal when one is "on" or "off" duty. Some clothing, such as a team jacket, serves as a group badge. Religious garments, such as a clerical robe, signal sacred roles or space. Uniforms announce occupational roles. The number of outfits in contemporary wardrobes reflects the complexity of modern social structure. Numerous roles and occasions require specialized outfits, ranging from swimming trunks and sweatpants to tuxedos. The simple Amish social structure requires few outfits. Amish dress is loosely organized around three social occasions: work, dress up, and church. A group's ability to dress its members in a "company uniform" reveals the strength and scope of the group's control. Because their entire world is sacred and they are always "on duty," the Amish always dress in uniform.

The Amish dress code serves a variety of social functions. The ethnic garb: (1) signals that a member has yielded to the collective order, (2) prevents dress from being used as a tool for self-enhancement, (3) promotes equality by keeping individualism in check, (4) creates a common consciousness that bolsters group identity, (5) increases social control because fellow members and outsiders relate to the Amish on the basis of ethnic membership, (6) projects a united front, which conceals variations in other areas of Amish practice, and (7) erects firm symbolic boundaries around the group—the equivalent of a cultural moat.

Giving up control over one's body and its presentation, ornamentation, and display is a fundamental offering—the supreme sign that the self has yielded to a higher authority. Dressing in prescribed clothing day after day is a public announcement of one's surrender to the supremacy of the group. Details of Amish dress provide subtle clues to an individual's conformity to church standards. The width of a hat brim, the length of hair, the length of a skirt, the size of a head covering, and the color of shoes and stockings all signal a member's compliance with group standards. Subtle variations quietly announce whether one is liberal or conservative, showing off or obeying the church, "jumping the fence" or falling in line.

Within Amish society, the form and color of dress signify sex, age, marital status, church membership, and leadership roles, as well as death and mourning. The language of dress enables rich communication without words. Common dress unites members—a twenty-four-hour reminder of identity and loyalty. Wearing ethnic clothing makes it easy to act, think, and feel "Amish" and impossible to fade into the mainstream. Dressed like their parents, children learn to act and think "Amish" from birth. Dress regulations have been encoded in the church's traditional customs and are usually not justified by moral or biblical arguments. The dress codes are simply accepted as "the way things are done among our people." Thoughtful leaders

Ethnic dress unites members and separates them from the non-Amish, as a crowd observes the filming of *Witness* in the village of Intercourse.

sometimes offer explanations based on modesty or simplicity. Central to both self and group identity, Amish dress is the language of belonging and loyalty.

The Woman's Wardrobe

Baby girls wear a head covering similar to that of adults when they are first brought to church at six weeks of age. At about the age of four, girls begin wearing an adult-style head covering.[7] The coverings are made of Swiss organdy and are always white, with one exception. From age thirteen until marriage, most girls wear a black covering when attending church services. The coverings vary slightly in style and size. Younger girls and more liberal women wear a covering with a larger back, narrower front, and longer, narrower tie strings. One member stated: "Ministers' wives and women age fifty and older wear the covering without the ruffle at the bottom of the back. Older women have the pleat through the middle of the back pressed in rather than sewn in. The covering is a symbol of subjection to God and to man. Amishwomen wear them, or at least a bandanna or scarf to cover the head at all times, especially while praying or in the presence of men."[8]

Small girls often wear their hair in braids, which do not hang loose but are fastened around the forehead. When the girls are eight or ten years of age, their hair is arranged into a bun at the back of the head. Adult women part their hair in the center and also wear it in a bun. Cutting or curling hair, shaving legs, and trimming eyebrows—viewed as irreverent tampering with God's creation—are prohibited by church regulations.

The dresses of little girls button in the back. Adult women close their dresses in the front with snap fasteners or straight pins. Sleeve lengths vary. Younger girls and more liberal women wear shorter skirts, lower necklines, and puffier sleeves. The skirts of older women may touch the top of their shoes, whereas those of younger girls are often just below the knees. Dresses are usually a solid color of gray, blue, green, purple, or wine. A black dress is worn by adult women to communion services, funerals, and to religious services during mourning periods (such periods may last as long as a year for close relatives).

Except for little girls at play, Amish females usually wear an apron over their skirts. A belt sewn at the top of the apron encircles the waist and is fastened with pins. The width of the belt varies from one to four inches; progressive women wear wider ones. Women also wear a cape that covers the top half of their dress. The cape is cut like a triangle, and its apex is fastened with pins at the waistline in back. The sides are brought over the shoulders, overlapped in front, and connected with pins.

A young girl begins wearing a cape and apron at about age eight. The cape and apron worn to church are white organdy, but those for other occasions are black. From age twelve to about forty, women wear the same color cape and dress. However, in church services, single girls wear a white cape and apron. At her wedding, the bride wears a white cape and apron, symbols of virginity. Single women wear a white cape and apron to church until about age thirty, when they begin wearing a colored cape and black apron, as do married women. After age forty a black cape and apron are worn over any color dress. Ministers' wives always wear a black cape and apron. Capes are worn mostly for dress, but aprons are worn at all times. Black stockings are worn by females, except babies under two years of age, who wear white ones. Teen-age girls and progressive women wear service-weight nylon stockings, but younger girls and older women often wear cotton stockings. Black tie shoes are usually worn. Brides and ministers' wives, as well as older women, always wear high shoes in

Two girls clean their shoes at the school door after recess in the fifties.

winter. In recent years, children, youth, and even some adults have begun wearing sneakers.

A shawl and bonnet complete the woman's distinctive wardrobe. Babies of both sexes wear a bonnet when they are first brought to church at six weeks of age. Little girls wear colored bonnets until age nine. Then they begin wearing black bonnets, as do adult women. Sunbonnets, however, may be colored. Ribbons tie the bonnet under the chin. The style of the woman's bonnet is fairly consistent, but slight differences in size signal traditional or progressive attitudes. There is a growing tendency for women to appear in public without a bonnet.

Woolen shawls are worn by Amish females of all ages—except girls, who usually wear a homemade coat for school. Black and rec-

An Amish teacher
with modern sneakers
and glove joins her
pupils in a game of
softball.

tangular, the shawl is draped over the shoulders and fastened in front at the neck with a hatpin or safety pin. A homemade woolen coat with a quilted lining is usually worn under the shawl by adult women. The coat is always black and is fastened with buttons or snaps in the front. Teens and some adults wear the coat without a shawl.

Most items in the Amish wardrobe are homemade. A member described the process: "The Amish mother sews all the dresses, capes, aprons, and head coverings for the girls and herself as well as the pants and shirts for the men and boys. Most of the underwear is bought except some slips and panties may be homemade for the girls. Men's overcoats and dress suits are made by a seamstress, usually an older single Amish lady who makes a living by sewing for other folks."[9]

Outfitting the Men

Baby boys wear dresses until about age one. Progressive mothers may outfit their child in pants and shirt by four months, whereas traditional mothers often wait until the boy is fifteen months old. The boy's first pants have buttonholes at the waistline, which fasten to large buttons on the shirt. At about four years of age, the boys wear adult-styled suits, which include a vest, suspenders, coat, hat, and "broadfall" trousers. The hair of Amish males is cut about even with the earlobe. Hair is not parted, and bangs are cut in front about halfway down the forehead. Sideburns without a beard are prohibited for members. Men shave until marriage, at which time they wear a beard, which in many ways serves the symbolic function of a wedding ring in the larger culture. Single men over forty also grow a beard. An untrimmed, full beard from ear to ear is required for adult men. The upper lip is shaved even after marriage, because the mustache, once associated with military officers, is forbidden by the church.

For males, the distinctive wide-brimmed hat is the foremost tag of Amish identity. The hat is to be worn whenever a male is outside the house. Amish boys begin wearing a hat at about age two. Straw hats are worn in the summer; black felt hats, in the winter. At about age ten, boys begin wearing a felt "telescope" hat, with creases pressed into the crown's inner edge. Little boys, older men, and ministers wear a black hat with a plain or rounded crown.

Sunglasses, gloves, and scarfs are worn seasonally. Wire hook-and-eye fasteners close the suit coats and vests worn at church services. Buttons are worn on work coats. In some cases, Velcro is used as a fastener. Shirts are usually pocketless. "Broadfall" trousers without hip pockets or zippers are the norm for males of all ages. The wide opening on the front of the pants is closed with buttons. Trousers are held by suspenders, for belts are prohibited. Men and boys wear a black sack coat for work. Men wear a frock coat with divided tails for church and special occasions. Boys receive a frock coat at age sixteen. A black vest is usually worn under the coat. In summer months, males may attend church or other dress-up occasions without a coat, but rarely without a vest. Vest, hat, and suspenders, minimal markers of ethnic identity, must never be left behind.

Although black is the dominant color for men, dress shirts are typically green, purple, blue, or wine. The color of death, however, is white. Both males and females are buried in white. Special white pants and a vest are made for the man; he is also dressed in his best white shirt. A special white dress is fashioned for the woman, and she also wears her white bridal cape and apron.

Dressing over the Decades

It is impossible to reconstruct the history of Amish dress. Some aspects can be traced back to European peasant traditions, others to early American customs. Some traits of Amish garb simply gelled over the years as the church tried to remain separate from the world, preempt pride, avoid fashions, and preserve tradition. The Amish dress code is justified by appeals to tradition, as simply the way things are, in a similar way that ties for men and skirts for women are justified in the larger culture. Modesty is often given as a reason for many of the practices. With few arguments to defend particular practices, Amish dress is seen as a sacred order that has, for whatever purpose, been blessed by the church and wisely passed on by the forebears of the faith. Conforming to the code is a redemptive ritual that binds one to the group and reveals a willingness to yield to history, to church, to God—a yielding that places one in touch with divine mysteries.

Some Amish leaders and thoughtful lay people offer religious reasons for some of the practices. A member stated:

There is significance in the Amish garb other than mere tradition. The broadfall trousers worn by the men are designed for the sake of modesty. Suspenders are worn so that the trousers need not fit so tightly. The head covering is a symbol of the woman's subjection to the man and to God. It is worn at all times, especially in the presence of men and while praying. The cape is designed for the nursing mother and the apron for the pregnant woman. So that no woman has to expose herself, all women wear clothes designed in this manner. The length of the hair for men and the width of the hat brim are established for the sake of uniformity.[10]

Although there have been minor changes in Amish dress over the last century, styles have been amazingly resilient. The dress code became more standardized after the turn of the century. An elderly member reported that around 1910 men wore different colors of corduroy trousers—brown, gray, and blue—and they rarely had a suit coat that matched their pants. Gradually, male dress suits became a uniform black. A sharper line between dress and work clothes emerged after the Depression. Until this time, many males had only one pair of shoes and would merely polish them before going to church. The separation of work and dress clothes reflects a growing distinction between work and other activities, as well as a more affluent lifestyle.

Although the broad contours of the dress code are firmly established, minor variations abound. Church leaders are unhappy that boys occasionally go hatless. Some girls have coverings that do not cover their ears, and strings that are rarely tied except for church. One layman worries about the shrinking size and shape of the head covering worn by teen-age girls. He believes it is a pattern that might follow the trend of some Mennonite groups, where, as the strings come off, more hair is exposed and soon the covering shrinks to a small "flat doily" on top of the head. However, he said: "We still have the strings on and the ear covered by the corner of the cap."

Some young men use their hair to taunt church authority and assert their independence. In the fifties and sixties, teen-age boys cut their hair short to defy church standards. More recently, young males have worn long hair to stir the ire of Amish elders. Several members date the flip-flop in hair length to the popularity of the Beatles. Leaders cite the change as an example of worldly influence. A minister stated: "We used to have trouble with short hair and now we have to tell them about long hair. As the world changes so we have to change our teaching."

The time when young men begin wearing the beard has also changed. In 1880, the beard was a requirement at baptism. By 1920, it was no longer required at baptism, but a young man had to have one before he could apply for marriage. Today the beard symbolizes marriage rather than church membership. Now young men are expected to have a "full stand" by the time of the first communion service *after* they are married, usually the spring communion. In the fifties, young men who trimmed their beards in defiance of church rules had to make public confessions. "Today," one leader said, "the beard isn't much of an issue since so many outside people have one. But we do have trouble with long hair, sideburns, and even the mustache sometimes. Some boys will go away deer hunting for a week and come back with a mustache on and be daring enough to come to church with it."

Amish dress symbolizes group membership at a farm sale in 1985.

Deer hunters have conformed to hunting regulations by wearing fluorescent orange vests and hats over their black coats and broad-
rimmed hats, making a colorful confluence of modernity and tradition.

One of the more subtle changes in dress has been a shift to
double- and single-knit polyester materials. There are no church restrictions on the type of material used for clothing, with the exception
of prints and certain colors. The acceptance of synthetic materials
saves considerable labor in washing and ironing. The traditional
styles and colors maintain a standardized "front" in the public eye.
Moreover, the use of common patterns on the front stage allows the
latest types of synthetic materials to be adopted back stage without
alarm. Striking a bargain, the Amish have accepted labor-saving, synthetic materials, but have insisted on making their own clothing so as
not to lose symbolic patterns, which protect their ethnic identity.

A threat to Amish identity appeared in the seventies, when a federal regulation required employees in construction industries to wear
protective hard hats. Although most Amish were in farm-related occupations, employees of public construction firms in several states were

affected by the regulation. The broad-brimmed hat served as the prime badge of ethnicity for men. Church leaders, dismayed by the regulation, feared that Amish men in nonconstruction jobs might also begin leaving their hats at home.

A Lancaster representative for the Amish National Steering Committee made several trips to Washington, D.C., to plead the case of the Amish with some of the "top men," including the secretary of labor and industry. The Amish representative explained to government officials that Amish dress is part of their religious testimony against worldliness and hence wearing the traditional hat was a religious issue. A firsthand Amish witness reported that the secretary asked the Amish representative to pass his hat around the table of bureaucrats. When it reached the secretary's hands, he tested its rigidity and wryly remarked: "That hat is pretty stiff by itself, it is no use in us fighting you. We'll see what we can do." The secretary's staff designed a written exemption form to excuse males from the regulation if they signed and presented it to their employer. And so, according to Amish lore, the traditional hat triumphed over bureaucratic regulation. Whether the negotiated settlement was indeed a concession by modernity or merely a playful quirk in the halls of bureaucracy is uncertain.

Although Amish dress is important throughout the life cycle, it is especially scrutinized at the time of baptism. Families vary a great deal in their enforcement of church regulations, but at baptism everyone must conform. One minister estimated that half of the families do not have to change the dress of their children at baptism. "But then," he said, "there are a portion that have to be kind of coaxed, kind of brought into line." The minister went on to state: "We have to work harder to get our young ladies in line with regulations than we do with the boys. Our girls get jobs away from home in restaurants and their coverings get smaller, dresses are shorter, stockings are almost flesh-colored, and the shoes get fancy."

Hair and dress styles are a barometer of church loyalty. A minister noted: "You can single your people out, your families out, which way they are leaning by the cut of their hair. After twelve years of age, you can just about tell what they're thinking by their hair. You can almost tell which boys are driving an automobile by the cut of their hair; they have it shingled, you know." "How a child is dressed," said one mother, "gives away the mother's heart."

The Amish version of dressing for success follows a different formula than the modern version, but, in both cultures, dress matters and communicates. In modern culture, dress fads, designer labels, and seasonal fashions provide symbols for conforming to consumer subcultures. In this sense, both modern and Amish wardrobes are tools of social conformity. There is a tinge of irony here, however. At first glance, the Amish seem preoccupied with dress. Their dress code appears complicated and restrictive to the outsider. This code does restrict individuality, but it also frees the Amish from the burden of choice. They do not sort through numerous outfits in a frenzy each morning or spend endless hours shopping to stay abreast of current fads. So, ironically, although the Amish appear to be engulfed by dress, they in fact spend much less time, money, and worry on clothing than do Moderns. Conformity to prescribed dress standards not only unites them and marks off their social turf, it also frees individuals from anxiety and incessant choice.

The Hoofbeats of Tradition

The horse and buggy are silhouetted on road signs, tourist brochures, and billboards as the archetypes of Amish identity. As society turned to cars and tractors in the twentieth century, the horse, by default, became a prime symbol of Amish life. Although the Amish do not worship the horse with cultic rituals or fetish charms, it does approximate a sacred symbol in several ways.

Lighter road horses pull buggies to town, and draft horses tow farm equipment across fields. The driving horses are often obtained from commercial race tracks. The heavier workhorses and mules are bought from jockeys, from horse dealers, or at public auction. Horseback riding is generally discouraged, because it borders on a form of worldly sport. Although young people occasionally ride horseback, the horse is primarily used for work.

The typical Amish farm family has one or two driving horses and six to eight horses or mules for field work. Families who no longer live on a farm have one or two horses for transportation. New Amish homes, built along rural roads or in villages, can be identified by their small horse barns. Although the Amish are not required to own a horse, it is an assumed mode of travel because car ownership is forbidden. Single adult sisters, for example, living together in a village home, stable their driving horse in a barn at the back of their property. Parents will often buy a driving horse for their son's sixteenth birthday. A good driving horse costs about $1,200.

As a symbol of Amish culture, the horse articulates several key values: tradition, time, limits, nature, and sacrifice. As a sacred link with history, the horse is hard evidence that modern Amish have not acquiesced to progress. It heralds the triumph of tradition and signals that one has been faithful to ethnic tradition. A counter symbol to the worldliness embodied in tractors and cars, the horse is tangible proof that the Amish have not sold out to the glamour and glitter of high technology. The horse, a striking symbol of nonconformity, separates the Amish from the modern world and anchors them in another one.

Some Amish display worldliness with fancy harnesses and decorative tack. Over the years, the church has forbidden such ornamentation in hopes of keeping the horse undefiled. Safeguarding the horse culture is a sure way of preserving the continuity of tradition. As one obeys the church and yields to communal wisdom, one offers a holy sacrifice. In this way, the horse becomes a sacred symbol.

Horses not only symbolize the slower pace of Amish society; they actually retard its speed. It takes longer to plow with horses. Driving time on the road increases fivefold. A horse culture places other limits on social life as well. Daily travel distance is drastically reduced. At best, on level roads, travel is limited to twenty-five miles a day by horse and buggy. Hilly terrain imposes additional limits. By restricting travel, the use of the horse curtails the outward expansion of the settlement and holds the community together. It intensifies social interaction in the small, local church districts.

Horses impose other curbs as well. Amish farmers yield to nature's clock, because horses cannot be used in fields at night. Using horses and mules for field work requires additional labor and slows farm work. It restricts the number of acres that can be plowed and controls both the size and the number of farms that one family can cultivate. Modern farmers with large tractors can till several hundred acres, whereas the typical Amish farm has less than fifty acres. The horse limits the expansionist tendencies of modernity. In all these ways, the hoofbeats of Amish horses slow the pace of Amish society.

The horse is also important in other ways. The Amish have always been a people of the land. By living close to nature, they believe they stay in touch with God. The Amish feel that the rhythms of nature, the changing seasons, and the struggle with weather all provide opportunities to experience divine presence. The horse preserves this link with nature in the midst of modernity. Horse care brings daily contact with nature—birth, death, illness, grazing, excrement, and unpredictable temperaments—a dialogue with the Creator. The horse has also held the Amish close to nature by keeping them out of cities.[11] With the rise of Amish shops and all their technological sophistication, the horse will likely become even more important. It may preserve one of the few bonds with nature for the rising commercial class.

The horse signals sacrifice and inconvenience. It takes time to hitch and unhitch horses. They must be fed morning and evening. Stables must be cleaned, and manure hauled to the fields. Horses must be shoed regularly. They also kick and bite. In some towns, it is difficult to find hitching posts. Driving a horse on modern highways is dangerous. Dependence on the horse requires daily sacrifice, a cogent reminder that identity and tradition supersede convenience in Amish life.

A mother makes her weekly trip to the bank in a spring wagon. Many Amishwomen are adept at handling horses.

The use of workhorses has taken an ironic twist in recent years. In speed and power, they obviously lag behind tractors. However, a different picture emerges when the financial return on the capital investment of small farms is considered. Draft horses have actually gained on tractors as the cost of modern farm machinery has soared since 1960. If labor costs are subtracted, Amish farmers, at least on small farms, are cost competitive with modern farmers, who use $40,000 tractors and $80,000 combines to harvest crops. The Amish contend that on small farms the horse is superior. An Amish farmer said: "Considering prices of grain, the horse farmers can produce milk, hogs, and poultry cheaper than the large tractor farmers."[12] Because horses pack the ground less than tractors, Amish farmers can begin plowing earlier in the spring. And though horses plow slowly, modern farmers marvel at how the Amish always seem to get their planting and harvesting done on time, if not first.[13]

The horse creates another benefit in Amish society—a subculture filled with lore and labor. Horse stories abound. Articles on horses appear in Amish publications. Horse tales preserve and perpetuate this distinctive symbol of Amish identity. But more importantly, the horse culture creates jobs. Cottage industries that manufacture, sell, and repair horse equipment provide jobs for many Amish.

As a front stage symbol, the horse projects a public image of conservatism, which conveniently camouflages differences in income, lifestyle, hobbies, and worldly involvements on the backstage of Amish life. The Amish businessman who travels in a hired car all week supervising a multimillion-dollar business also bends to tradition by driving his horse to Sunday worship services. Progressive Amish who read *Newsweek*, limit the size of their families, and landscape their homes can nod with affinity to conservative Amish as their horses pass each other on the road. And though the conservatives may not eat in modern kitchens, play baseball on Sunday, or dine in restaurants, they can return a cordial greeting. The horse offers compelling proof that the Amish are still Amish while permitting the benign neglect of worldly behaviors in other areas of Amish life.

The horse slows things down, imposes limits, and symbolizes some of the deepest meanings of Amish life. Riding in a horse-drawn carriage is a visible symbol of ethnic identity, unmistakable to insider and outsider alike. As a good ethnic badge, the horse both integrates and separates. It leaves no doubt about the boundary lines of Amish society. As the blinders over the horse's eyes shield out roadside distractions, so the horse has blinded Amish society from worldly distractions and kept it bound to tradition. It would be foolish to concede the horse to modernity. A cherished symbol that has served the community well in practical ways should not be placed carelessly on the bargaining table. The Amish have refused to concede the horse, but they have been willing to negotiate under the table with the car and tractor.

The Carriage of Simplicity

The carriage symbolizes the essence of Amish identity in several ways. Some other plain churches have horses for pleasure, work, and riding, but not an Amish carriage. Like the car in modern society, the Amish buggy provides conveyance and performs symbolic functions. Six different vehicles are used by the Lancaster Amish: the open buggy, the spring wagon, the market wagon, the cab wagon, the two-wheeled cart, and the standard carriage. Each is pulled on the road with a single driving horse and rolls on wooden wheels wrapped in a steel band. Sleighs are also used in winter.[14]

The term *buggy*, often used for many of these vehicles, technically only designates the open, one-seat vehicle. The open buggy, sometimes erroneously called "the courting buggy," is used by young and old alike, but its use has declined in recent years. The spring wagon, so called for its extra spring suspension, is an open wagon used for hauling heavy supplies on the road. The market wagon, an enclosed carriage, is the Amish version of the station wagon, with a tailgate that swings upward, a removable back seat, and heavier suspension. It traditionally was used to haul produce to city markets. Its roof and enclosed sides protect both driver and produce from the weather. The cab wagon, the Amish edition of the pickup truck, has an enclosed cab for the driver and an open bed for hauling materials. The basic and most widely used vehicle is the standard carriage. Having undergone several changes in the twentieth century, the standard carriage today is a gray, enclosed, boxlike, two-seat vehicle.[15]

The carriage functions as the family car for most Amish families. Its two seats may carry six or more passengers. Sliding doors with glass windows provide openings on both sides near the front of the carriage. The front is enclosed by a glass windshield. In contrast to design fads in modern cars, the exterior form of the carriage has resisted change. Gray became the standard color in the early twentieth century, and, with the exception of the enclosed front, the basic form and style were also shaped at that time. Today's carriage is equipped with battery-operated front lights, turn signals, flashing rear lights, and a large triangle reflector. All these modern accouterments are required by state law.

Older carriages were open in the front and had no dashboard, windshield, or sliding doors. Roll curtains covered the open doorways, and a canvas tarp was fastened across the front to shield the driver from flying mud. Sliding doors and permanent windshields, called storm fronts, began appearing on a few carriages in the late twenties. The expanding settlement required longer trips in harsh weather, which encouraged the use of enclosed carriages. Storm fronts and sliding doors on carriages eased into use over some thirty years and were officially permitted in the sixties. As the enclosed carriage gained acceptance, the open front became a symbol of conservatism. Ministers were not permitted to enclose the fronts of their carriages. However, by the eighties some ministers with small children were permitted to have enclosed carriages. The conservative districts in the settlement's southern region have been slower to accept the fully enclosed carriage. In the mid-eighties, some bishops in this area permitted enclosed carriages as long as a family also kept an open-front carriage for church services.

The Symbolic Buggy

The Amish buggy serves a variety of social functions. Its gray color and boxlike form are public symbols of Amish identity. Gray symbolizes Gelassenheit, for it quietly blends into the immediate surroundings; it is the unpretentious color of modesty. Ironically, however, there is nothing quite as obtrusive on a modern highway as a horse-drawn vehicle. When some buggy makers began producing darker buggies in the thirties, Amish leaders insisted on the traditional gray as the best expression of Gelassenheit. There was another reason as well for staying with gray: Old Order Mennonites had blacktop buggies. Retaining gray was the surest way of preserving Amish identity for tourist, neighbor, and fellow Amish alike.[16]

Like garb, the buggy is a visible ethnic badge that constrains social interaction in public. Stepping out of a buggy in front of a store is a public announcement of one's ethnic identity. The carriage provides a mobile stage for enacting the drama of separation. On the road, the mobile stage separates the Amish from the larger world. With few windows, the ethnic travelers are barricaded from the outside world, even while in transit. When the Amish venture into public, their garb and carriage control social interaction. This social harness not only restrains them from assuming public roles and blending into the social mainstream but also influences the content of conversation.

Whereas the car in modern society accentuates social status and inequality, the Amish carriage is a symbolic equalizer. It signals the egalitarian nature of Amish society. The church has staunchly prohibited ornamentation and ostentatious display on buggies. Although there are minor variations, carriages are quite uniform. People of all sorts—farmer, homemakers, businessman, laborer, and millionaire alike—must drop the trappings of status and prestige as they step into similar buggies. And, for the moment at least, the carriage levels them symbolically. Unlike the car in modern society, the Amish carriage imposes a community standard that transcends individual choice, preference, and status.

Although the carriage suppresses individuality, it is not unusual to find the carriages owned by teen-agers decorated with creative designs of plastic reflectors. A leader described some buggies owned by Amish youth:

> Some have wall-to-wall carpeting, insulated woolly stuff all around the top, a big dashboard, glove compartment, speedometer, clock, stereo radio, buttons galore, and lights and reflectors all over the place. There's one that even has little lights all the way around the bottom. They even have perfumed things hanging up front, and at Christmas time, some have tinsel and little bells. If they have the money, that's what they do and that's pride. Some of the members even have some of this stuff, but not a radio. These are Cadillacs and some members don't put their Cadillacs away even though they get a little faded.

The carriage serves as a boundary marker in many ways.

On the outside, at least, the carriage is a social statement that summarizes Amish values: separation, simplicity, frugality, tradition, equality, and humility. The carriage protests the fads and fashions of modern transportation. Its stark rectangular form, which clashes with the sleek styles of modern cars, symbolizes the stalwart nature of Amish society. It epitomizes local control, for its form and accessories are governed by local tradition rather than by market research conducted by the giant car makers. Like the horse, the carriage has spawned a variety of Amish shops. These shops manufacture, repair, and service carriages. Locally manufactured, the carriage transcends the flux of oil prices, imports, and labor strikes. It is, in short, a collective statement of Amish values and identity.

The Changing Buggy

On the outside, the carriage appears resilient to change. But there have been discreet intrusions of modernity beneath its austere shell. These changes in the buggy are, in many ways, a paradigm of social change in Amish society at large. Whereas the external image remains firm, various changes have penetrated the subterranean level—some forced by legal requirements, and others welcomed by default. The buggy has been a bargaining table of sorts where the forces of tradition and technology have waged a quiet debate. In the early twentieth century, Amish carriages were rarely driven at night. When they were, a kerosene lantern provided light. After World War I, enterprising Amish youth began hooking up electric lights, powered by small batteries. Church leaders were adamantly opposed to the use of electric lights, believing they would speed the use of lights in homes and that the lights made the buggies look too worldly, too much like cars. Upon baptism, many youth had to scrap the electric lights on their buggies.

In the twenties, to the church's consternation, state laws required electric lights on vehicles at night. Oral historians report that the use of lights became a contentious issue, because church rules forbade them. The church gradually acquiesced to the forces of modernization, and, in the thirties, most Amish carriages traveling at night had battery-powered lights. In the fifties and seventies, flashing red lights and large reflective triangles, respectively, were required by state law.[17] For a people who detest publicity, these requirements were most unwelcome. Flashing lights and bright triangles mocked the modest spirit of Gelassenheit. But acknowledging the need for safety and respecting the public welfare, the Amish agreed to use them. In 1987 state legislators made a slight concession by permitting the flashing lights to be turned off during the daytime.[18]

Safety concerns prevailed, but public officials did not want to run the Amish out of town, for they were becoming a prime tourist attraction. So, over the years, a bargain was struck. The Amish could drive buggies on public roads without paying gas taxes or license fees but they would carry the trappings of modernity—electric lights, turn signals, flashers, and fluorescent triangles. Amish buggies would not be inspected or licensed, and their operators would not need a driver's license. Steel horseshoes could continue to chop up public roads at considerable expense to taxpayers. This was tolerated because the Amish were attracting tourist revenues and boosting agricultural productivity.[19] The Amish would contribute nothing to the public road system, apart from regular taxes. Tourists would pay gas taxes and spend enough money to offset the Amish "freeloading." Representatives on either side of the bargaining table knew they had struck a good deal.

The buggy is a metaphor of social change in Amish society. Although the buggy's exterior has stabilized over the years, its interior has undergone a variety of discreet changes. Hidden to the outsider, these discreet changes make today's buggy a rather up-to-date vehicle. In addition to the safety features forced by state law, other technological enhancements have slipped into the carriage. Beginning in the mid-seventies, fiberglass replaced wood in the bottom shell of many buggy frames, as well as in the shafts that are connected to the horse's harness. Vinyl tops, in gray of course, cover the newer buggies. The wheels spin on modern ball bearings, and hydraulic brakes slow down the carriage. Some carriages have battery-operated windshield wipers. Thermopane windows, which deter fogging in cold weather, are also an option. The young male purchasing his first buggy can select carpet in four colors and several textures. He also has a choice of at least six colors of upholstery in two textures of crushed velvet. Other colors and textures can be ordered by catalogue. These modernized buggies cost about $2,500 and will last from ten years to a lifetime, depending on their use and care. The Amish, in essence, have refused to concede the traditional form and color on the carriage's exterior but have accepted modern technology under the surface. In this sense, the buggy is a paradigm of social change in Amish society. Some changes are induced by legal regulations but others, by default, sneak in behind the stalwart public symbols of tradition.

Thus, dialect, dress, horse, and carriage—symbols of integration and separation—provide the community with a common currency. They are daily reenactments of Gelassenheit—of surrender to communal values. Unlike symbols reserved for historical festivities, dialect, dress, horse, and carriage are concrete expressions of ethnicity which shape everyday behavior in real ways. They link the subculture together in a common history and a common mission against worldliness. As armaments of defense, they draw the boundary lines between church and world. As badges of ethnicity, they announce Amish identity to insider and outsider alike. They are sacred symbols, which the Amish have guarded vigilantly. Their public visibility conveniently masks a multitude of discreet changes on the backstage of Amish life.

4

The Social Architecture of Amish Society

> Our discipline thrives on the man walking behind the plow, not the man traveling by train all over the country trying to build a superstructure.
> —Amish farmer

Social Building Blocks

Social life is shaped not only by cultural beliefs and symbolic meanings but also by patterns of behavior. Societies, as well as buildings, have distinctive architectural styles. Like building blocks, social relations are arranged together in unique ways by different groups. In some societies males dominate, whereas in others females do, and in still others neither dominates. Each set of human arrangements has a structure, a distinctive social architecture. Growing up in an Amish family with dozens of first cousins nearby is quite different from living in a modern nuclear family with two cousins living five hundred miles apart. Child-rearing practices in Amish families, where both parents usually work at home, differ radically from dual-career families whose children play in day-care centers. A society's architectural design shapes human behavior in profound ways. What features distinguish the social architecture of Amish society? What is the organizational shape of Gelassenheit?

Demographic factors, birth rates, sex ratios, marital status, and family size are the building blocks of a society's social structure. Table 4-1 compares the demographic differences between the Amish and non-Amish population in Lancaster County. The Amish are more likely than their neighbors to marry, live in larger households, terminate school earlier, and engage in farming. A striking feature of Amish society is the large proportion (53 percent) of people under the age of eighteen. With only 5 percent of its members over sixty-five, Amish life tilts toward child rearing. Schools, rather than retirement villages, dominate the social landscape.

Table 4-1 Demographic Characteristics of the Amish and Non-Amish Population in Lancaster County

	Amish (%)	Non-Amish (%)
Sex		
Male	47	48
Female	53	52
Age		
Under 18 years	53	28
18–44 years	32	40
45–64	9	20
65 and over	5	12
Marital Status of Adults[a]		
Single	23	39
Married	77	61
Education		
Eighth grade or less	100	23
High school attendance	—	17
High school graduate	—	37
More than high school	—	10
College diploma or more	—	13
Occupation		
Professional	—	27
Farming	64	4
Household Size		
Single-person households	7	20
Mean number of people per household	5.0	2.8
Mean Family Size		
Number of children and adults	8.6	3.3

Sources: Amish profile of 382 adults (eighteen years and older) described in Appendix A. 1980 U.S. Census summarized by the Lancaster County Planning Commission.
[a] Eighteen years and older.

The individualization of modern society, characterized by spiraling percentages of single people and single-parent homes, is largely absent from Amish society. Whatever the Amish do, they do together. Only 7 percent of Amish households are single-person units, compared to 20 percent for the county. Virtually all of the single-person households adjoin other Amish homes. In fact, 43 percent of all households are on the same property as another Amish household. Many of these double homes are farmhouses with a smaller adjacent house for grandparents. Five people live in the average Amish household—nearly double the county rate of 2.8. The vast majority of Amish reside in a household with a half-dozen other people, or at least live adjacent to one. Moreover, additional members of the extended family live across the road or beyond the next field.

Age and Sex Roles

Age and sex roles are essential building blocks in Amish society. The Amish identify four stages of childhood: babies, little children, scholars, and young people.[1] The term *little children* is used for children between the time that they begin walking and until they begin school. Children between the ages of six and fifteen are often called *scholars. Young people*, from mid-teens to marriage, explore their independence by joining informal youth groups that crisscross the settlement.

Social power increases with age. In a rural society where children follow the occupations of their parents, the elderly provide valuable advice. Younger generations turn to them for their expertise in treating an earache, making pie dough, training a horse, predicting a frost, buying a cow. In a slowly changing society, the seasoned judgment of wise elders is esteemed by younger members. This contrasts sharply with rapidly changing societies, in which children often teach new technological skills to their parents. The power of age also engulfs the Amish church, where the words of an older minister count more than those of a younger one. The chairman of the ordained leaders is traditionally the oldest bishop. Wisdom accumulated by experience, rather than professional or technical competence, is the wedge of power in Amish society.

While power increases progressively with age, sex role distinctions are also a prime source of inequality in Amish society. In the realm of church, work, and community, the male voice carries more influence than the female one. Age and sex combine to produce a patriarchal hierarchy that gives older men the most social clout and younger females the least.

Amish families are organized around traditional sex roles. As in most marriages, a variety of power equations emerges, depending on the personalities of the partners. For the most part, the Amish husband is seen as the spiritual head of the home. He is responsible for its religious welfare and has the final word on matters related to the church and the outside world. The husband's role requires him to deal with strangers that appear on the Amish homestead. Among farming families, husbands organize the farm operation and supervise the work of children in barns and fields. Some husbands assist their wives with gardening, lawn care, and child care, but others do little. Amish children are usually born at home with the assistance of a certified midwife. The husband is often nearby to welcome the new child.[2] One father was called a "good Christian husband" because "he starts and tends the fires in the stove and helps with the children." Husbands rarely help with household work—washing, cooking, canning, sewing, mending, cleaning. The visible authority of the husband varies by household, but Amish society is primarily patriarchal and vests final authority for moral and social life in the male role.

Feminism has not changed the role of Amishwomen. Amish wives believe that, in the divine order of things, they are expected to submit to their husband's authority, but that does not mean they are docile.[3] Entrusted with the responsibility of raising a large family, they become efficient managers. Married women rarely have full-time jobs outside the home. In fact, only 3 percent of married women hold part-time jobs away from home. Even with ample help from children, it is difficult to manage a household of eight or more people without electrical can openers, blenders, mixers, dishwashers, microwave ovens, clothes dryers. In addition to providing child care, the wife normally oversees the garden, preserves food, cooks, cleans, washes, sews, mends, supervises yard work. Many women mow their lawns with push mowers, without engines. Moreover, those who live on a farm often assist with barn chores, milking cows, gathering eggs, pulling tobacco plants in the spring, stripping leaves from tobacco stalks in the winter. The work is hard and the hours are long, but there is quiet satisfaction in nourishing thriving families, tending productive gardens, canning fruit, baking pies, sewing colorful quilts, and watching grandchildren find their place in the Amish world. There are also pleasant moments of reprieve, a quilting "frolic," a sale, a wedding, and, of course, perpetual visiting.

Women are able to vote in church business meetings and nominate men for ministerial duties. They do not, however, participate in the community's formal power structure as ordained leaders or as members of special committees. Virtually all Amish schoolteachers are single women, but they are also on the fringe of the formal leadership structure. Without the prod of economic forces, labor-saving changes have come more slowly in the kitchen than in the barn. The ban on electricity has, of course, eliminated many appliances from Amish homes. Washing machines powered by gas engines, air pressure, or hydraulic pressure are widely used. Treadle sewing machines are typical. Some sewing machines are powered by air pressure. The kitchens and bathrooms in newer Amish houses have a modern appearance, with Formica counters, vinyl floor coverings, and fine cabinetry. Gas stoves and refrigerators of recent vintage have eliminated wood cookstoves and iceboxes, although kerosene space heaters are still used. Permanent-press fabrics, disposable diapers, cake mixes, and the latest cleaning detergents have lightened the load of household work. Nevertheless, some Amishwomen think the acceptance of labor-saving devices has favored the men.

One young woman described the tilted balance of power in detail:

> The joke among us women is that the men make the rules so that's why more modern things are permitted in the barn than in the house. The women have no say in the rules. Actually, I think the main reason is the men make the living and we don't make a living in the house. So you have to go along with what they need out there. You know, if the public health laws call for it, you have to have it. In the house you don't. Even my Dad says that he thinks the Amishwomen get the brunt of it all around. They have so many children and are expected to help out with the milking. Some help for two hours with the milking from beginning to end and they have five little children. That's all right if a man helps them in the house and puts the children to bed, but a lot of them don't. I don't think it's fair that we have the push mowers to mow the lawns with. It is hard work on some of these lawns. We keep saying that if the men would mow the lawns there would be engines on them, and I am sure there would be. Years ago they used to mow the hay fields with an old horse mower, but now they have engines on the field mowers so it goes easier for the horses, but they don't care about the women.

It would be wrong to conclude that Amishwomen are discontent. They are not liberated by modern standards, but their roles are stable and well-defined. They know who they are and what is expected of them. One husband said: "A wife is not a servant; she is the queen and the husband is the king."

As self-employed people, Amish wives, ironically, have greater control over their work and daily affairs than do many modern women who hold full-time clerical and nonprofessional jobs. Unfettered by the pressure to succeed in a career, Amishwomen devote their energies to family living. And while their work is hard, it is *their* work and it brings as much, if not more, satisfaction than a professional career. The Amish see the professional woman as a negative role model, a distortion of God's created order. Their role models are other Amishwomen who have managed their families well. Happiness, after all, depends on one's values and social point of reference. Amishwomen succeed well in comparison with their reference group—other Amishwomen—and are relatively happy. Liberated women in modern society, often burdened by conflicting role expectations and strong pressures to excel professionally, may experience greater anxiety over their roles than unliberated Amishwomen.

Family Ties

When Amish leaders tally up the size of their churches, they count families instead of individuals.[4] The family, the keystone of Amish society, is large in size and influence. Amish youth marry between the ages of twenty-two and twenty-five, on a Tuesday or Thursday in November, after the harvest season comes to a close. It is rare for someone under the age of twenty-one to be married. Marriage is highly esteemed, and raising a family is the professional career of Amish adults. Nine out of ten adults are married. Marriage vows are rarely broken. In extreme cases, couples may live apart, but divorce is taboo. Divorced people are automatically excommunicated.

Believing that birth control is tampering with God's will, couples yield to the law of nature and produce large families.[5] Including parents and children, the average family has 8.6 members, compared to the county norm of 3.3. By age forty-five, the typical Amishwoman has given birth to 7.1 children, whereas her modern neighbors average 2.8. Death and disease reduce the number, so completed families average 6.6 children. Slightly over 13 percent of Amish families have 10 or more children, and while Amish children are numerous, the expense of their upbringing is relatively low. There are no orthodontia payments, swimming pool memberships, tennis lessons, stereos, summer camps, sports cars, college tuitions, or designer clothes.[6] Amish children assume daily chores by five or six years of age, and their responsibilities in the barn and house grow rapidly. They are not seen as economic burdens but welcomed as blessings from the Lord and as members who will contribute their fair share to the family economy.

The power of the family extends beyond sheer numbers. The family's scope, influence, and control dwarfs that of the modern nuclear family. Amish life is spent in the context of the family. Social functions in modern families, from birth to death, from eating to leisure, are often staged outside the home. In contrast, Amish activities are anchored at home. Children are usually born there. They play at home, and school is within walking distance. By age fourteen, children work full-time at home. Amish children are taught by their extended family, not by television, babysitters, popular magazines, or nursery school teachers. Teen-age recreational activities, such as sledding, swimming, skating, baseball, volleyball, barn tag, and corner ball, are centered at or near home, without admission fees.

Young couples are married at home. Church services rotate from home to home. Meals are eaten at home. In recent years church leaders have urged families not to eat in restaurants. Social events, singings, "sisters' days," quilting parties, and work "frolics" are staged at home. Occasionally, small groups of men slip away for a day of deep-sea fishing or, on the sly, even play a game of golf, but the

Amish boys walk toward the house for a wedding.

majority of Amish recreation is close to home and nature.[7] Adults work at home or nearby. Vacations to "get away from home" are rare, although some elderly couples vacation in Florida for several winter months.[8] Out-of-state travel by van, train, or bus for medical or business purposes often includes visiting in other settlements. These journeys are called "trips," not vacations.

Hair is cut at home. Many table games are homemade. The Amish do buy groceries and purchase commercial products, but much of their food and clothing is homemade. Instead of eating at a pizza shop or buying frozen pizza, Amish families make homemade pizza. Time and money spent on shopping trips are minuscule compared to the American norm. There are no visits to the health spa, pet parlor, hairdresser, car wash, or sports stadium, and thus there is more time for "home work" and "home play." Staying home is not a dreaded experience of isolation for the Amish. It means being immersed in the chatter, work, and play of the extended family. The Amish use modern medicines and health services, but they are more likely to rely on home remedies and visit the doctor only as a last resort. All of these centripetal forces pull the Amish homeward most of the time. Retirement occurs at home. Funerals are held at home, and the deceased are buried in nearby cemeteries.

There are, of course, trips to town for business, shopping, and errands, as well as for social events in the Amish community. But most dramas of Amish life are staged at home or in a nearby Amish home. The Amish have not allowed industrialization to oust major life functions from their home. In this regard, they have certainly not joined the modern world.

In sharp contrast to mobile contemporary families, Amish families are tied to a geographical area and anchored in a large extended family. Many Amish live on or within several miles of their childhood homestead. Others may live as far as fifteen miles away. After a new family "settles down" in a residence after marriage, its members typically live there for the rest of their lives. Thus geographical and family roots are strong. A mother of six children explained that all of them live within Lancaster County and that she delights in visiting her thirty-six grandchildren at least once a month. Those living on the other side of her house she, of course, sees daily. With families averaging nearly seven children, it is not unusual for a couple to have forty-five grandchildren. A typical child will have two dozen aunts and uncles and as many as seventy-five first cousins. Although some of these relatives are scattered on the settlement's fringe, many live within a few miles of home. To be Amish is to have a niche, a secure place in this network of relatives. Embroidered or painted rosters of the extended family hang on the walls of Amish homes—a constant reminder of the individual's notch in the family tree.

The Church District

The Amish families who live near one another form a church district or congregation—the chief social unit in Amish society beyond the family. The number of households per church district in the Lancaster settlement ranges from twenty to forty-six, with an average of thirty-three. With many double households, the average district has about twenty extended family units. Some 76 adults and 87 youths under eighteen years of age give the typical district a total of 163 people.[9] Church services are held in homes, and, as congregations grow, they divide. A district's geographical size varies with the density of the Amish population. On the edge of the Lancaster settlement, church districts stretch twelve miles from side to side, but they shrink dramatically in the settlement's hub. Families in the center of small districts are within a half-mile walk of other members.

Roads and streams frame the boundaries of most church dis-

A barn dance takes place near home, as does most Amish recreation.

tricts. Like members of a traditional parish, the Amish participate in the church district that encircles their home. The members of a district worship together every other week. They often attend the services of adjoining congregations on the "off Sunday" of their congregation. The residents of one district, however, cannot become members of another one unless they move into its territory. There are no church buildings, and the homes of members become the gathering points not only for worship but also for socializing.

Because families live in close proximity, many members of a district are also blood relatives. Throughout the settlement six surnames—Stoltzfus, King, Fisher, Beiler, Esh, and Lapp—account for over 70 percent of the households. The rank order of household sur-

Table 4-2 Rank Order of Household Surnames

Name	Number of Households	Percentage
Stoltzfus[a]	938	25.3
King	449	12.1
Fisher	408	11.0
Beiler	352	9.5
Esh[b]	253	6.8
Lapp	215	5.8
Zook	197	5.3
Glick	135	3.6
16 names with 11–72 households	696	18.8
12 names with 10 or fewer households	59	1.5
Total	3702	100.0

Source: Directory (1987).
Note: This tabulation also includes households in settlements that originated from the Lancaster Community.
   [a]63 of these households spell their name "Stoltzfoos."
   [b]27 of these households spell their name "Esch."

names is displayed in table 4-2. Kinship networks are thus rather dense both within and between church districts. One rural mail carrier had to distinguish among sixty Stoltzfus families. Moreover, he had three Amos E. Stoltzfuses and three Elam S. Stoltzfuses on the same route.

The district is the social and ceremonial unit around which the Amish world orbits. Self-contained and autonomous, the congregations are tied together by a network of bishops. Districts ordain their own leaders and, on the recommendation of their bishop, have the power to excommunicate members. Baptisms, weddings, and funerals take place within the district. Errant members must confess their sins publicly before other members. Local congregations under the leadership of their bishop vary in their interpretation of religious regulations. Decisions to aid other districts financially and to participate in community-wide Amish programs are made by the local district. Congregational votes are taken on recommendations brought by the bishop. Hostetler has aptly called this sytem a "patriarchal democracy."[10] Although each member has a vote, it is usually a vote to accept or reject the bishop's recommendation. The authority of the bishop brings compelling pressure to comply with proposed actions. Fellowship meals after worship services and other social activities, such as Sunday evening "singings," take place in the district. Hence members play, socialize, worship, and work together in a dense ethnic network. The church district is factory, church, club, family, and precinct all wrapped up into a neighborhood parish.

Leadership Roles

Leadership in each district is consolidated in three male roles: bishop, minister, and deacon. The leaders are viewed as servants of God and of the congregation. In fact, their German titles translate literally as "servant."[11] The bishop serves as the church's spiritual head and often presides over two districts.[12] One district is usually the bishop's "home base." Congregations meet every other week, and their bishop is able to attend each of their regular meetings. The bishop officiates at baptisms, weddings, communions, funerals, and members' meetings of the congregation. As spiritual head of the leadership team, he interprets and enforces church regulations. If disobedience or conflict arises, it is his responsibility to resolve it. Neighborhood, family, and church networks are often entangled in local controversies that require delicate diplomacy. The bishop is responsible for recommending excommunication or, as the case may be, the reinstatement of penitent members. While considerable authority is vested in the office of bishop, final decisions to excommunicate or reinstate members require a congregational vote. Diverse personality styles among the bishops lead to diverse interpretations of church rules. Some leaders are "open-minded," whereas others take firm doctrinaire positions. The bishop is the incarnate symbol of church authority. One member remarked that every time she sees a policeman, he "reminds me of the bishop." She added, however, that her bishop is a kind person, more concerned about the inner spiritual life of people than about external regulations.

If the office of bishop is vacated by death or illness, another bishop is given temporary oversight of the congregation. Eventually one of the ministers in the congregation is ordained bishop. The ordination of a bishop may be delayed several years if the eligible ministers are too young or inexperienced. A senior bishop explained that he prefers to ordain bishops who have demonstrated their ability to raise a family dedicated to the church. The plans to ordain a bishop are approved by the local congregation as well as the other bishops in the settlement. One of the eligible ministers is made bishop by the "casting of lots."

The minister, or preacher, fills the second leadership role in the local district. A congregation of seventy-five members usually has two preachers and sometimes three, depending on their age and health. Preaching long, extemporaneous sermons in the worship service without the aid of notes is the minister's primary responsibility. Ministers also assist the bishop in giving spiritual direction and leadership to the congregation. Without professional credentials or training, the ministers are selected from within the congregation and serve unpaid for life, earning their own living by farming, carpentry, or other typical Amish occupations.

A deacon's public duties are limited to reading Scripture and leading prayers in the worship service. He supervises an "alms fund" for the needy in the congregation. He attends to the material needs of families in the congregation which require mutual aid. The deacon also assists with baptism and communion. Social control in the local district also hinges on the deacon's office. At the request of the bishop, the deacon, often accompanied by a minister, makes investigative visits to the homes of members who are flouting or violating church regulations. The outcome of the interview is reported to the bishop, who takes appropriate action. The deacon also carries messages of excommunication or reinstatement to members from the bishop. One bishop called this aspect of the deacon's role "the dirty work." The deacon represents the congregation when young couples plan to marry. The groom brings a church letter of "good standing" to the deacon of the bride's congregation, who then meets with her to verify the marriage plans. The bride's deacon then announces, or "publishes," their plans to the local congregation. The deacon does not arrange marriages, but he does symbolize the church's supervision of them.

The bishop, minister, and deacon form an informal "executive committee" that guides and coordinates the activities of the local district. During the first phase of the worship service, while the congregation is singing, this leadership team of four or five men meets for consultation. They decide who will preach the "main" sermon later that morning, and they also discuss other issues. Additional meetings are held as necessary. The power consolidated in the ordained leaders rests primarily with the bishop.

The Mobile Sanctuary

The rotation of worship services from home to home shapes Amish identity and forms the bedrock of their social organization. In the local area, the Old Order Amish are sometimes called House Amish, in contrast to the more liberal Church Amish, who worship in church buildings. While the Old Order Amish share some cultural traits with other plain people in the region, the Amish are *not* "meeting house people." Their mobile "sanctuary" distinguishes them from Old Order Mennonites, who worship in meeting houses but, like the Amish, drive horses and speak Pennsylvania Dutch. The Amish view a permanent church building or meeting house as a symbol of worldliness.

The Amish were tempted to use church buildings about the time of the Civil War. This issue hovered over the 1877 division in the Lancaster area. In 1862, a national series of ministers' meetings grappled with some of the thorny issues tormenting the Amish church. The meetings, held every year until 1876, discussed, among other things, lightning rods, insurance, photographs, baptizing in streams, and holding worship services in meeting houses.[13] The Lancaster bishops refused to participate in these meetings because they were afraid that liberal changes in the Midwest would drift eastward and stir up controversy in their churches.

Progressive-minded members in two districts of eastern Lancaster County soon began pressing for changes. The internal strife forced a stalemate that delayed the observance of communion for seven years (1870–77). The discord came to a head in the late fall of 1876 when preacher Gideon Stoltzfus in the lower Pequea district was "silenced" from preaching by his bishop. He was charged with fellowshipping with liberal Amish in the Midwest. About two-thirds of his district, some seventy-five progressive members, left the Old Order Amish and formed what eventually became a Mennonite congregation. Within several years, the progressives fulfilled the Old Order's worst fears by building a meeting house.

A few miles to the east and a few months later, in the spring of 1877, a similar division erupted in the Conestoga district, leaving only eight families with the Old Order Amish. And as the sages predicted, the progressives in this area also erected a meeting house by 1882.[14] These ruptures in two Lancaster districts within six months stunned the small Amish community, which contained only six districts and less than five hundred members.

Thus 1877 marks a pivotal point in the Amish saga in Lancaster County—a landmark that still casts a shadow over Amish consciousness. From that juncture to the present, the Old Order Amish have observed what happens when a progressive group drifts off and builds a meeting house. Eventually they hold Sunday school and soon they drop the German language. In time, they accept cars and electricity and before long they wear fancy clothes and attend high school. The 1877 division has served as a timely reminder of the inevitable, long-term consequences when liberal groups become enchanted by such worldly things as meeting houses.

Worshipping in homes is a prudent way of limiting the size of Amish congregations. The physical size of houses controls the numerical size of church districts. It guarantees that each individual has a social home in a relatively small congregation. So while the Amish sanctuary floats, the individual is securely anchored. People are known by first name. Birthdays are remembered, and illnesses are public knowledge. In contrast, Moderns often anonymously float in and out of permanent sanctuaries. The mobile Amish sanctuary affirms the centrality of the family by keeping religious functions literally at home, integrated with family life. This is a radical departure from modern religion, with its specialized services in a sanctuary cut off from the other sectors of life.

The mobile meeting house not only assures individuals a secure niche in a small social unit but also enhances informal social control. Close ties in family networks place informal checks on social behavior. The mobile sanctuary assures that, on the average, members will visit the home of each family once a year. These annual visits, subtle inspection tours, stymie the proliferation of worldly appliances. The visits also shore up social cohesion and solidarity. How many people in a modern congregation have toured the homes of *all* other members in the past year?

The mobile sanctuary protests the sanctuaries of modern Christendom, which the Amish view as ostentatious displays of pride that point not heavenward, but earthward to the congregation's social prestige. The financial resources used by modern congregations for buildings, steeples, organs, and pastors are used by the Amish for mutual aid. With geographically determined boundaries, there is little need for evangelism. Expansion, fueled by biological growth, is not dependent on novel programs and modern facilities that compete with other churches. The Amish are baffled as to why Moderns build opulent homes but do not worship in them. Although Amish homes are not luxurious, they are used for worship, work, eating, and socializing. The mobile sanctuary, while not a public symbol, is deeply etched in Amish consciousness. Small, local, informal, lowly, and unpretentious, it is the structural embodiment of Gelassenheit—a major clue to the riddle of Amish survival.

The Organizational Chart

The organizational structure of Amish society is ambiguous. There are no headquarters, professionals, executive directors, or organizational charts. Kitchens, shops, barns, and home offices provide office space for this religious organization. The nebulous structure confounds outsiders. On one occasion, public officials in a heavily populated Amish township were distressed by rowdy Amish youth. Not knowing who to contact in the Amish community, the township supervisors finally expressed their concern in a letter to an Amish layman who sometimes serves as public spokesman.[15] The vitality of Amish culture is a remarkable achievement, despite the lack of experts, corporate offices, memos, computers, and elaborate flow charts. Apart from schoolteachers, there are no paid church employees, let alone professional ones. Amish society is linked by a web of interpersonal ties which stretches across the community. How do the

In newer homes, church services are often held in the basement. A traditional wagon is used to haul benches from house to house.

Amish manage to retain uniformity with nearly ninety loosely coupled church districts?

The solution to this riddle lies in the flat leadership structure. Each bishop typically serves two districts. The seventy-five adult members in each district are only one step away from the top of the church hierarchy. The flat, two-tier structure links grass-roots members directly to the citadel of power and has several benefits. Each bishop personally knows the members of his districts and in this way monitors the pulse of the community. Members feel a close tie to the central decision-making structure because their bishop attends bishops' meetings and may provide feedback on the discussion. The bishop, in turn, understands the larger concerns of all the bishops across the settlement and can personally enforce and explain church regulations to the members of his two districts. With some 150 members in both districts, he is able to regulate and monitor social change effectively on a first-name basis.

A seniority system based on age and tenure undergirds the power structure of the bishops. A young minister described the decision-making process among the bishops: "The five oldest have priority. It tends to point to the oldest one. If they want a final decision they say to him, 'Let's hear your decision.'" If health permits, the senior bishop presides over the bishops' meeting, as well as a ministers' meeting a few weeks later. The diplomatic skills of this highly esteemed elder statesman are critical for upholding harmony. A minister described the seniority system: "Many bishops have told me that they are going to the oldest bishop to ask for his advice on a certain issue. And he will not hesitate to give his opinion, based on Scripture. Then he will conclude and say, 'Don't do it that way just because I told you, go home and work with your church.' So it is not a dictatorship by any means; it works on a priority basis and a *submitting* basis" (emphasis added).

Twice each year, the bishops confer on problems, shape informal policies, and discuss social changes that threaten the church's welfare. A leaders' or ministers' meeting, involving bishops, ministers, and deacons, follows the bishops' meeting each fall and spring. This combined group of ordained leaders, numbering several hundred men, meets in a large home, shop, barn, or machinery shed. The bishops report on issues from their bishops' meeting and solicit the ministers' support. Other issues of concern or special problems are also handled. The leaders' meeting plays a significant role in maintaining cohesion and harmony across the settlement.

The number of districts grew from eleven in 1920 to fifty-two by 1975, stretching the older organizational pattern. The leadership structure was revised in three ways to fit the prolific settlement. First, despite growth, the span of each bishop's control remained the same. In pyramid fashion, growing organizations tend to add rungs in their hierarchy as well as to widen the control of top managers. The Amish have resisted this pattern. Instead of adding more congregations to each bishopric, they simply increased the number of bishops as districts multiplied. Limiting the number of districts per bishop may have been encouraged by the restrictions of horse travel. Keeping two districts per bishop and allowing all bishops to participate in the bishops' meeting prevented the development of new rungs in the hierarchy. The flat architecture enhances social control, as well as the church's ability to monitor social change.

Multiplying the number of bishops led to other problems. With eighteen districts in the forties, nine bishops could easily meet and conduct their business informally. As the number of bishops increased to several dozen, the leadership became consolidated in an informal "executive committee" of senior bishops. The sentiment of this catchment of wisdom is a compelling, but by no means final, authority in the bishops' meeting. Participation in this caucus of a half-dozen bishops is based on age and tenure rather than on election or appointment. Members of this inner circle do not supervise other bishops, for even these senior members continue to supervise their own districts. Although the appearance of an elite group of senior bishops represents a consolidation of power, it did not add a new rung on the ladder of authority. Without the benefit of professional consultants or middle managers, the bishops serve, in their words, as "watchmen on the walls of Zion," looking out for the church's welfare.

The growing number of districts precipitated a third change in organizational structure. By 1975 the community had expanded to fifty-two districts. It was difficult to find a meeting place to accommodate the large leaders' meeting, which by then consisted of some two-hundred bishops, ministers, and deacons. Conducting business with such a large group was hampered without a loudspeaker system and formal parliamentary procedures. Thus, in April 1975, the leaders were divided into north and south subgroups, as shown in figure 4-1.[16] Route 340, an east/west road through the heart of the settlement, became the dividing line. A northern leaders' meeting on Monday is followed by a southern leaders' meeting on Wednesday. Bishops from the entire settlement continue to meet twice a year. The inner circle of senior bishops attends both the northern and southern leaders' meet-

Figure 4-1 Organizational Structure of the Lancaster Settlement

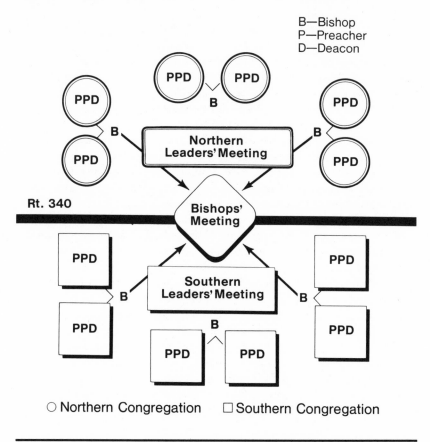

ings to encourage uniformity of practice. Many members credit the leaders' meeting as the key factor that enabled the Amish to avoid schisms and maintain uniformity despite a host of social changes in the past twenty years.

The Shadows of Bureaucracy

No formal committees report to the Amish bishops. Over the years, as laymen have formed committees for special projects, they often have involved bishops as a goodwill gesture. In general, the ministers and bishops, guardians of tradition, are reluctant to initiate or endorse new ventures. The formal power structure, slanted toward tradition, reacts to threatening social changes but rarely exercises a leadership role in establishing new programs. Although the bishops' body has steered clear of formalized procedures, several groups show traces of bureaucracy. In each case, interested laymen, sometimes with and other times without the blessing of the bishops, have established organizations to coordinate activities that require resources beyond the scope of local districts. Six organizations cast hazy bureaucratic shadows across the settlement.[17]

1. Amish Aid Society. Community barn raisings have been a long-time public symbol of mutual aid among the Amish. An informal plan pays for replacement materials and property destroyed by a fire or storm. Begun in the 1870s, the Amish Aid Society assesses members so that the costs of recovery from a disaster are shared throughout the community.[18] Members who join the plan are assessed $1 per $1,000 of property valuation. Each district has a director, who records property assessments and collects the "fire tax." When the central treasury becomes depleted, the committee asks the director in each district to collect a new assessment. Collections vary by the frequency of fires, but average about one a year. This modest system of fire and storm insurance operates without paid personnel, underwriters, agents, offices, computers, or profits. Its sole purpose is to provide a network of support for members. Manual labor for clean-up and rebuilding is freely given by members far and wide when a fire or storm strikes.[19]

2. School Committee. In 1937, in response to the consolidation of public schools, a group of laymen organized a School Committee, which sought to have Amish children excused from public school after the eighth grade. Eventually Amish schools were built and administered by local Amish school boards. The School Committee evolved into a statewide organization known as the Old Order Book Society, which coordinates Amish schools today. The society maintains a liaison with state education officials and provides guidelines for the administration of one-room Amish schools. Representatives from

The community offers mutual aid in times of despair.

different settlements in Pennsylvania attend the society's annual meeting.[20]

    3. Liability Aid. In the sixties, Amish businessmen began purchasing commercial liability insurance to protect themselves from lawsuits. The church opposed participation in worldly insurance programs, which use the force of law. To resolve the dilemma of providing protection against lawsuits without being "unequally yoked" with commercial insurance, Amish Liability Aid was established in 1965. According to one member, this plan "protects you from others when there's an accident and you're not protected for yourself." Within ten years of its origin, the plan had 824 participating members, who were assessed $10 per year to cover the cost of liability cases paid by the program.[21]

    4. Amish National Steering Committee. In the early sixties, some Amish conscientious objectors served in hospitals as an alternative to military service. These young men frequently became worldly, some-

The community turns despair into hope.

times married non-Amish nurses, and often did not return home. If they did, they found it difficult to fit into their rural communities. In an effort to solve this problem, Amish leaders across the nation met in Indiana in 1966. This meeting gave birth to a National Steering Committee, which has become a broker of sorts between the Amish community and government officials. In its early years, the committee was concerned with draft legislation and alternative service programs. More recently, the committee has mediated legal disputes between the government and the Amish on Social Security, hard hats, unemployment insurance, workmen's compensation (an insurance plan for disabled workers), and other matters. In the role of a meek lobbyist, the committee chairman stays abreast of legislation that might impinge on Amish life. He also provides feedback to legislators who want Amish reactions to pending legislation. The committee has three members, fourteen state directors, and a network of local representatives. An annual meeting reviews the work of the committee, whose chairman lives in the Lancaster settlement.[22]

The committee functions as a self-perpetuating body outside the formal structure of the church. Some individual bishops support the committee, whereas others fear that it will become too powerful.

Some Amish have accused the committee of "trying to run the churches." But the committee contends that it "is only the voice of the churches combined and the churches are the backbone."[23] In terms of structure, procedures, size, and written guidelines, the committee reflects the greatest imprint of bureaucracy on any Amish organization to date. Despite this bureaucratic stamp, the committee operates from a home office with voluntary labor.

5. *Church Aid.* Caught between the rising costs of hospitalization and their reluctance to accept Medicare, some Amish families began buying hospitalization insurance in the late sixties. Fearing that commercial insurance would undercut the community's reliance on spontaneous mutual aid, the Amish have always frowned on commercial policies. Rising hospital costs threatened to bring a fuller embrace of commercial insurance and "yoke" Amish "unequally" with an evil world. Thus, a group of Amish laymen initiated Amish Church Aid—an informal version of hospitalization insurance. The program began in January 1969, and within four years 1,450 members from thirty-six districts were participating in the program.[24] Those who join the plan pay an initial fee and then "are assessed for additional payments as the need arises." After a $1,000 deductible per family, Church Aid reimburses members for their expenses. Amish may join Church Aid only if the ordained leaders in their district support the plan. Some districts have not subscribed to Church Aid because of its costs and its similarity to commercial insurance. Nonparticipants with large medical bills are usually assisted by alms funds from their own district as well as from adjoining ones. Church Aid guidelines make it clear that if members are involved in motor vehicle accidents in which they are the driver or owner they will not be reimbursed for medical expenses.[25]

6. *Bruderschaft Library.* Following the example of other Amish communities, the Lancaster Amish decided to organize a historical library in May 1979. The project blossomed, and in August 1984 the Pequea Bruderschaft Library was incorporated northeast of the village of Intercourse. Established by a board of seven directors, the historical library exists "to assist members of the Amish Church and others in learning about the historic beliefs and practices of the Amish Church."[26] A part-time librarian maintains the collection and aids researchers.[27]

The six organizations float on the fringe of the formal community structure. For the most part, the committees have co-opted ordained leaders to build ties of understanding and to gain their tacit endorsement. A central board or director does not appoint or oversee these floating bodies. They have arisen spontaneously to meet needs that transcend the resources of the local district. While some of these committees show traces of bureaucracy, they are for the most part

The austere office of the Pequea Bruderschaft Library. The trunk was brought to America by an early Amish immigrant.

Table 4-3 Amish Organizations by Date of Origin and Function

Date of Origin	Name	Function
1870s	Amish Aid Society[a]	Fire and Storm Aid
1913	Amish Book Committee	Book Publishing
1937	Old Order Book Society[b]	Coordination of Schools
1965	Amish Liability Aid	Liability Assistance
1966	National Steering Committee	Government Liaison
1969	Amish Church Aid	Medical Assistance
1979	Pequea Bruderschaft Library[c]	Historical Resources

[a]Date of origin is uncertain. It was functioning by 1879.
[b]Called the School Committee prior to 1957.
[c]Incorporated in 1984.

informal, flat, decentralized, small, and obedient to tradition. Although their loose structure would create nightmares for modern bureaucrats, they have served the Amish community well.

Architectural Summary

The social architecture of Amish society is small, compact, local, informal, and homogeneous—features that clash with the design of modern societies. Amish social structure embodies Gelassenheit and bolsters the groups' defensive strategy against worldliness. A brief synopsis of the distinctive features concludes our architectural tour.

1. *Small.* From egos to organizational units, Gelassenheit prefers small-scale things. The Amish realize that larger things bring specialization, distance, divisive subgroups, and often remove average people from power. Meeting in homes for worship limits the size of congregations. Ironically, this commitment to small-scale units makes individuals "big" in the sense that they are known intimately by a small, stable group. It is impossible to get lost in the crowd in an Amish congregation. The security and identity provided by small congregations lessen the pressure for individuals to "make it on their own." Small farms are preferable to large ones. Large craft and manufacturing shops are frowned upon. Big operators garner attention to themselves, establish a threatening power base, and insult the egalitarian community with excessive wealth.

An Amish businessman explained:

> My people look at a large business as a sign of greed. We're not supposed to engage in large businesses, and I'm right at the borderline now and maybe too large for Amish standards. The Old Order Amish don't like large exposed volume. You don't drive down the road and see big Harvestore silos sitting on Amish farms, you don't see one of these big thousand-foot chicken houses. I can easily tell you which are the Mennonite farms. They'll feed 200 head of cattle, have 50,000 chickens, and milk 120 cows. They're a notch completely ahead of us. We stop at the point of a herd of 50 cows, and 10,000 chickens. We farm with horses, so that we're satisfied with eighty acres of land, where a Mennonite, hey, he can't afford to pay $40,000 for a tractor and only farm eighty acres. He's got to farm half of the neighborhood to make it pay. Then he needs some bigger equipment, he needs a combine, and then he needs the whole bit. That also applies to business, and my business is just at the point right now where it's beyond where the Old Order Amish people think it should be. It's just too large.

Another businessman expressed the fear of large organizations: "Our discipline thrives with a small group. Once you get into that big superstructure, it seems to gather momentum and you can't stop it." Criticizing the growing size of an Amish organization that the bishops curbed, he said: "It became self-serving, like a pyramid. Suppose we get a rotten egg leading it sometime? He can do more damage, and wreck in one year, what we built up in twenty years. That's why the bishops curbed it." The Amish have not reviewed the scientific literature describing the impact of size on social life but realize that, in the long run, the modern impulse for large-scale things could debilitate their community.

2. Compact. The Amish have resisted the modern tendency to specialize and separate social functions. Unlike most religions in modern society, Amish religion is not partitioned off from other activities. Work, play, child rearing, education, and worship, for the most part, are neither highly specialized nor separated from one another. The same circle of people interacting in family, neighborhood, church, school, leisure, and work blends these functions together in a compact network. Members of these overlapping circles share common values. The dense webs of social interaction decrease privacy. Gossip, ridicule, and small talk become informal instruments of social control as networks crisscross, and, in the words of a member, "everybody knows everything about everyone else."

If modernity separates through specialization and mobility, it is not surprising to hear Amish pleas for social integration—"togetherness," "unity," and a "common mind." In a formal statement, the bishops admonished teen-agers to stay home more on weekends and urged parents to have morning worship with their families as "a good way of staying together."[28] A young woman explained why the church frowns on central heating systems: "A space heater in the kitchen keeps the family together. Heating all the rooms would lead to everyone going off to their own rooms."

Another member described the compact structure of Amish society: "What is more scriptural than the closely-knit Christian community, living together, working together, worshipping together, with its own church and own schools? Here the members know each other, work with and care for each other every day of the week."[29] A bishop, arguing against the use of modern combines to harvest wheat, said they would eliminate binding up sheaves of wheat during the summer harvest. This practice, he said, reminds members anew each year of how the church is bound in unity like a sheaf of wheat. These symbolic descriptions illustrate how the overlapping spheres of Amish life merge together in a compact structure that has remained immune from the fragmentation of modern life.

3. Local. Amish life is staged in a local arena. Largely cut off from mass communication, rapid transit, geographical mobility, and national organizations, Amish life revolves around the immediate neighborhood. Businessmen are often conversant about national affairs, but the dominant orientation is local, not cosmopolitan. Things close by are known, understood, and esteemed. Typical phrases in Amish writings—"home rule," "home community," "local home standards"—anchor the entire social system in the local church district. The local base of Amish interaction is poignantly described in an Amish view of education: "The one-room, one-teacher, community school near the child's home is the best possible type of elementary school. Here the boys and girls of a local community grow up and become neighbors among each other."[30]

4. *Informal.* With few contractual and formal relationships, Amish life is fused by informal ties anchored in family networks, common traditions, uniform symbols, and a shared mistrust of the outside world. The informality of Amish society expresses itself in many ways. Social interaction is conducted on a first-name basis without titles. Oral communication takes precedence over written. Few written records are kept of the meetings of ordained leaders. Organizational procedures are dictated by oral tradition, not policy manuals and flow charts. Although each bishop wields considerable influence in his districts, the congregations are loosely coupled together by family networks rather than by formal policies.

5. *Homogeneous.* The conventional marks of social class, education, income, and occupation have little validity in Amish society. Ending school at eighth grade homogenizes educational achievement. Farming, the traditional vocation, levels the occupational structure. In recent years, shop owners and craftspeople have emerged as a new occupational grouping. Similar occupational and educational levels have minimized financial differences in the community in the past. Some Amish own several farms and display discreet traces of wealth in their choice of farm equipment and animals. Historically, however, the common agricultural base has homogenized wealth. Recent changes threaten the historic equality. Farms are typically valued at over $300,000, and it is not uncommon for an Amish business to have annual sales exceeding $1 million.

Thus the financial resources of farm and shop owners exceed that of shop workers, who earn hourly wages. High land values and new sources of revenue will likely, in the long run, disturb the egalitarian nature of Amish society. One member, describing a certain rural road, said: "Three Amish millionaires live up there, but they don't drive around in Cadillacs, own a summer home at the bay, or have a yacht." Wealth in Amish society is held modestly, not displayed conspicuously. Despite growing inequality, there is, at least on the surface, an attempt to maintain homogeneous symbols of faith and ethnicity. Both the well-to-do businessman and the farm laborer dress alike, drive a horse to church, and will be buried under similar gravestones. On the whole, the economic structure of Amish society is relatively flat, in contrast to the hierarchical class structure of postindustrial societies. In all of these ways, Amish architecture exudes an elegant simplicity—small, compact, local, informal, and homogeneous—that embodies Gelassenheit and partially explains the riddle of Amish survival.

5

Rites of Redemption and Purification

Shunning works a little bit like an electric fence around a
pasture.
—former Amishman

Ritual: The Music of Interaction

Social life balances on a tripod of culture, structure, and ritual.
In order to survive, societies must develop cultural blueprints for social behavior. These collective guidelines translate values and beliefs
into expectations for daily behavior. Norms for expected behavior
range from informal folkways to formal legal codes. Groups encourage their members to fall in line with normative or ideal behavior in at
least three ways. Childhood socialization is the primary and most
powerful form of social control, because it teaches the young a culture's unique view of the world. Second, informal social controls—
gossip, ridicule, embarrassment—encourage conformity. Finally, formal social control in the form of police, courts, and prisons springs
into action when informal controls break down. The Amish, like other
societies, have a cultural blueprint—a normative order and rituals
that help enforce it. This chapter explores the religious rites that reaf-
firm and preserve the Amish moral order.

Religious rituals fuse culture and structure into social music.
Without the music of ritual, a group's culture and structure are
static—like an orchestra frozen on a concert stage. Culture exists in
the minds of the players; the players understand musical notations
and know how to play their instruments. Structure is present as well.
Seated in their proper sections, the musicians face the conductor. But
there is no ritual, no interaction, no music. The cultural knowledge
and the social architecture blend into music as the conductor's baton
signals the start of the performance—the ritualized interaction. In a
similar way, rituals of interaction combine culture and structure into

a social symphony in Amish life.

Social rituals—handshakes, birthday greetings, graduations, weddings—organize everyday routines. Religious rites rejuvenate the moral order of a group and place its members in contact with divine power. Amish rituals are not hollow. From common meals to singing, from silent prayer to excommunication, the rites are filled with redemptive meanings. As sacred rituals, they retell the Amish story, recount God's redemptive acts, recharge group solidarity, and usher individuals into divine presence.

Ordnung: The Grammar of Order

The Amish blueprint for expected behavior, called the *Ordnung,* regulates private, public, and ceremonial life. *Ordnung* does not translate readily into English. Sometimes rendered as "ordinance" or "discipline," the *Ordnung* is best thought of as an ordering of the whole way of life. Gingerich defines it as a code of conduct which the church maintains by tradition rather than by systematic or explicit rules.[1] A member noted: "The order is not written down. The people just know it, that's all." Rather than a packet of rules to memorize, the Ordnung is the "understood" behavior by which the Amish are expected to live. In the same way that the rules of grammar are learned by children, so the Ordnung, the grammar of order, is learned by Amish youth. The Ordnung evolved gradually over the decades as the church sought to strike a delicate balance between tradition and change. Specific details of the Ordnung vary across church districts and settlements.

A young minister describes the Ordnung as an "understanding": "Having one understanding, getting together and discussing things and admonishing according to that understanding and punishing according to that understanding, getting principles built up on an even basis, you know, can be beneficial." In some areas of life, the Ordnung is very explicit; for example, it prescribes that a woman's hair should be parted in the center and that a man's hair should be combed with bangs. Other facets of life, left to individual and family discretion within limits, include food preferences, types of crops grown, job choice, style of house, place of residence, and hobbies. The Ordnung contains both prescriptions—you ought to wear a wide-brimmed hat—and proscriptions—you should not own a television.

Children learn the Ordnung from birth by observing adults and by hearing parents and others talk about it. It gradually becomes the definition of reality, "the way things are," in the child's mind. In the same way that modern children learn that women, rather than men, wear lipstick and shave their legs, so Amish children learn the ways of the Ordnung. To the outsider, the Ordnung appears as a maze of legalistic rules. But to the child, growing up inside the world of the Ordnung, wearing an Amish hat wherever one goes is just the normal thing to do. It *is* the world—the way things are supposed to be, the way God intended them.

The Ordnung defines certain things as simply outside the Amish world. Asked whether an Amish person could be a real-estate agent, a member replied: "Well, it's just unheard of, a child wouldn't even think of it." All in all, the Ordnung represents the traditional interpretations—the rules, regulations, and standards—of what it means to be Amish. Although children are taught from birth to follow the Ordnung, it is not until baptism that they make a personal vow to uphold it.

The Ordnung is the reservoir of "understandings" that have accumulated in Amish culture over time. A minister described the evolution of the Ordnung: "Our fathers' church leaders had a strong desire to hold on to the old way of life, and although much has changed over the years they have been successful in holding the line to the point that we have been separated from the world, which, in time, created a culture different from that of the world. This did not come on overnight, nor did it come through rash or harsh commands of our bishops, but by making wise decisions to hold firm to the old-time religion from one time to another, from one generation to another."[2]

Core understandings of the Ordnung regarding education, divorce, cars, and so forth are fairly stable and need little verbal reinforcement. The outer edges evolve, however, as the church faces new issues. Some technological innovations, such as calculators, are permitted by default. Embryo transplants in dairy cows are strictly forbidden. Other issues, such as using phones in machine shops, may fester for several years. When new practices, such as eating in restaurants, become "an issue," they are discussed by the ordained leaders, and, if a consensus develops, it is grafted into the Ordnung.

In response to the rowdy behavior of some Amish youth on weekends, the bishops developed a list of "working ordinances" for the churches and young people. These were printed, a rare occurrence. Offering guidance for the weekends, the Ordnung, in part, said:

> Saturday: On the whole there is to be no going away on Saturday night by the young or old people, with the exception of a genuinely good reason. Birthday parties or others are not to take place on Saturday night. There is the exception that boys may go to visit their girls once every two weeks as is customary among us, but they are not to go with them to meetings and they are to be home again by a prescribed time. If a boy has his own horse this does not mean that he may leave home without his parent's approval. Sunday: No

The Ordnung permits an Amish carpenter to use a state-of-the-art forklift in his shop, but also requires him to drive a traditional carriage to church services.

drinks are to be bought and there is to be no handling of money on Sunday. Parents, take the time to read with your children and to instruct them.[3]

The Amish are reluctant to change their minds after a cultural practice is ingrained into the Ordnung. Changes require a "loss of face," and, rather than lose face, the Amish may develop ingenious detours to get around an old-fashioned practice. For instance, freezers are not permitted in Amish homes but are sometimes placed in the home of a non-Amish neighbor. Because changing the Ordnung is difficult, the Amish are slow to outlaw novel things at first sight. If seen as harmless, a new practice (for example, the use of chain saws or instant coffee) will drift into use with little ruckus.

Adherence to the Ordnung varies among families and church districts. Some bishops are more lenient than others in their enforcement of it. The Ordnung is enforced with leniency under special circumstances (for example, a retarded child may be permitted to have a bicycle, which is usually off limits). If a person conforms to the symbolic markers of the Ordnung, there is a great deal of "breathing space" in which to maneuver and still appear Amish.

Examples of Practices Prescribed by the *Ordnung:*

    color and style of clothing

    hat styles for men

    the color and style of buggies

    use of horses for field work

    steel wheels on machinery

    use of the German dialect

    the order of the worship service

    kneeling for prayer in worship

    the menu of the congregational meal

    marriage within the church

Examples of Practices Prohibited by the *Ordnung:*

    using tractors for field work

    owning and operating an automobile

    electricity from public power lines

    central heating in homes

    wall-to-wall carpeting

    pipe line milking equipment

    filing a lawsuit

    joining worldly (public) organizations

    entering military service

    owning computers, televisions, radios

    high school education

    air transportation

    jewelry, including wedding rings and wrist watches

    divorce

A labyrinth of capricious rules to the outsider, the Ordnung feels like stuffy legalism to some Amish. But for most Amish it is a sacred order that unites members and separates them from the world. "A respected *Ordnung* generates peace, love, contentment, equality, and unity," says one minister. "The latter is the key effect of church *Ordnung*. It will focus an individual to a group of one body, one flesh, one mind, one state. It creates a desire for togetherness and fellowship. It binds marriages, it strengthens family ties, to live together, to work together, to worship together, and to commune secluded from the world."[4] Following the Ordnung—wearing the proper clothing, plowing with horses, shunning publicity, avoiding worldly pleasures, and singing the hymns of the *Ausbund*—is a sacred ritual that symbolizes one's faithful obedience to the vows of baptism, to the brotherhood, and to God. Abandoning self and bending to the collective wisdom place the obedient in touch with God.

Baptism: The Permanent Vow

Small children accept and practice the Ordnung as they receive it from their parents. Before they are baptized, Amish youth are under the care of their parents, and the church has no official jurisdiction over them. Thus Amish teen-agers may or may not conform to the Ordnung. Some youth rebel or "sow wild oats" in their late teens. During this ambiguous period, when they are neither in nor out of the church, teen-agers face the decision of whether they want to kneel for baptism and join the church. It is not a trivial matter. Those who make this major promise must submit to the Ordnung for the rest of their lives. If their obedience to the church falters, they could be socially ostracized forever. Young adults who choose not to be baptized eventually leave the Amish community. However, they need not worry about being shunned, because they have not broken the baptismal pledge.

Romantic ties may add an incentive for church membership, for Amish ministers only marry church members. "We have no weddings for someone who is not a member of the church. It's as simple as that," said one young husband. For some young people, the rite of baptism is an easy decision, the natural climax to a streamlined socialization program that nudges them in the direction of church membership. For others, it is a difficult choice. Some leave home and flirt with the world, while others flirt with it behind their parents' back. But in the end, four out of five promise to embrace the community for life. A young married husband described the tug of romance, land, family, and community which pulls youth toward baptism:

Most of the youth sowing wild oats are just out there to put on a show. It's just something that kind of comes and goes. If they have well-established roots, most of them kind of have their mind set on a particular girl. There is something there that really draws them back. Now, I haven't been one of the wilder guys, but I sowed plenty of wild oats as far as that goes. The best I can explain is that it is strong family ties that really do pull. I had the world in front of me, but the other thing that I had, too, was the farm. I had the cows since I was eighteen and was kind of tied down. Some of the young people know that they are going to come back to the church and some of them don't. I will admit, I was rebellious enough. Like I say, the close family ties are the thing that really draws you back. I still think it [Amish life] is a better lifestyle, I really think so. If you grow up with it, there really is something here that just kind of draws. If you do a lot of this running around and going on, it kind of makes you feel foolish after awhile.

The typical age of baptism ranges from sixteen to twenty-one. Girls often join at a younger age than boys. A series of instructional classes during the five months preceding the ceremony places the stark implications of baptism before the candidates. During the first hour of the church service, over the summer, the novices meet with the ministers for instruction. The ministers and bishop review the Confession of Faith and emphasize selected aspects of the Ordnung.[5] On the Saturday before the baptism, there is a special wrap-up session when candidates are given their last chance to turn back. Hostetler states: "Great emphasis is placed upon the difficulty of walking in the straight and narrow way. The applicants are told that it is better not to make a vow than to make a vow and later break it."[6]

The baptismal rite follows two sermons during a regular Sunday morning service. The deacon provides a small pail of water and a cup. The bishop tells the candidates to go on their knees "before the Most High and Almighty God and His church if you still think this is the right thing to do to obtain your salvation." The candidates are then asked three questions:

(1) "Are you willing, by the help and grace of God, to *renounce* the world, the devil, your own flesh and blood, and be *obedient* only to God and his church?" (Yes)
(2) "Are you willing to walk with Christ and his church and to remain faithful through life and until death?" (Yes)
(3) "Can you confess that Jesus Christ is the Son of God?" (Each candidate repeats, "I confess that Jesus Christ is the Son of God.")[7]

The congregation stands for prayer while the applicants remain kneeling. Then the bishop lays his hands on the head of the first applicant. The deacon pours water into the bishop's cupped hands. It drips over the candidate's head. The bishop then extends his hand to each new member as he or she rises. The bishop says: "May the Lord God complete the good work which he has begun in you and strengthen and comfort you to a blessed end through Jesus Christ. Amen." The deacon's wife greets new female members with a "holy kiss," and the bishop likewise greets new male members and wishes them peace. In a concluding word, the bishop admonishes the congregation to be obedient and invites other ministers to give testimony. The ritual of baptism places the new members into full fellowship, with the rights and responsibilities of adult church membership.[8]

Amish youth drag race their horses. The lone church member is dressed according to the Ordnung. With wrist watches, store-bought shirts, and shingled hair, the other four enjoy their independence before baptism.

Worship: A Plain Liturgy

The worship service dramatically reenacts the Amish moral order. Social structure and beliefs coalesce in a sacred ritual that embodies the core meanings of Amish culture. The worship service imprints the "understandings" of the Ordnung in the collective consciousness. This redemptive ritual reminds members who they are and from where they have come, and it ushers them into divine presence. With simple props and scripts, the drama of worship reaffirms the symbolic universe of Amish culture.

Each district holds services every other Sunday in the home of a member.[9] Services begin early, with some members arriving before half past seven in the morning. Members either drive by horse and buggy or walk to the service. The sacred prelude for the day is played out on the keyboard of country roads, as the rhythmic clip-clop of hoofbeats advances toward the meeting site. The three-and-a-half-hour service culminates in a noon meal, followed by informal visiting throughout the afternoon. The local congregation swells in size, as friends and family from a distance often join the service. Unlike modern congregations, where half or less of the members attend worship, everyone shows up and packs into several rooms of a member's home. It is not unusual for 125 adults and 125 children to attend the service. Partitions between rooms are opened. Backless benches and some folding chairs face a central area, where the preacher stands. Benches and songbooks are transported from home to home in a special wagon.

The service is organized around congregational singing and two sermons. The main sermon lasts about an hour and fifteen minutes. Illustrations are taken from the Bible, farm life, and local events. Sermons often include references to accounts of suffering in the *Martyrs Mirror*. These references replay the persecution drama and remind the Amish of their past. Preachers tell members that they are pilgrims and strangers traveling in a different direction than the rest of the world. Obedience is a key theme in the service.[10] Ministers urge members to obey the commandments of the Scripture, the vows of baptism, and those in authority over them. After reading the Scripture, the deacon may also admonish the congregation to be obedient to the Lord. The following is the traditional order of service:

fellowship upon arrival

silence in worship areas

congregational singing

leaders meet in separate room

opening sermon

silent kneeling prayer

scripture reading by deacon

main sermon

affirmations from ordained leaders

kneeling prayer, which is read

benediction

closing hymn

members' meeting

meal

fellowship

The Amish have no organ, offering, church school, ushers, professional pastors, printed liturgy, pulpit, cross, candles, steeples, robes, flowers, choirs, handbells, altar. The props of modern worship are absent. Plain people gather in a plain house and worship in simplicity. A traditional, unwritten "liturgy" regulates each moment of the service. The ceremony symbolizes the core values of Amish society.

The congregation sings from the *Ausbund*—a hymnal with only printed words.[11] Tunes, learned by memory, are sung in unison. Many of the *Ausbund* hymns were written by persecuted Anabaptists in the sixteenth century. A song leader sits among the congregation. In a spirit of humility, he is selected on the spot. A member described the selection process: "You'll see men whispering, 'You do it, you do it,' until someone finally goes ahead and does it."

A brief members' meeting may follow the last song. Church affairs involving mutual aid, discipline, and plans for district activities are discussed. A light lunch, with a traditional menu, follows the service. In the afternoon, visiting cliques emerge around age, family, and sex, but, for the most part, the day is a common experience. From beginning to end, the worship symbolizes waiting, unity, and humility, a ritualistic reenactment of Gelassenheit.

Sex, age, and leadership roles shape the worship in several ways. Men and women enter the house by separate doors and sit in separate areas of the "sanctuary." Women do not lead any aspect of the worship, but after the service they prepare and serve the meal. They eat at separate tables from the men and are responsible for cleaning up. Age characteristics are pronounced in the ordering of social behavior. The eldest members enter the house and worship areas first, followed by others in roughly descending age. Seating in the worship areas is dictated by age and sex, with spaces designated for older and younger members.

Leadership status is also visible. The ministers shake hands with the women in the kitchen before entering the worship area and taking their seats in the "ministers' row." The men shake hands with the ministers outside as they assemble or as they find seats in the house. The handshake, which often is not accompanied by words, is an act of deference to the minister's authority. As the young unmarried men enter the house, the older men, who are already seated, take off their hats. As the first song begins, the ministers take off their hats in one sweeping action. On the first word of the third line of the first song, the ordained leaders stand and walk to another room in the house to counsel together and select the preacher of the morning. Ordained men are the only ones who stand or speak in the service. Afterward, they sit at the head table, which is served first.

The cultural values embedded in the ritual's structure stun modern consciousness. The entire service creates a radically different world—a world of waiting. There are no traces of rushing. The day of worship stretches from half past seven in the morning to about half past three in the afternoon. The slow tempo of singing ushers in a dif-

Members of a church district gather for worship on an Amish homestead.

ferent temporal order. One song may last twenty minutes. In a rising and falling chant, each word stretches out like a miniature verse in itself. The slow and methodic chantlike cadence reflects a perspective that stretches back to the sixteenth century in image and mood.

The lengthy service is conducted without coffee breaks, worship aids, or special music. Very young children sleep, wander among the aisles, or occasionally munch crackers. Four- and five-year-olds sit patiently on backless benches and on the lap of their parents. The service trains children in the quiet discipline of waiting. It is a lesson in Gelassenheit—waiting and yielding to time, parents, community, and God.

The grammar of the worship incorporates humility and submission. It would be considered pretentious for a minister to prepare a written sermon or even bring a polished outline. Ministers do not know who will preach the morning sermon until they meet as the congregation sings the first hymn. The preacher is chosen by a consensus of the ordained leaders. The spontaneous selection preempts pride. As he begins his sermon a few minutes later, the preacher reminds the congregation that he is a servant of God ministering in his "weakness."

This rite of humility is described by a member: "The one who has the main sermon will often begin by saying, 'I'm not qualified to preach, but I preach because God called me to preach. I wish that someone else, a visiting minister, or someone who would be more capable of delivering the sermon, would preach but because that's not the case, I will *give myself up* to be used by God to preach the sermon today'" (emphasis added). The member continued: "I never cease to be amazed how they can get up and preach for a whole hour without referring to notes or their closed Bible." By yielding in humility to others and giving himself up in front of the congregation, the preacher reenacts the essence of Gelassenheit.

The congregation kneels twice in prayer. The first prayer, a silent one, follows the opening sermon and lasts several minutes. The entire congregation waits on God quietly, in humility, on their knees on a hard floor. The Amish believe that it would be preposterous for someone to offer a spontaneous prayer or to write one. It is better to wait together in silence. The congregation kneels a second time near the end of the service and a minister reads a traditional prayer.

Symbols of collective integration unite the ritual. Singing in unison prevents showy displays that accompany solos, choirs, and musical performances. The praise song "Lob Lied" is the second song in each service.[12] Thus, on a given Sunday morning, all congregations holding services sing the same song at roughly the same time, an experience one member described as giving a beautiful feeling of unity among all the churches. From the elderly bishop to the youngest child, kneeling together in prayer and singing in unison create a shared humility. Children are not shuttled off to church school, and adults are not given a chance to select a stimulating adult elective class. The common worship does not cater to special-interest or -age groups. The specialization of modernity is simply not present in these worship services.

There is little individual expression in the service. One does not choose a special pew. Seating patterns are determined by age and sex, and one simply follows in line and fills in the bench. Ministers give brief affirmations to the main sermon—in essence, endorsements of it. Lay members rarely share personal testimonies in the worship service. Solos and individual interpretations of Scripture are unheard of because choice and individual expression yield to the common message, the common song, and the common experience.

Simplicity pervades the service, from backless benches to bare walls and black vests. The uniform dress code prevents ostentatious display. Members dress in full conformity with the local district's Ordnung. Some young men may sport sideburns or styled hair to show off their last month of independence before joining the church and submitting to the Ordnung. But they also kneel in humility. Members dress appropriately for their age and sex, because this is the sacred moment of the religious week, when even the careless are careful to follow the Ordnung. The uniformity is a statement of conformity to group values—a sign of unity—for all are together in time, space, and symbolism as they enter the presence of God.

Fitting some two hundred people into several large rooms of a house forces a physical closeness. Chairs and benches are packed tightly together. A young minister reported the surprised reaction of visitors to the kneeling: "They said, 'Everyone squats, bangs, crashes, and suddenly goes down, and where's the kneeling pads?' We don't have them, you know, and it's nothing to us because it's our tradition." Confining to Moderns, the physical closeness symbolizes the unity of the tight-knit community, close to one another and close to God, in worship. For some, the ritual of worship becomes an empty protocol on Sunday. But for most, it is a redemptive heartbeat that reaffirms the moral order twenty-six times a year.

The continuity of Amish worship over the decades is striking. A description of an Amish service written more than a century ago is virtually identical to today's format.[13] Members born at the turn of the twentieth century report few changes in the unwritten liturgy of the service. An old-timer reports two changes in the worship service over the past eighty years: "It might be a little shorter and the singing might be a little faster! The sermons are very similar. There has been very little change in the Scripture that is quoted. Each minister is different, but, as a whole, it's the same meaning expressed in different words." Compared to other spheres of Amish life, the worship service has remained remarkably unchanged by modernity.

Communion: A Unifying Experience

Communion and the ordination of leaders are ritual high points that underscore the lowly posture of Gelassenheit. The fall and spring communion services are rites of intensification. They revitalize personal commitment and fortify group cohesion within each district and throughout the settlement. A sequence of meetings regulates the period of preparation prior to the communion service each fall and spring: bishops' meeting, congregational council meetings, and leaders' meetings.

An all-day meeting of the bishops in September and March deals with controversial issues stirring in the community. Contentious issues, such as eating in restaurants, installing telephones in shops, using computers, changing hair styles, and troublesome youth, are discussed. If a consensus among the bishops emerges, it becomes embedded into the "understanding" of the Ordnung.

Following the bishops' meeting, a "preparatory," or council, meeting is held in local districts in conjunction with the regular worship service. This service of self-examination is held two weeks before communion. The day's sermons create an emotional build-up to the council service, when members are asked to affirm the Ordnung, indicate peace with God, and express a desire to partake of communion. Sometimes the council service is a tense time when sin and worldliness are purged from the community. A member said: "Twice yearly, you know, they have their bishops' meeting and then they come back to the church and announce what's up, you might say. Then the church, everybody, is given a voice to say yes or no. And you can say, 'No, I'm not agreed,' but you better have good documentation, and that's the way it should be."

The length of the council sermon, often two and a half hours, signals the meeting's importance. Children and nonmembers usually are not present. The sermon traces the Old Testament story from Genesis to the conquest of the Promised Land. The pivotal moment is the defeat of Joshua's army by the people of Ai. Amish ministers stress that hidden plunder had to be confessed and given up before Joshua's army could proceed to victory. The sermon then turns to the New Testament and shows how the golden thread of the Bible leads to Christ. Ministers plead with the congregation to destroy the "old leaven" so that the body can be healthy and grow. They reiterate that hidden sins of pride and disobedience, if not confessed, will, like the hidden sins of Israel at Ai, lead to the church's defeat.

After the sermon, the bishop presents the church's position on issues that are "making trouble at the time," or things that "the bishops are not allowing yet." The dress code is reaffirmed, and questionable social practices are discouraged. "We are asked to work against these troubles," a young minister explained, "and clean ourselves of them, and then we expect a testimony from each member to see if he is in agreement with that counseling." A member explained the procedure: "Two of the ministers go around, one with the men and one with the women, and they go around and ask each one, 'Are you agreed?' and everybody says, 'I'm agreed,' and you better be, too! Or have some grounds for it, which is right. This is done in front of the entire congregation." In cases of disagreement, members are asked to come to a front bench and explain their position.

If a serious impasse cannot be resolved, communion is postponed until the congregation is "at peace"—meaning that all members are in agreement with the Ordnung. The council service is a critical moment for purging sins of selfishness, pride, and self-will —moral decay that might disrupt the common life. The special service is also a moment when the moral order, the Ordnung, is reaffirmed and the collective will prevails. It is an especially moving moment if repentant offenders are reunited with the fellowship. If harmony is achieved in the council meeting, communion follows in two weeks. A day of fasting is normally held between the council service and communion.

The observance of communion begins about eight in the morning and continues until four in the afternoon, without a formal break. During the lunch hour, people quietly leave the main room in turns to eat a light meal in an adjoining room. The service peaks as the minister retells the suffering of Christ and then the congregation shares the bread and wine. Some ministers pace their sermons so that the passion story occurs at about three, to coincide with the supposed moment of Christ's death.

The bishop breaks bread to each member. The congregation drinks grape wine from a single cup that is passed around to commemorate the suffering and death of Jesus Christ. The sacrifice and bitter suffering of Christ are emphasized and held up as models for members. When speaking of the wine and bread, the bishop stresses the importance of individual members being crushed like a grain of wheat and pressed like a small berry to make a single drink. A bishop explained: "If one grain remains unbroken and whole, it can have no part with the whole . . . if one single berry remains whole, it has no share in the whole . . . and no fellowship with the rest."[14] These religious metaphors legitimize the importance of obedient yielding to the whole body.

The service culminates in foot-washing, as the congregation sings. Segregated by sex and arranged in pairs, members dip, wash,

Community solidarity is expressed at death as a funeral procession follows a hearse.

and dry each other's feet. Several tubs of warm water and towels are placed throughout the rooms. Symbolizing extreme humility, the washer stoops rather than kneels to wash the foot of a brother or sister. One bishop reminds his members that they are "stooping to the needs of their brother." The ritual of humility concludes with a "holy kiss" and an exchange of blessing between the two partners. At the end of the foot-washing, alms are handed individually to the deacon for the poor fund, the only type of offering ever taken in an Amish service. Having affirmed the moral order, the purified community turns to another six months of life together.

Ordination: Divine Lottery

The ordination of leaders is an emotional high point in the life of the community. The customary practice of leadership selection mirrors the Amish value system in several ways and stands in sharp contrast to the selection of professional pastors.[15] Only married men who are members of the local church district are eligible for ministerial office. The personal lifestyle of candidates is valued far above training or competence. There is no pay, training, or career path associated with the role of minister. It is considered haughty and arrogant to aspire for the office. Ministers are called by the congregation in a procedure known as "the lot," in which they yield to the mysteries of divine selection. The term of office is for life. If a minister is needed because of the illness or death of his predecessor, or the formation of a new church district, a unanimous congregational vote is required to hold an ordination.

The ordination service is typically held at the end of communion. Male and female members proceed to a room in the house and whisper the name of a candidate to the deacon, who passes it on to the bishop. Men who receive three or more votes are placed in the lot. Typically, about a half-dozen men receive enough votes. At the last instruction class before baptism, men pledge to serve as ordained leaders if called upon by the church. Thus, personal reasons for being excused from the lot are unacceptable. Those in the lot are asked if they are "in harmony with the ordinances of the church and the articles of faith." If they answer yes, they kneel for prayer, asking God to show which one he has chosen.[16]

The lot "falls" on the new minister with only a few minutes of warning. A slip of paper bearing a Bible verse is placed in a song book. The book is randomly arranged with other song books, in a number equal to the number of candidates. Seated around a table, the candidates each select a book. The bishop in charge says: "Lord of all generations, show us which one you have chosen among these brethren." The candidates then open the books, looking for the fateful paper. The lot "falls on the man as the Lord decrees."[17] The service is packed with emotion. Like a bolt of lightning, the lot strikes the new minister's family with the stunning realization that he is about to assume the high calling of ministerial responsibilities for the rest of his life. In the spirit of Gelassenheit, the "winner" receives neither applause nor congratulations. Rather, tears, somber silence, and sympathy are extended to the new leader and his family, who must bear the heavy burden of servanthood as they give themselves up to the church.

This simple ritual, based on biblical precedent, is an astute mechanism for leadership selection.[18] Once again, personal desires are surrendered to the common welfare. The leader and his family yield to the community "by giving themselves up" for the larger cause. No perks, prestige, financial gain, career goals, or personal objectives accrue to the officeholder. Although it would be haughty to seek ordination, some individuals may privately hope for the office, or at least enjoy the respect given their role after ordination. Core values are reaffirmed, for only local, untrained men are acceptable candidates. The permanency of the lot underscores the durability of commitment and community. The entire ritual is a cogent reminder that leadership rests on the bedrock of Gelassenheit.

Although this simple ritual may resemble a divine lottery to the outsider, it has profound social consequences. The abrupt "falling of the lot" prevents "campaigning" beforehand. All members may nominate candidates, but in the final analysis the leader is "chosen by the decree of the Lord." In a critical moment that will shape its life for years, the community yields and "accepts the Lord's will." Being selected by divine choice is quite different from being invited to serve a congregation by a sixty-to-forty vote. The minister may not be the first choice of some members, but his authority is legitimated by a divine mandate unequalled by seminary training and theological degrees. Members who are unhappy with the choice can only quarrel with God, not a faulty political process, or a power play by a search committee. Furthermore, only God fires Amish ministers. It is, in short, an ingenious solution to leadership selection that in a rather plain and simple manner confers stability, authority, and unity to community life.

Confession: Amish Therapy

Baptism, worship, communion, and ordination are sacred rites that revitalize the Amish moral order. But they are not enough to preserve the Ordnung. The Amish, like other people, forget, rebel, experiment, and, for a variety of reasons, stray into deviance. Formal social controls swing into action when informal ones fail. Beyond the aid of gossip to keep folks on the "straight and narrow way," the Amish have developed rituals of confession. These rites punish deviance and reunite backsliders into full fellowship. Confessions diminish self-will by reminding members of the supreme value of submission. Some members play the confessional role without remorse. Nevertheless, most confessions are cathartic moments, when the power of the corporate body unites with divine presence to purge the cancerous growth of individualism.

The form of the ritual depends on the seriousness of the deviance. Four levels of confession can be identified: private, "sitting," "kneeling," and a six-week ban. Level one involves a personal visit by the leaders of the congregation. Through personal observation or by hearing gossip, the bishop or ministers become aware that a member has violated the Ordnung. A member may have used a tractor in the field, cheated in a business deal, installed a silo unloader, joined a local planning commission, filed a lawsuit, attended a dance, participated in a Bible study group, or be planning to open a questionable business.

Following a pattern based on procedures outlined in Matthew 18, the bishop typically asks the deacon of the congregation to visit the wayward member. A minister usually accompanies the deacon. If the offense is a relatively minor matter that has drawn little attention in the church, and if the member displays an attitude of sorrow and contrition, the matter may be dropped at this stage. Issues solved in the privacy of barns and homes do not require public confession. The errant member simply acknowledges the wrong to the leaders and promises to stop the insulting behavior or to "put away" the offensive item. The deacon then reports the outcome of the meeting to the bishop.

Levels two and three involve public confessions. If the transgression was a public offense, in obvious violation of the Ordnung, the offender may be asked to make a confession at a members' meeting in order to appease the complainant. Moreover, members who spurn the leaders' advice and refuse to cooperate will likely be asked to make a confession before the congregation. Depending on circumstances, it may be a "sitting" or "kneeling" confession, representing levels two and three, respectively. The deviant member is asked to come to the next worship service, when the issue is brought to the congregation in a special members' meeting. The following sequence of events is typical.

The ministers discuss the problem in private during the first part of the regular worship service. The bishop "makes the layout of the situation," proposes a punishment for the person, or tries to strike an agreed plan of action among the ministers. At the end of the service, a hearing is held in front of all members. The bishop asks the defendant several questions about the incident. Defendants are given time to explain their side of the story and to correct the facts. After the hearing, the offender steps outside. If the hearing does not produce new information, the bishop presents the congregation with the punishment agreed upon by the ministers earlier in the morning. Members are asked if they agree with the proposed punishment. A minister said: "The congregation usually agrees with the bishop's layout, except if they know things that the ministers don't, and then they may have to recounsel the whole thing again." The unanimous consent of the congregation is sought before the individual returns to hear the verdict. The congregation usually consents to the bishop's proposal. The offender is then called back into the meeting and the punishment is announced publicly.

For a small offense—wearing jewelry or joining a public baseball team—a "sitting" confession (level two) can be made. For more serious offenses—such as traveling by airplane or hiring a car on Sundays—the person may be asked to make a "kneeling" confession (level three) in front of the congregation and to promise to abide by the Ordnung in the future.

The most severe form of punishment (level four) is a six-week ban.[19] During this time, the congregation avoids social contact with the wayward person. Offenders usually come to the three church services during this period and meet with the ministers for admonition. They leave immediately after the service, before the meal and fellowship. The exile allows them time to reflect on the seriousness of their transgression and to taste the stigma of shunning. It is hoped that all of this will produce repentance and a contrite spirit. At the end of the ban, offenders are invited to make a "kneeling" confession in a members' meeting. They are asked two questions: Do you believe the punishment was deserved? Do you believe your sins have been forgiven through the blood of Jesus Christ? Those who confess their sin and promise to "work with the church" are reinstated into it. The meeting concludes with some fitting words of comfort.[20]

For the "headstrong" who will neither submit nor confess to the church, the six-week probation leads to full excommunication. In any event, errant members are invited and urged to come to church. "If they don't come," explains a member, "then the church, you might say, subpoenas them; they must be there in two weeks and if they don't come then they lose their membership." This places the burden of responsibility on the offender.

In each situation there is considerable freedom to improvise. Ministers try hard to "work with the church" and resolve conflict in peaceful ways. There is, however, a firm resolve to seek solutions that will maintain harmony and save the "face" of the Ordnung, as well as the authority of Amish leaders. The entire process hinges on an attitude of submission—of Gelassenheit. Individuals who display an attitude of contrition are quickly forgiven and reinstated into the fellowship. The obstinate who mock the spirit of Gelassenheit will feel the harsh judgment of the congregation. A petty, tit-for-tat syndrome, fueled by envy, sometimes sours the confessional process. In one case, a member pressed for action against a bishop's son who was attending films and flaunting a car. In due time, the bishop sought his revenge by threatening to excommunicate the member for installing a telephone in his barn.

The ritual of confession is filled with humility and healing. A member sketched the confessional sequence that occurred after young church members attended a wild party hosted by Amish youth who had not joined the church:

> They go before the church and they must make a confession depending on the severity of what happened, and they may even lose their membership. They hardly ever refuse to make a confession. Can you picture this, after the church service, after these long sermons, we have a song, and then all the nonmembers go out quiet as a mouse, and can you imagine yourself, a young boy or girl, and you have to get off your seat and walk up and sit right in front of the ministers and you're supposed to talk so that the whole church hears you and you get questioned about this thing. Can you imagine not *giving up?* [emphasis added]. That's pretty impressive, it gets pretty strong.

The social pressure to confess is strong, but confession can also be a moment of healing that unites the congregation. A young couple, married for several years, asked the church to exclude them for six weeks because they felt guilty about their premarital behavior. A member described the experience: "They asked to be expelled and so there was this six-week period of repentance. Then they were reinstated as members and it was such a sensational thing, and everybody felt that this young couple really wanted to expose themselves and let the church know that they were sorry for what they had done and wanted to lead a better life. Everybody felt so good about it. It was really a healthy thing for the church. It was really a good feeling."

The practice of confession in front of the gathered congregation ritualizes the individual's subordination to the group. It strikes at the heart of individualism and heralds the virtues of Gelassenheit. In cathartic value, it bears a rough resemblance to modern psychotherapy, but it is less expensive and a bit more humiliating. In contrast to psychotherapy, most Amish confessions are initiated by the call of the church, not the individual. Amish confession, one of the costs of community solidarity, has been largely untouched by modernity. An Amish minister emphatically claimed that "not a thing has changed" in the confessional procedure over the years.

Expulsion: The Moral Purge

Corporations are not afraid to dismiss insubordinate employees. Modern churches, however, in the name of tolerance and love, are reluctant to dismiss deviant members. When confession fails, excommunication is the final recourse among the Amish. If baptism is the entrance to Amish life, excommunication is the exit. The door, however, is not slammed quickly. It can only be closed by the congregation's unanimous vote, after efforts to win back the deviant have failed. The German word *Bann* means "excommunication."[21] The English word *ban* is also used. From the internal perspective of Amish culture, the ban is designed to purify the body and redeem the backslider. The separation unites the community against sin. Ritual purges of deviance revitalize and affirm the moral order. In the same way that the punishment of criminals reaffirms the legal code of modern societies, so the expulsion of sinners rejuvenates the Amish Ordnung.

Although the process of expulsion sounds harsh to Moderns, who generally value tolerance, the Amish demonstrate considerable patience and leniency. A young farmer is given six months, until the next communion service, to remove the rubber tires from his tractor, because the purchase of steel wheels will cost $500. A businessman using a computer is allowed to complete a major eight-month project before he must "put it away." In the case of adultery, divorce, or purchase of an automobile, excommunication is virtually automatic. But in most cases leaders display considerable patience as they "work with" their members and "try to win them back."

If all else fails, the back door to the Amish house will close. A bishop is fond of saying: "The ban is like the last dose of medicine that you can give to a sinner. It either works for life or death." Leaders believe that errant members bring excommunication upon themselves by their stubbornness. But the door is always open a crack. Expelled members are welcomed back and will be reinstated if they are willing to kneel and confess their error. One man, excommunicated for dishonest business practices, decided to repent and confess his faults after nearly a year of exile. A senior bishop, in explaining the ban, emphasized the importance of love: "If love is lost, God's lost too. God is love, doesn't the Bible tell us God is love? And I sometimes think that love is worth more than fighting about this and that. You lose friendship through it."

The doctrinal statement of the Amish emphasizes the importance of maintaining the church's purity. "An offensive member and open sinner [must] be excluded from the church, rebuked before all and purged out as a leaven and thus remain until his amendment, as an example and warning to others and also that the church may be kept pure from such 'spots' and 'blemishes.'"[22] The theological intent of excommunication is to purge sin, but its social consequence is maintenance of the Ordnung. The ban is the ultimate form of social control. When mavericks sidestep the Ordnung or "jump the fence too far," the group disowns them to preserve the integrity of the common order. Community order, authority, and identity take precedence over tolerance. Even Moderns who cherish tolerance are often ready to expel dissidents, political traitors, illegal aliens, and insubordinate employees.

Meidung: Social Quarantine

A unique feature of Amish excommunication is the practice of Meidung, often called "shunning." As a reminder of the seriousness of their infractions, expelled people are ostracized in everyday life. "Compared to other church disciplines, ours has teeth in it," said one member. Meidung, the "teeth" of Amish discipline, is a cultural equivalent of solitary confinement, designed to preserve the well-being of the larger community.

Lack of agreement on the practice of Meidung triggered the Amish separation from the Swiss Anabaptists in 1693, and it has remained a distinguishing feature of Amish life. An Amish bishop explained the reason for shunning: "In the *Martyrs Mirror*, you read that if there's a ban and no shunning, it's like a house without doors or a church without walls where the people can just walk in and out as they please. That's what we hold to." The application of shunning varies in Amish communities but, in principle, remains the symbolic and substantive cornerstone of Amish church polity.[23]

A doctrinal statement on shunning spells out its theological justification:

> If anyone whether it be through a wicked life or perverse doctrine is . . . expelled from the church he must also according to the doctrine of Christ and his apostles, be shunned and avoided by all the members of the church (particularly by those to whom his misdeeds are known), whether it be in eating or drinking, or other such like social matters. In short that we are to have nothing to do with him; so that we may not become defiled by intercourse with him and partakers of his sins, but that he may be made ashamed, be affected in his mind, convinced in his conscience and thereby induced to amend his ways.[24]

A statement by the Lancaster bishops calls for shunning members "if they behave in a way that is offensive, irritating, disobedient or carnal, so that they may be caused to turn back, or till they come out of their disobedience."[25]

Excommunicated people are shunned until they repent. Upon confessing their sins, they are reinstated into the church. But, for unrepentant people, shunning becomes a lifetime quarantine. Amish-born people who have never joined the church are not shunned. Only those who break their baptismal vow by leaving the church or falling into disobedience are ostracized.

Shunning places a heavy moral stigma on the expelled. These "blemished" ones have forfeited their baptismal vows and turned their back on the church and God. Although interaction with expelled people is severely restricted, it is not completely terminated. Limited social conversation is permitted, but church members are advised not to deal directly with the outcasts or to accept anything from them. For instance, members will not accept a ride in the car of a former member who joins the Mennonites. Members avoid business dealings with those "under the ban." If a member sells something to an outcast, the member does not accept payment directly from the other person's hand. Sometimes a third party will handle a necessary business or social transaction. In other cases, the stigmatized person places the money on a table or counter, after which the church member picks it up.

The practice of shunning makes family gatherings especially awkward. The banned person may attend but will likely be served food at a separate table, or at the end of a table covered with a separate tablecloth. When family members are permanently excommunicated, they are, for all practical purposes, disowned. In one case, an adult male was excommunicated and shunned. He then was excluded from plans for his father's funeral. Soon afterward, he decided to make amends with the church and returned to the fold. A wife who persists in attending small group Bible studies with Christians of another denomination may be placed under the ban. Although continuing to live with her Amish husband, she must eat at a separate table and abstain from sexual relations. Parents must avoid adult children who are excommunicated. Brothers and sisters are required to shun each other. Church ties take precedence over family ones.

Families and congregations vary somewhat in how strictly they enforce social avoidance. Church members who refuse to ostracize the moral culprits are themselves expelled and shunned. The threat of social isolation is a powerful deterrent to disobedience in a community where everyone is linked by family ties. Meidung cautions those who would mock the church, scorn its Ordnung, or spurn the counsel of ordained leaders. To be socially quarantined for life is no small matter when it means separation from family, friends, and business colleagues. Meidung is a potent tool for social control. "It has holding power," an Amish minister said.

A former Amishman, shunned for more than fifty years because he joined a liberal church, described Meidung: "Shunning works a little bit like an electric fence around a pasture with a pretty good fence charger on it." While it packs a potent jolt for wayward members and their families, it is the cornerstone of social control in Amish society. Baptism, communion, and confession are redemptive modes of social control to keep folks in line with the Ordnung. When other means fail, the Meidung is there—a silent deterrent that encourages those who think about breaking their baptismal vows to think twice! Indeed, it is one of the secrets of the riddle of Amish survival. When asked about the ability of the church to hold its members, one person said: "That's easy to answer, it's the *Meidung*. If it weren't for shunning, many of our people would leave for a more progressive church where they could have electricity and cars."[26]

These rites of redemption and purification have stood the test of time and show few, if any, traces of erosion. They symbolize, rehearse, and communicate the essence of Amish culture. The kneeling posture in the rites of baptism, prayer, ordination, foot-washing, and confession portrays the stance of Gelassenheit. The Amish have refused to yield their sacred ritual to modern individualism, with its tolerance of deviant behavior. Such a concession would surely lead to the disintegration of their moral order. Their attempts to preserve order may seem legalistic and suffocating when compared to those of mainline churches. Yet the personnel policies that shape the organizational life of corporate and government bureaucracies are hardly less restrictive. The regulatory mind-set is not unique to the Amish; they have simply applied it to the moral bedrock that undergirds their entire way of life.

6

Passing on the Faith

Too much worldly wisdom is poison for the soul.
—Amish minister

The Riddle of Amish Education

Groups threatened by cultural extinction must indoctrinate their offspring if they want to preserve their unique heritage. Socialization of the very young is one of the most potent forms of social control. As cultural values slip into the child's mind, they become personal values—embedded in conscience and governed by emotions. Personal conscience, legitimated by religion, is more powerful than law in constraining behavior. Believing that the dominant culture threatens their traditional values, the Amish carefully socialize their young.

The Amish contend that the Bible commissions parents to train their children in religious matters as well as in the Amish way of life. For example, day-care centers, nursery schools, and kindergartens are not permitted, because children are to be instructed by their parents. As in most cultures, child rearing is an informal process where children learn the ways of their culture through interaction, observation, and modeling. Unlike modern children, however, Amish children have little exposure to diverse ideas and experiences. An ethnic nursery, staffed by extended family and church members, molds the Amish world view in the child's mind from the earliest moments of consciousness. Given the importance of ethnic education, it is surprising to discover that no Amish schools existed before 1938 and, in fact, very few existed before 1960.

The rise of the Amish school system chronicles a fascinating dialogue between the Amish and modernity. The Amish were willing to negotiate on some issues, but on this one they refused to budge. Many parents paid for their intransigence by imprisonment. Why were these gentle people so willing to snub progressive education? Why did they resort to courts, petitions, and politics to preserve humility? That is the riddle of Amish education. The forces of progress, trumpeting the virtues of education, were not about to be insulted by a motley group of peasant farmers. Through a variety of legal actions, the Amish were subpoenaed back to the educational bargaining table again and again.[1] Finally, in 1972, the Supreme Court ruled in their favor, stating that "there can be no assumption that today's majority is 'right' and the Amish and others are 'wrong.' A way of life that is odd or even erratic but interferes with no rights or interests of others is not to be condemned because it is different."[2] But that is getting ahead of our riddle.

The Little Red Schoolhouse

Publicity surrounding some of the court cases gave the erroneous impression that the Amish despised education. "We're not opposed to education," said one Amishman, "we're just against education higher than our heads, I mean education that we don't need." In the early days, Amish youth were as well-educated as the children of other early settlers.[3] When one-room public schools were established in 1844, the eldest son of an esteemed Amish bishop was a member of the school board.[4] The enforcement of compulsory attendance laws in 1895 stirred up some criticism, but, for the most part, the Amish supported public education in the rural one-room schoolhouse.[5] In the twentieth century, Amish children attended public elementary schools and their fathers frequently served as board members. In some schools Amish children were in the majority. Policies and curriculum were tailored to local sentiment. Teachers affirmed the rural culture, often their own, and complied with local requests. At the turn of the century, rural children attended school only four months out of the year. Passed in 1925, legislation required attendance until age fourteen, but local boards freely granted permits for farm work.[6] Providing a practical education in basic skills, the local schoolhouse dovetailed smoothly with Amish culture. The spirit of progress, however, continued. Over the years, the state legislature lengthened the school year, raised the compulsory attendance age, and enforced attendance. For the most part, the Amish accepted the changes in stride.

In 1925 rumors of school consolidation agitated a heavily populated Amish township. A candidate for public office declared his opposition to consolidated schools and promised not to close any of the one-room buildings.[7] Fears of consolidation were not illusions. The state was already paying school districts $200 each time they closed a

Amish children in a one-room public school ca. 1945.

one-room school. In a twenty-year period (1919–39), 120 one-room schools were abandoned in Lancaster County.

Mushrooming interest in education prompted an Amishman to write four articles debunking "excessive" education in a county newspaper in 1931. In a rare public outcry, he contended that a common elementary education was enough for an agricultural people. "Among all the Amish people in Lancaster County," he said, "you couldn't find one who ever took any high school, college or vocational school education. Yet I don't believe there's a class of people in the entire world that lead a happier life than do our people on the average. For pity's sake, don't raise the school age for farm children . . . for if they don't do farm work while they're young they seldom care for it when they're older." Complaining of rising school taxes, he asserted: "I am in favor of public schools, but I am not in favor of hiring teachers at twice the salaries that farmers are making to teach our girls to wash dishes and to dance." He described a young, educated female acquaintance who could not boil an egg as "a bright scholar, a good dancer, busy attending parties, in fact very busy equipping herself to be a modern flapper with lots of pep. Brother, if you want an educated modern wife, I wish you lots of wealth and patience and hope the Lord will have mercy upon your soul."[8] Experience, he concluded, is a better teacher than higher education.

The Tumult of 1937

The farmer's fear of encroaching education was an omen of a bitter confrontation that flared up in 1937. A plan to abandon ten one-room schools in one sweep and replace them with a consolidated elementary building sparked the controversy. Induced by a federal grant, officials in East Lampeter Township, home of many Amish, began building the new school despite local protests. Incensed that the consolidation would place their children on school buses and in classrooms with strange teachers, a coalition of citizens, largely Amish, organized themselves. Without the blessing of the church, but with the help of Philadelphia lawyers, they obtained a court order in April 1937 to halt construction of the new building. The two-month building recess was soon overturned by a higher court. Construction resumed, and the "newfangled" school opened in the fall of 1937. Some Amish children attended a one-room school that remained open, but others simply stayed home from school.[9]

In a surprising display of stubbornness, attorneys for the Amish renewed their fight in court. After meeting a delegation of Amish parents, Governor George H. Earle declared that he would reopen the ten one-room schools. The local school board balked, and the matter was tossed back and forth for another nine months. The legal matter was finally settled when the U.S. Court of Appeals blessed the consolidated school. In a conciliatory gesture, public officials maintained a one-room school for the Amish, but it only accommodated a few of them. The widely publicized dispute bitterly divided the larger community, as well as the Amish themselves.[10] Such aggressive use of the law was rare, if not unprecedented, in Amish history.

In the spring of 1937, as the East Lampeter dispute intensified, a more ominous cloud loomed over the Amish throughout the county.[11] School codes required attendance until age sixteen, but farm hands and domestics could drop out at age fourteen. In an effort to keep youth from snatching the few existing jobs from adults, legislators considered stretching the school term from eight to nine months, as well as raising the required attendance age for farm youth to age fifteen. Such talk, on top of the consolidation strife, frightened Amish leaders. Raising the compulsory age to fifteen years for farm hands and extending the school year would deprive parents of valuable help. Moreover, Amish youth would be bussed to consolidated schools and might need to attend a large, worldly high school for a year until they turned fifteen.

Frightened by the rumors, eight Amish bishops representing all sixteen districts petitioned a state legislator in March 1937 to "oppose all legislation" extending the school year and raising the compulsory attendance age.[12] The proponents of progressive education were not intimidated, however, by the views of a few farm folk. On 1 July 1937, as the Amish began a new harvest season, state legislators raised the compulsory attendance age for rural youth to fifteen years and lengthened the school term to nine months. This action mobilized the Amish in a massive protest that dwarfed the ongoing dispute in East Lampeter Township. After finishing their harvest and seeing the near-completion of the consolidated building, the bishops met in September to chart their course. They believed that the revised school code would "lead our children away from the faith." Each of the sixteen church districts asked a member to tap congregational sentiment.[13] Most members supported making a plea to state officials if it could be done in a "gentle way." The opinion of a hesitant minority was articulated by preacher Jacob Zook: "Better leave our fingers off; the Amish have stirred up enough stink for the present."

Most of the Amish, however, wanted action. With tacit support from the bishops, the sixteen delegates, preachers, and laymen met on 14 September 1937. They organized themselves and began a two-year struggle that would take them to legislative halls and the governor's office. Calling themselves the Delegation for Common Sense Schooling, they hammered out a bargaining position with two key features. First, they would not send their children into the nurture and teaching of the world until they were grown. Second, they would send their children to public schools on four conditions: an eight-month school year, exemption after eighth grade, one-room schoolhouses, and teaching children the truth.[14] After polishing a formal petition, the delegates launched a plan to gather sympathetic signatures and agreed "not to go to law, nor court, nor hire a lawyer."[15]

Armed with one thousand copies of their petition, the Amish canvassed for signatures in numerous townships. Public opinion split in response to the Amish plea. To haggle over one additional year of schooling seemed petty to many, but others lauded the Amish. In any event, the plain folk were able to garner over 3,000 signatures of support, which they pasted into a 130-foot scroll. Moreover, prominent businessmen from several communities rallied in support of the Amish with their own petition. Armed with the signed petitions, Amish representatives visited Governor Earle. Surprised by the public outcry, he stalled and asked Attorney General James H. Thompson to investigate whether the new school law did violate religious freedom. Shifting their tactics during the Thanksgiving season, Amish delegates decided to try some rural diplomacy on the governor. They presented him with a basket containing a dressed turkey, a gallon of cider, and an ear of corn—symbolic first fruits of the flock, orchard and field—hoping he would reciprocate with leniency.

Additional visits with state officials convinced the Amish that their only recourse was to petition the General Assembly of Pennsylvania for a revision of the law. So the Delegation for Common Sense Schooling wrote a new petition, "To Our Men of Authority," hoping to persuade the legislators to change the school law. They pleaded again to have Amish children exempt from schooling after the eighth grade regardless of their age. "We do not wish to withdraw from the common public schools," they concluded, but "at the same time we cannot hand our children over to where they will be led away from us."[16] Some Amish were critical of the school delegation's political activity, so, to solicit the support of their own people, the delegation sent a pamphlet explaining their goals to all their congregations in December. Members of the delegation promised that they would defend themselves "with the word of God rather than trying to defend [themselves] with the services of a lawyer."[17]

The Political Struggle

In December 1937, three events shrouded the traditional gaiety of the Amish wedding season. First, the consolidated elementary school had opened its doors despite Amish protests. Second, despite the Thanksgiving offering, formal petitions, personal meetings with top state officials, and pleading letters, Amish fourteen-year-olds had not been exempted from school. Many were hiding at home. Third, the Amish learned that modern culture cherished education and would not cater to them. Amishman Aaron King, who lived on the settlement's eastern fringe, was jailed for refusing to send his fourteen-year-old daughter to high school. King was convicted after a federal district court turned down his appeal in December 1937.[18]

The Christmas present the Amish delegation had hoped to receive in return for their Thanksgiving offering did not arrive. Instead, they were asking themselves if they would be willing to be imprisoned for the sake of their children's education. The new year opened on a bleak note. Attorney General Thompson declared that religious freedom and the rights of conscience could not obstruct the enforcement of school laws. In a blunt assessment of their bargaining clout, the Amish school committee concluded in January 1938 that "we got nothing."[19]

Writing a letter to Attorney General Thompson the next day, the head of the Amish delegation, Stephen F. Stolzfus, said that his impatient delegates wanted "to take a stand." "But," he continued, "I tried to cool them down and got them persuaded to just keep quiet and see what we get." He ended by saying: "If we get nothing from our men in authority, we must do something ourselves. Why can't the Board of Public Instruction show us leniency and exempt our children when they have a fair education for farm and domestic work? If we educate them for businessmen, doctors or lawyers they will make no farmers."[20] Hoping to avoid a public confrontation, Attorney General Thompson urged the Amish not "to do something drastic such as take a stand, as you call it." Citing the rumors and publicity that would surely come if they "took a stand," he admonished them to have "patience as taught in the Bible."[21]

By the late spring of 1938, Amish patience was dwindling. The Amish discussed setting up private schools and decided to consult state officials.[22] Public officials discouraged such schools and urged the Amish to bring their plea to the legislative assembly. So in the midst of the July wheat harvest, the Amish were busy drafting a new petition. After the bishops' blessing was received, five hundred copies were sent to legislators and other public officials. Included with the petition was an amendment to the school code prepared for the Amish by Attorney General Thompson's staff which would allow fourteen-year-olds to obtain work permits.[23] In May 1939, state legislators passed a measure permitting fourteen-year-olds to quit school for farm and domestic work. But the Amish had opened their first private schools in November 1938. The two Amish schools had opened nearly the same day that ten one-room public schools were sold at auction.[24]

After two years of strenuous effort, the Amish had achieved only one of their goals—work permits for fourteen-year-olds who had completed eighth grade. Accordingly, fifty-four permits were granted to Amish youth in the fall of 1939. The two-year battle had not achieved many Amish goals, but it brought a gift in disguise. The struggle had forced the Amish to hone their educational philosophy for the first time. The intense bargaining forged a philosophy of education that anchored the Amish outlook for the rest of the century.

Ralph T. Jefferson, an "educated" state representative from Philadelphia, wrote to the Amish and declared that "education is the greatest gateway to knowledge." Displaying gross ignorance of Amish culture, he urged them "to turn on your radio, the water, the light, the heat, the gas, the electric, and turn your mind again to the electric churn, milker, sweepers, irons, and washers . . . " as evidence of the fruits of education.[25] Such counsel to the Amish was a superb example of the folly of higher ignorance! The demand for farm products in the war years handed the Amish a brief respite. In May 1943, new legislation gave local school boards more flexibility to issue work permits.[26] The war also stalled construction of new Amish schools for another decade. Apart from minor skirmishes in local school districts, the education dispute was eclipsed by the war and leniency prevailed.

Imprisonment

The educational peace that the Amish had enjoyed during the war years vanished in 1949. In April, new legislation raised the compulsory school age to sixteen, unless the child was excused for farm or domestic work. A hidden clause gave the state superintendent of public instruction new power over work permits. The new law also required districts to bus students to high schools in neighboring townships if the district did not have a high school of its own. The sudden turn of events incited a bitter dispute between the Amish and state education officials. Dozens of Amish parents were jailed until a compromise was struck in the fall of 1955.

Brandishing the new regulations, the superintendent restricted work permits to "dire financial circumstances." The permits had to be approved not only by local and county educators but also by the superintendent himself. As a final gesture of his determination to enlighten Amish citizens, he threatened to withdraw state subsidies from school districts that overlooked the new regulations.

At least two dozen Amish fathers were arrested in the fall of 1949 for refusing to send their fourteen-year-old children to school. Two fathers appealed the conviction, but a court decision upheld the Amish arrests by ruling that religious sects were not immune from compliance with reasonable educational duties.[27] Provided with such legal ammunition, the Pennsylvania Department of Public Instruction opened a vigorous campaign to keep Amish youth in school.[28]

Meeting in February 1950, Amish bishops issued a fifteen-point statement, once again reiterating their traditional opposition to education beyond eight grades and fourteen years of age. Unlike earlier statements, this one was not addressed to legislators and did not plead for leniency. It merely spelled out their position and implied that this time they "would take a stand." They would do what was right according to their conscience. And like the martyrs of old, they were willing to suffer the consequences. One thing was certain in this round of negotiations—they would go to jail before acquiescing to educational progress.[29]

The bishops' statement fell on deaf ears. In the fall of 1950, 98 percent of the work applications from Lancaster County were rejected by the Department of Public Instruction.[30] Realizing that the state's threat to withdraw financial subsidies was not a bluff, local school districts began arresting Amish fathers who refused to send fourteen-year-olds to school. Within a three-day period in September 1950, thirty-six fathers were prosecuted. Refusing to pay fines because they argued they were innocent, thirty-one spent several days in jail until they were bailed out by non-Amish sympathizers.[31] Front-page photos showed the Amish entering the Lancaster County Prison. Bold newspaper headlines declared: "Dozens Go to Jail," "20 Amish Violators Prosecuted," and "Two Ministers among 19 Sent to Jail." In many cases, local sympathizers paid fines and bailed out the Amish after an overnight stint.

Fathers face arrest in an alderman's office ca. 1950 for refusing to send their children to consolidated schools for ninth grade.

Arrests and jailings continued intermittently for five years. An Amish father, arrested seven times, appealed his conviction as a test case in February 1954. Once again, a higher court sustained the conviction. This spurred a new round of arrests in the fall of 1954.[32] The five-year confrontation was bitter. Public opinion split. Amish members of local school boards, as well as non-Amish sympathizers, resigned. Still other local and county officials were miffed that the obstinate Amish were making such a ruckus over one year of schooling.

In order to keep their fifteen-year-olds out of public high schools, some parents made them repeat eighth grade. Others held their children back from first grade so that they would be fifteen years old when they completed eighth grade. Still others decided to take a stand and suffer arrest and brief imprisonment. One township developed an "eighth-grade-plus" program for Amish students who were not permitted to go to public high schools. One Amishman recalled his experience as a fourteen-year-old after his father had taken him out of school: "We were in the field one day and the constable came and served dad some papers. I had three days to appear in school. The next morning Pop said, 'You are going to school. I have neighbors all around me and I am not going to sit in jail, I just can't.' He was looked down on by some. After returning to eighth grade again, I read a hundred books, everything from classic literature to a series of biographies of the leaders of our country. And the irony of it

Newspaper headlines report Amish arrests and imprisonment for school violations in the early fifties.

was, that when we had to take our high school entrance tests, I had the highest mark in the whole county."

The Vocational Compromise

Was there no escape from this excruciating battle between modernity and tradition? After his adamant stand on work permits, the superintendent could hardly renege on his policy. But he was also tired of the rancorous public opinion that scorned his interpretation and conceded that "something might be able to be worked out within the law for both."[33] The Amish had chosen martyrdom over political action and were not about to lose face. As the arrests continued in the fall of 1953, the Amish bishops endorsed a statement that promised to save face for everyone around the bargaining table. The bishops agreed that the Amish would educate their own children beyond the eighth grade.[34]

The Amish position congealed in December 1953, when the bishops and the Amish School Committee approved a proposal for a vocational training program for children after they had completed eighth

Table 6-1 Turning Points in the Amish School Controversy

East Lampeter consolidation dispute	March 1937–May 1938
Bishops protest pending legislation	March 1937
School Committee[a] organizes	September 1937
School Committee protests legislation	1937–1941
Two Amish schools open	November 1938
Coexistence during war years	1942–1948
Enforcement and imprisonment	1949–1955
Bishops' eighteen-point statement	1950
Vocational school compromise	1955
Amish schools increase	1955–1975
U.S. Supreme Court decision	1972

[a]Sometimes called the School Delegation, this group evolved into the Old Order Book Society in 1957 and currently coordinates Amish schools.

grade in public school.[35] The solution appeased both parties. The state could say that Amish fourteen-year-olds were indeed in school, and the Amish were able to control the place and the content of the education.

Under the vocational program, an Amish teacher held classes, three hours per week, for a dozen or so fourteen-year-olds in an Amish home. The youth submitted diaries of their work activities around the farm and home and studied English, math, spelling, and vocational subjects. Attendance records were submitted to the state. But, in essence, the children were under the guidance of their parents for most of the week, an astonishing victory for the Amish.[36] With the state's blessing, the Amish ended the six-year struggle by opening their first vocational school in January 1956 in an Amish home.[37] Although voided by the 1972 Supreme Court ruling, the program still continues.

The inauguration of the program silenced debate on high school attendance, but it camouflaged a more serious problem stalking the Amish—the consolidation of public elementary schools. Elementary consolidation was gaining momentum by the mid-fifties. The Amish refused to send their children to consolidated elementary schools or, in some townships, to new junior high schools.[38] They had always resisted busing children to faraway classrooms with strange teachers and children, but it was the use of television in public elementary schools that incensed them at this moment, according to one Amishman. Beleaguered by political fights and imprisonment, the Amish decided to withdraw from the bargaining table once and for all and build their own schools. Thus, since the late fifties, the Amish have built and operated their own elementary schools.

The Fear of Education

Back to our riddle—Why did the Amish, in the words of preacher Jacob Zook, make such a "big stink" about education? Why were these gentle people willing to be arrested, fined, imprisoned, and mocked? What provoked them to hire attorneys, lobby legislators, solicit signatures, and circulate petitions? A scrutiny of the statements written in the heat of the struggle reveals objections that the Amish recited again and again in their pleas for leniency. For religious endorsement, they appealed to the Bible, the teaching of Christ, the examples of the Apostles, Anabaptist martyrs, Amish forefathers, tradition, experience, conscience, as well as religious liberty as granted by the Constitution.

Numerous themes echoed in the litany of protest:[39] (1) Location. The Amish wanted a local school, preferably one within walking distance. They did not want their children bussed. (2) Size. They objected to large consolidated schools, where pupils were sorted into separate rooms and assigned different teachers each year. They repeatedly pled for the one-room school, which had served them so well in the past. (3) Control. They believed that schools should be under the local community's control. According to their interpretation of the Bible, parents were responsible for nurturing and training their children. (4) Length. While they supported local one-room elementary education, the Amish felt that children belonged at home after the elementary grades. Parents also campaigned for a short, eight-month school year so that children could help with spring planting. (5) Teachers. They wanted teachers who were trustworthy and also sympathetic to Amish values and rural ways. The Amish refused to just "hand their children over" to professional educators. (6) Curriculum. They argued that high schools lauded "worldly wisdom," a phrase they borrowed from the *Martyrs Mirror*. "Worldly wisdom" clashed with "wisdom from above." A favorite Scripture stated clearly that the wisdom of man was foolishness in the eyes of God (1 Cor. 1:18–28). Furthermore, knowledge "puffeth up" and makes one proud (1 Cor. 8:1). Citing still another Scripture, they insisted that philosophy would spoil their children (Col. 2:8). Sex education, science, and evolution in the school curriculum symbolized the vanity of worldly wisdom. (7) Mode. Although they use textbooks in their own schools today, the Amish have always stressed the limits of "book learning." They repeatedly argued for practical training guided by example and experience. They stressed learning manual skills, for they believed that they should earn their bread by the sweat of their brow. Book learning, they feared, would lead their youth away from manual work. They wanted an Amish equivalent of internships and apprenticeships supervised by parents. (8) Peers. Too much association with worldly friends would corrupt their youth and lead to marriage and other forms of "unequal yoking" with outsiders. (9) Consequences. The paramount fear lurking beneath all the other concerns was that modern education would lead Amish youth away from farm and faith, and undermine the church. The wisdom of the world, said Amish sages, "makes you restless, wanting to leap and jump and not knowing where you will land."

Religion undergirded Amish objections to consolidated, modern education. But could not these spiritual explanations be brushed aside for economic ones? Weren't children essential to the maintenance of a labor-intensive farm economy? Religious and economic factors partially explain Amish resistance to modern education. However, a deeper reading of the transcripts of these bargaining sessions provides clues to why these gentle people resorted to political action to preserve humility.

Solving the Riddle

An Amish school leader provided hints of the deeper reason for rejecting progressive education. He described Amish opposition to high school: "With us, our religion is *inseparable* with a day's work, a night's rest, a meal, or any other practice; therefore, our education can much less be *separated* from our religious practices."[40] An Amish farmer said: "They tell me that in college you have to *pull everything apart*, analyze it and try to build it up from a scientific standpoint. That runs counter to what we've been taught on mother's knee" (emphasis added). Although few articulated it as eloquently as these people, the Amish realized that the consolidated high school, an embodiment of modernity, was a great separator.

The engineering logic of the assembly line, specialization, and efficiency—so successful in producing radios and Model T Fords—had been applied to education. The result was large consolidated schools. Having rejected the Model T, the Amish also feared this new educational model. They intuitively grasped that modern schools are social separators that fragment both social structure and human consciousness. The schools would assimilate minority youth into mass culture, but that assimilation would divorce them from their ethnic past. Despite their sixth-grade education, Amish parents knew that progressive education could fracture their traditional culture. One-room Amish schools, embodiments of social integration, stand today as the antithesis of modern education.

How was the modern school a separator? The Amish felt that high school education would separate children from their parents, their traditions, and their values. Education would be decontextualized—separated from the daily context of Amish life. The Amish

Many Amish children live within walking distance of their one-room school.

world, laced together by religious threads of meaning, would be divided into component parts: academic disciplines, courses, classes, grades, and multiple teachers. Even religion would be studied, analyzed, and eventually separated from family, history, and daily life. It would become just another subject for critical analysis. Professional specialists—educated in worldly universities and separated from the Amish in time, culture, and training—would be entrusted with nurturing their children. Such experts would encourage Amish youth to maximize their potential by pursuing more education to "liberate" themselves from the shackles of parochialism. By stirring aspirations and raising occupational hopes, the experts would steer Amish youth away from farm and family, or certainly lead to their restlessness if they did stay home.

Passing from teacher to teacher and from subject to subject in the educational assembly line, Amish students would encounter bewildering ideas, often at odds with their folk wisdom. Teachers would be unable to trace a child's performance in several subjects, or to have the delight of seeing the student gradually mature over the years. Moreover, Amish parents would be severed from the curriculum, policies, and administrators that would indoctrinate their youth. Abstract textbooks, written by distant specialists, would encourage intellectual gymnastics that surely would turn manual labor into drudgery. Most importantly, high school would separate Amish children from humility. In an environment that championed individuality, they would become self-confident, arrogant, and proud. Academic competition would foster individual achievement and independence, which in turn would sever their dependency on the ethnic community.

The consolidated school would also plunge Amish youth into a diverse setting teeming with non-Amish. High school friendships with outsiders would make it easier to leave the church in later years. The high school, a merchant of modernity, would sell young Amish a new set of values that would separate them from their past. The intellectual climate—rational thought, critical thinking, logic, scientific methods, symbolic abstractions—would breed dissatisfaction with the slow pace of Amish culture and erode the authority of Amish tradition. Amish youth would learn to scrutinize their life and culture with an analytic coolness that would threaten the bishops' power. In all of these ways, the high school would cultivate a friendship with modernity and encourage Amish youth to sever ties with the culture of their birthright. The Amish did not define the threat in such rational ways, but they understood its menace.

The Amish school system is a massive effort in social engineering which controls social interaction and the flow of ideas. Amish schools stifle relationships with the outside world. They inhibit the development of interpersonal skills necessary for comfortable relations with nonethnics—all of which increases dependence on the church. The Amish boycott of high schools obstructs the path to marriage with outsiders, professional careers, and social participation in mainstream organizations. More importantly, the Amish schools are an effort to manage consciousness, to set and control the agenda of ideas. Abstract and rational modes of thought are simply not entertained in the Amish school. The uniform world view propagated by Amish education funnels ideas in prescribed channels that undergird the ethnic social system.

Overlapping networks of like-minded others in the small Amish classroom insulate the child from rival explanations of reality and keep Amish ideology firmly intact. The schools, an important link in the chain of socialization, pass on a constricted view of the larger world. To Moderns, it is indeed a provincial education that restricts consciousness. But in a society where an expanded consciousness is not the highest virtue, Amish schools have ably passed on the traditions of faith to new generations. And that is the solution to our riddle. In order to protect the ways of Gelassenheit, these normally gentle people had to bargain aggressively with the imperialistic forces that sought to enlighten them with worldly education.

Amish Schools Today

Today, with few exceptions, Amish children attend one-room private schools staffed with Amish teachers.[41] In some cases, the Amish bought one-room schoolhouses when the public townships discarded them. Most recently, they have built their own schools. However, the twenty-year transition to Amish schools (1955–75) provoked considerable internal debate. Some parents wanted to send their children to public elementary schools to give them opportunities to interact with outsiders. The enthusiasm of some Amish parents for public education quickly waned upon the arrival of sex education, television, video, drug busts, and the teaching of evolution in the public schools. In 1950 there were only three Amish schools; by 1975 there were sixty-two. Today the Amish community wholeheartedly supports its private schools.

Today more than three thousand Amish pupils attend over one-hundred one-room private schools in the Lancaster settlement.[42] On the average, thirty-one students attend the schools, which often are built on the edges of Amish farms. Throughout the eight grades they learn spelling, English, German, mathematics, geography, and health. Although taught by Amish teachers, classes are conducted in English. Practical skills, applicable to everyday Amish life, are emphasized rather than abstract and analytic ones. Neither science nor religion is taught. Devotional exercises—Scripture reading, singing, and repeating the Lord's Prayer—are held each morning. To teach religion as an academic subject would objectify it and open the door for critical analysis. The Amish believe that formal religious training belongs in the domain of the family and church. According to a school manual, they hope that religion permeates the school "all day long in our curriculum and in the playgrounds." This goal is accomplished "by not cheating in arithmetic, by teaching cleanliness and thrift in health, by saying what we mean in English, by learning to make an honest living from the soil in geography, and by teaching honesty, respect, sincerity, humbleness, and the golden rule on the playground."[43]

Amish schools lack the educational trappings often taken for granted in public schools—sports programs, dances, physical education, cafeterias, field trips, clubs, bands and choruses, computers, guidance counselors, and principals. Battery-operated clocks, gas lanterns, wood stoves, hand-pumped water, and outdoor toilets are typical in the Amish school. Some of the textbooks are produced by Amish

Figure 6-1 Amish Schools, 1935–1990

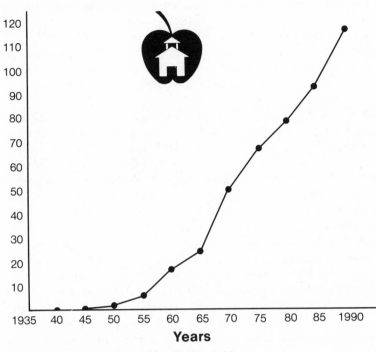

Years

Sources: Directory (1973), *Blackboard* (1986: 9–23).

publishers. Recess breaks in the morning and afternoon provide "time-out" from learning. Spelling bees and recitation by class groups are common. The children usually carry their lunch. Research evidence from other settlements suggests that, on the average, Amish students perform as well as other rural, non-Amish students in basic quantitative skills, spelling, and word usage.[44] The vitality of the Amish settlement certifies the ability of its schools to prepare pupils for a successful life in Amish culture—a more critical output measure than comparing them to non-Amish students. Moderns want to know if Amish schools compare favorably with public ones. The important question, however, is how well an education prepares pupils for adulthood. On that issue, Amish schools fare as well if not better than public schools.

Amish parents control their schools. They elect a three-member school board that oversees the school's operation. In some cases a five-member board may administer up to three schools. The school board hires, fires, and pays teachers (typically $20 per day). It also maintains the building and advises on curriculum. Other parents are involved with the school through visits, work "frolics," and special programs. In addition to paying public school taxes, the Amish support their own schools through a tax collected by the board's treasurer. A family with three children in school may pay as much as $250 in Amish school taxes per year. In all ways, the schools are locally owned and operated. In contrast to some public schools, where parents are kept at arm's length by professional educators, Amish schools give parents free access to the curriculum, instruction, and administration.

Teachers, typically single Amishwomen, have been educated through the eighth grade in the Amish school program. They are not state-certified but are selected on the basis of their natural interest in teaching, academic ability, and esteemed Amish values—faith, sincerity, and willingness to learn from pupils.[45] Whereas modern school administrators recruit teachers on the basis of degrees, certification, and professional skills, the Amish believe the foremost qualification for teachers is "good Christian character."[46] Ironically, the nonprofessional Amish teachers—free of the typical restrictions imposed by principals, professional organizations, and bureaucratic policies— have great latitude to shape curriculum, discipline, and policies according to their best judgment. The Old Order Book Society provides guidelines for curriculum and administration to encourage uniformity.[47] Amish teachers must cooperate with the church but, in contrast to professional teachers, have an astonishing amount of freedom to shape their instructional setting. Typically, teachers are on probation for three years.[48] Several county-wide teachers' meetings each year provide opportunities for the exchange of ideas and teaching tips. In addition, an Amish teachers' magazine, the *Blackboard Bulletin*, is a source of ideas and encouragement.

The Amish school buffets the tentacles of modernization. Cultural integrity triumphs over specialized expertise. Continuity reigns supreme. In some instances, all the children in a family have the same teacher for all eight grades. Parents relate to one teacher, who over the years develops a keen understanding of the family. A teacher may relate to as few as ten families in a school year, for there are four or five children from some households. Older children tutor younger ones. On the playground, like-minded Amish play together with relatives, neighbors, and church members, insulated from the contamination of outside culture. In the Amish school, sacred and secular, moral and academic, spiritual and intellectual, public and private spheres are not mixed together; they have simply never been separated. Obedience, tradition, humility, and religious values eclipse rationality, competition, and diversity. Whereas modern high school students write analytical essays, conduct scientific experiments, and learn to think critically, Amish youth leave the eighth-grade classroom for apprenticeships in farming, crafts, shop work, and manual trades—where experience rather than a degree counts.

The Mellow Years

The relationship between the Amish and public education officials mellowed after the Amish received the blessing of the Supreme Court in 1972. Some legislators share pending regulations with Amish leaders for reaction and counsel. In some cases, informal agreements spell out mutual expectations. Amish schools, for instance, are heated by wood or coal furnaces in the classroom, because they rarely have basements. However, state fire regulations prohibit furnaces in open classrooms. Building basements for the sole purpose of housing furnaces would have been quite costly. After several discussions, state officials agreed to overlook the furnace infractions.

In the mid-eighties, new regulations called for schools to be state-certified. This was a rather perfunctory process for the Amish. According to an Amish spokesman, state officials agreed to honor past informal agreements and not impose new regulations if the Amish, in turn, would agree not to obstruct the pending legislation. Setting their own standards, the Amish designed and printed their own certification forms. A few descriptive facts on each school are reported on the certification form, which also states that the school is open 180 days. "For many things," the spokesman said, "it is better if we don't even ask state officials because it just puts them on the spot." The bitter struggles of early years have been replaced with benign neglect and mutual respect.

Although some may occasionally take high school correspondence courses, Amish children rarely attend public high school. Even Amish teachers are urged to prepare for teaching through self-education rather than correspondence courses. Young shop workers occasionally take short courses in specialized mechanics, but few Amish youth aspire to go to high school. Describing high school, a minister said: "There's no longing for it, no call for it, it's rarely mentioned. I don't know of anybody that would want to go." For the occasional youth who attends high school or college, separation from the church is painful, especially if the youth is a member. A professional social worker, excommunicated by the Amish church prior to her senior year in college, described trying to dissuade her bishop from excommunicating her: "He was a just and deeply caring person. I met him out in the field. I asked questions about education and sin and tried my best to make him understand that I wanted to continue both my education and my membership in the Amish community. He would not say that further education was sin and he agonized in his efforts to explain why excommunication was necessary if I would not repent. Both of us were sensitive and hurt deeply; we cried unashamedly."[49]

All things considered, the Amish have held the upper hand in the thirty-six-year dispute that ended with the Supreme Court decision in 1972. The only issue that they had conceded was the shortened school year. Even so, with fewer holidays and shorter vacations, Amish schools end before public ones, to honor the spring planting season. On all the other issues—location, size, control, compulsory age, and curriculum—Amish convictions held sway.

Sowing and Reaping Wild Oats

There is even a more perplexing riddle than the Amish use of force to protect humility. Why do the Amish, who fought so hard for the right to teach their children humility, permit rebellious teen-agers to flirt with the world? And why do some youth, educated in the ways of obedience, suddenly turn to mischief a few years later? The rowdiness of Amish youth is an embarrassment to church leaders and a stigma in the larger community. Before baptism, many of the boys own cars on the sly and others drive them with and without licenses. One leader claims that the baptismal age is higher for boys than girls because the boys do not want to give up their cars. Another member estimates that 30 percent of the young males own cars, 40 percent have a driver's license, and as many as 70 percent drive at one time or another.

Amish youth typically join one of several groups of Amish youth known as "crowds." Ranging from one hundred to three hundred people, the "crowds" crisscross the settlement. These groups vary considerably in their conformity to traditional Amish values. Some are fairly docile, but others engage in boisterous behavior that occasionally makes newspaper headlines. Membership often follows family tradition and is a prime source of identity for Amish youth prior to marriage. The reputation of the "crowd" signals whether a young person is liberal or conservative. The groups engage in recreation—baseball, swimming, ice-skating, roller-skating, singings, parties, and barn dances called hoedowns. A group sometimes rents a public roller-skating rink for a party. In addition to the large group activities, smaller clusters of Amish youth attend films in public theaters and travel to the shore or to cities, such as New York.

For many of these activities, Amish youth, especially boys, shed their sectarian garb. Hatless, and wearing styled hair and store-bought jackets, they "pass" as typical youth. Hair styles often signal the extent of their deviance. Many parties involve the use and abuse of alcohol. In one case, alcohol abuse was so consistent and flagrant that public officials wrote to church leaders asking for help in curbing it.[50]

An Amish teenager keeps his car by two corncribs, a respectful distance from the house.

Youth are sometimes arrested for drunken driving and, in other cases, have been involved in fatal accidents. The rebellious antics, often called "sowing wild oats," have come to be expected behavior for Amish youth. On some occasions, the mischief is carefully hidden from parents, but in other instances church rules are openly mocked. It is a liminal stage in Amish culture when youth are neither in the church nor out of it. They are truly betwixt and between. Thoroughly socialized in an Amish environment, they have not yet taken the baptismal vow. Many Amish leaders are chagrined by the worldly behavior of the teen-agers, but quickly point out that there is little they can do, because the unbaptized youth are not yet under the church's control. Leaders attribute this slippage in the cultural system to poor enforcement by parents.

To both insider and outsider, teen-age rowdiness appears at first as a tatter on the quilt of Amish culture. There is, however, a compelling sociological explanation for this persistent tradition. These rowdy youth usually settle down to become humble Amish adults. There are exceptions, but, for the most part, the flirtation with worldliness does not lead them away from the church. Tampering with the world is a form of social immunization. It provides some teen-age excitement, but also a minimal dosage of worldliness that strengthens resistance in adulthood. This quirk in Amish culture has a redeeming function in the social system, which may explain why it persists.

Flings with worldliness give Amish youth the impression that they have a choice regarding church membership. The loophole conveys the perception that they are free to leave the Amish if they so choose. The evidence, however, suggests that the perceived choice is partially an illusion. Amish youth have been thoroughly immersed in a total ethnic world with its own language, symbols, and world view. Moreover, all of their significant friendships are within the Amish community. To leave the Amish fold would mean to sever all cherished friendships and family ties—although if not baptized, they would not be shunned. Rejecting their birthright culture would thrust them into an entirely different world. Even on escapades to faraway cities Amish youth travel together. These reference groups insulate the rebels from the terror of a solitary encounter with the real world.

In many ways, Amish youth do not have a "real" choice. This is likely one of the reasons why over 80 percent of them do, in fact, embrace Amish ways. For the majority who join the church, the illusion of a choice serves a critical function in adult life. Thinking they had a choice as youth, adults are more likely to comply with the demands of the Ordnung. Members might reason this way: "If, after all, I chose to be baptized and vowed on my knees to support the church with the full knowledge of its requirements, then I should be willing to obey the demands of the Ordnung." Without the perception of choice—the sowing of wild oats—adult members might be less willing to comply with church rules, and in the long run this would weaken the community's ability to maintain social control. The wild oats are reaped by the church, in the form of obedient adults who willingly comply with the Ordnung because they believe they had a choice. The wild oats tradition yields a rich harvest for the church—a cornerstone in the group's ability to elicit obedience from adults. And that may be the reason why parents who will suffer imprisonment for the education of their youth will also let them flirt with the world.

7

The Riddles of Technology

The telephone is still on probation.
—Amish grandmother

The Breach of 1910

The positive marks of Amish identity—horse, buggy, dress, windmill—also have their negative counterparts. Radios, televisions, cars, and tractors became profane symbols in the Amish mind in the twentieth century. However, faced with modernization, the Amish have been willing to negotiate the *use* of telephones, electricity, cars, and tractors. The bargaining sessions, stretching over the decades, have produced what appear today as perplexing riddles. This chapter explores the riddles surrounding the use of telephones and electricity. Solving them requires a brief look at their historical context. This backdrop involves the breach of 1910—a turning point in the Amish saga which sets the stage for the riddles.

The roots of the 1910 schism go back to the early 1890s. An Amish minister, Moses Hartz, had a son by the same name who became a traveling agent for a milling company. Finding the Amish environment too constricting, the son stopped attending services and, among other things, began wearing pockets on the outside of his coat—a convenience forbidden by the Amish. In April 1895, without the unanimous consent of his congregation, the presiding Amish bishop excommunicated the son and placed him under the ban. As an Amish minister, his father was expected to uphold church rules. However, he balked and refused to shun his offspring. After futile efforts by the church to change the father's mind, he was "silenced" as a minister and, with his wife, was placed under the ban.[1]

Eventually the Hartzes were received as members in a progressive Amish-Mennonite congregation, after making a "kneeling" confession. Upon hearing of their confession, Amish leaders called a special meeting and decided to lift the ban. A minister who missed the special meeting was perturbed by the decision. He promptly contacted other Amish leaders and persuaded them to renew the ban. The Amish leaders eventually reversed their decision, and the Hartzes were, once again, shunned. They remained in social exile for the rest of their lives.[2] This action, in the late 1890s, marked the strict use of shunning on members who joined similar but more progressive churches. The episode triggered intense debate on the practice of shunning, which smoldered for twenty-five years, until the bishops released a special statement in 1921, hoping to put the issue to rest.[3]

The Hartz incident, however, is only the prelude to the real story. The controversy brewed for over ten years until 1909—a time of rapid social change—when cars, telephones, and electricity were making their debut. The strict shunning of members who joined progressive Amish-Mennonite churches kindled the ire of some members of the Amish church. The disenchanted families had already been dabbling with progressive changes, but the strict enforcement of shunning in the Hartz case galvanized their dissent. In the fall of 1909, about thirty-five Amish families who had been disturbed by the Hartz incident began holding separate services every three or four weeks for singing and Bible reading. The group petitioned the bishops for a more lenient use of the ban and announced their intention "to withdraw" if the request was not granted.[4] Meeting on 12 October 1909, the Amish bishops denied their request. The splinter group, of some eighty-five people, represented about one-fifth of Amish membership at the time. The new group held its first worship service in February 1910, and it ordained two ministers at its second communion service in April 1911.[5]

The progressive faction was eventually dubbed the Peachey church, for it was assisted by two ministers named Peachey from an Amish congregation in central Pennsylvania.[6] In contrast to the mild separation of 1877, the breach of 1910 stirred strong emotional feelings. Even some seventy-five years later, an Amish minister still contends that the dissenting group was "just a bunch of hotheads." Although its dress and cultural practices remained Amish for some time, the Peachey church accepted new technology more readily than the Old Order Amish. Soon its members were using telephones, tractors, and electric lights. They were permitted cars by 1928, and by 1930 they were worshipping in a church building. In 1950 the Peachey church became affiliated with a larger national body, the Beachy Amish church. Today six congregations are affiliated with the Beachy Amish church in Lancaster County.[7] They conduct their worship services in English, hold Sunday school, drive cars, and use electricity. The men wear an abbreviated beard, and members dress in plain garb, although not as plain as that of the Old Order Amish.

An intriguing aspect of this milestone in Amish history is the contrasting interpretations that the two factions use to explain the schism. Most printed interpretations were written by those on the progressive side, Beachy Amish or Mennonites. These accounts attribute the 1910 split to the strict shunning of the Hartzes.[8] An Old Order Amish document verifies that shunning was central in the dispute.[9] However, as often happens in oral history, other explanations evolve over time. It is striking that Amish leaders, some seventy-five years later, insist that telephones and the use of electricity were key issues, or "handles," in the 1910 cleavage. While acknowledging that shunning was an issue, the Old Order Amish contend that the technological changes were also key irritants. Other members suggest that although the telephone may not have been the catalytic factor, the Peachey church began to use telephones about the same time that the Old Order Amish forbade them. Regardless of the historical facts, what is important for our purposes is that the Amish still perceive the telephone as a symbol of the breach of 1910. The division cast a shadow over the telephone and shaped the Amish attitude toward it in the twentieth century.[10]

The Telephone Riddle

The use of phones has been a contentious issue among the Amish in recent years. Phones are forbidden in their homes. Why would the phone—that indispensable modern mouthpiece—take on moral connotations? Why should it receive the stigma of worldliness?

Invented in 1876, the phone gradually entered American homes after the turn of the century. But as late as 1940, only half of Pennsylvania farmers had one.[11] Rejecting it early in the century, the Amish have gradually "allowed it to creep in," and one informant says that "now everybody uses them, well at least 99 percent!" The phone saga provides a fascinating insight into the Amish ordeal with modernity.

Surprisingly, a number of Amish purchased phones as they appeared in rural areas in the first decade of the century. Some early phones were merely homemade concoctions of lines strung between neighboring homes. One Amishman said: "I remember when the phones came. The church didn't say anything about them. It was thumbs up. Two of my wife's uncles had the phones in and there were quite a few others that had them and then an issue came up. Two people talking on the phone were gossiping about someone else and it went so far that it became a church issue. They were asked to come to church and make a confession about it. Then the church decided that we just better not allow these phones."[12] An Amish historian estimates that "around 1908 the bishops decided that the phone should be put away and those involved in it just dropped it and tore the lines out."

Today's Amish are not entirely sure why the bishops outlawed phones, except that they made gossip too easy, were too handy, and were worldly. Apart from the tag *worldly*, no religious injunctions are cited against the phone. However, its *use* was never banned. The Amish have readily used a neighbor's phone for emergencies and have had standing agreements to borrow phones in nearby garages or shops. Installing phones in houses, however, has been a firm taboo since the Ordnung forbade it around 1910.

A complicating but crucial factor in the phone decision was the formation of the Peachey church. An Amish minister stated: "A group of people got a bit rebellious and they started to get telephones and this dragged along until 1909." An Amishman who was thirteen years old at the time said: "The phone was one of the issues [in the division]."[13] Whether phones helped to provoke the division or whether the dissidents started installing them after they split with the Old Order Amish is unclear. What is certain is that the bishops rejected phones about the same time that the progressive Peachey church left the Amish fold. And, among other things, the Peachey church installed phones, which was reason enough for the Amish to permanently outlaw them. When asked about the reason for prohibiting the phone, an Amish leader said: "It's something that's left over from 1909." Compared to the divisions of 1877 and 1966, the split of 1910 was especially bitter. Regardless of the sequence of events, it was obvious that the liberals had adopted the phone and that the Old Order Amish could never accept it again without a severe loss of face. Permitting phones would be a de facto endorsement of the insurgents. In essence, the Peachey church functioned as a negative reference group—a model of worldliness, which the Amish hoped to avoid.

To explain the phone taboo solely as an intergroup, face-saving ploy overlooks deeper social meanings. The phone is a tool of modernity, in both symbolic and substantive ways. It ties one to the outside world. A social analyst noted: "The telephone was a major means of alleviating the isolation of country life."[14] Lacking automobiles, good roads, electricity, radios, mass media, and regular postal service, rural areas were insulated from urban influences. The telephone line was the first visible link to the larger industrial world—a real and symbolic tie that mocked the Amish belief in separation from the world. Thus, in the context of an isolated, rural subculture bombarded with new inventions, it was not a stupid or thoughtless reflex to dub the phone "worldly."

In modern information societies, media images, data printouts, and electronic communications are major conduits of social interaction. They allow people in vastly different settings to communicate with one another. The messages, however, are decontextualized, detached from their immediate surroundings. In a highly mobile society, the phone connects people separated by thousands of miles, and yet, for the Amish, bonded by face-to-face interaction, it was a separator.

The phone decontextualizes conversation by extracting it from a shared social context filled with symbolic codes. Although close friends can discuss intimate matters on a phone, such conversations lack the rich nuances of body language, facial expression, and eye contact. In contrast to the spontaneity and immediacy of face-to-face conversation, phone talk is more formal, abstract, distant, and mechanical. Young children find telephone conversation baffling because it requires greater abstraction than face-to-face chatter. One must imagine the other person in a different context removed from the immediate setting.[15]

One clue to the uniqueness of phone talk is that it must be learned. Amish unfamiliar with the phone speak with awkward pauses and uncertain sentences when they call a nurse or physician.[16] As the phone came into wider use among the Amish in the seventies, an Amish publication provided instructions on how to make phone calls to other settlements to report a death.[17] Readers were given instructions that would be taken for granted by Moderns: "When you are making a call give your name and the location that you are calling from. If a child answers, ask for a parent or older person. Tell the person you have a death message for: name and address. Ask if they will please deliver it as soon as possible." Phone talk is learned, segmented, rational, and impersonal—an idiom that in form, tone, and structure is the mechanical language of modernity.

Phone conversations reflect distant, secondary relationships in several ways. The old adage "It's easier to say 'no' on the phone than in person" captures the greater social distance and lower personal accountability underlying phone conversations. They obviously unite people. But one is never sure if the person on the other end of the line is mocking, laughing silently, or, worse yet, doing things to relieve boredom, while giving the impression of "listening." One has to imagine the other person's location and appearance. Dress clues, so critical in Amish society for assessing a person's attitude, are impossible to see. In this sense, phone conversations are "half messages" stripped of body language and contextual symbols.

Phones separate in other ways. Face-to-face talk and spontaneous visiting are the chief forms of social interaction in Amish society. While visiting, the Amish share death, birth, and wedding announcements, as well as everyday news. Calling reduces visiting. If one can phone, why visit? Hostetler has shown that silence is an important form of communication in Amish society.[18] Silent messages do not transmit well on phones. In the long run, the phone threatened to alter Amish communication patterns. The Amish never developed elaborate arguments against the phone, but they understood that a ban of it would reinforce face-to-face communication. Although quicker and handier, the phone would eventually erode the core of Amish culture: face-to-face conversations.

In 1910, as the Peachey church was splitting off from the Amish church, the phone's fate was sealed. Modernity, however, was not ready to take an Amish "no." Pressures to accept phones have plagued the Amish, and, in recent years, phones have been "creeping in" around barns and shops. An older minister said: "They are being smuggled into shops and they're getting out of hand." Caught between their historic taboo on the phone and increasing business pressure, the Amish have negotiated some ingenious compromises.

The Telephone Shanty

As the Depression was easing in the mid-thirties, several Amish families approached church leaders and requested permission to share a phone. According to oral tradition, they argued that "in case of a fire or something, or an emergency, if someone needs a doctor, there's no telephone nearby." They pleaded with the ministers to have a "community phone." "It was tolerated," said an Amish leader, "and that was the beginning of the 'community phone.' They had a phone in someone's building but it had to be taken out and put into a phone shanty like the ones we have today."

Over the years, community phones have gradually appeared in small shanties at the end of farm lanes. The upsurge in such phones came after 1960. Telephone shanties—which often resemble outhouses in size and appearance—are typically found at the end of lanes or beside barns and sheds. Several families share the phone and its expenses. With an unlisted number, the phone is primarily used for outgoing calls to make appointments and conduct farm business. Loud call bells that amplify the phone's ring are prohibited by some bishops to restrict incoming calls. In recent years, the Amish have begun calling one another. Friends or business associates schedule routine times when they are "handy" to receive calls, and often special "appointments" are set up in advance. The principle of separation from the world is expressed by using unlisted numbers.

Various reasons are given for permitting the community phones: (1) the lack of nearby non-Amish neighbors in densely populated areas, (2) the embarrassment of farmers dragging barn dirt and smells into non-Amish homes, (3) the need to make appointments with doctors, (4) the need of farmers to call veterinarians and feed dealers,[19] (5) the need of businessmen to order supplies, and (6) the need to

A community phone shanty shared by several farmers.

call family members living in other settlements or on the outer edge of the Lancaster community.

Convenience, economic necessity, and a sprawling settlement have created ingenious arrangements that bring phones within easy reach yet preserve the ban on home phones. But the transition to the phone was not easy. "We had a good bit of trouble with these telephones," said a bishop. "It's cooled down pretty well just now since we got these community phones. That was a pretty big thing to get over. They started putting them in and we didn't like it." Another member said the phone had the potential to cause a split in the church. "The telephones are still on probation," said a wise grandmother.

Community phones in public shanties were widely accepted by 1980. Today heated discussions focus on the use of phones in Amish shops. Church districts vary widely on the use of phones in shops and barns. The settlement's conservative, southern part, with a high proportion of farmers, has a strict policy on phones. But in the heart of the settlement, with shops galore, they abound. It is not unusual to find farmers with a private phone in the barn, tobacco shed, or chicken house, usually tucked away from public view. Lacking a radio, some farmers routinely call the national weather service for forecasts each morning.

The strongest pressure for phones has come from small shop owners and businessmen. Some bishops permit phones in shops, but others do not. A bishop allowed a phone inside one business because he felt it was rude to make customers order merchandise by mail. Some church districts permit phones in shanties built adjacent to shops, allowing the caller to literally reach out the window to use the phone. A few bishops benignly permit loud "call bells." Some businessmen use an informal answering service provided by a non-Amish neighbor. In other districts, phones are routinely found in shops. Phone numbers are usually unlisted, but some young entrepreneurs print their number, or answering service number, on their business cards.

A successful businessman who uses a state-of-the-art electronic cash register explained why he does not have a telephone: "The bishop said that he'd really rather that I didn't have one if it's just for the sake of convenience, unless I have to. So I use a neighbor's answering service since [a phone] isn't really necessary and since the bishop is on top of the list of the people that I respect." Some people who do not own shops or major farming operations also have private phones. An Amish family living in a double house rents a phone in the basement on the "English" side of their house. Another shop owner has a phone in a shanty built against the back porch of his house. Two single sisters living in a small village installed one in their small horse barn. One person said her uncle has a hidden one in his home and "his father would turn in his grave if he saw it."

The Telephone Bargain

Apart from the historic forces that shaped the interdiction against phones, present-day explanations for banning them from homes hinge on two issues: separation and community integration. The Amish believe that a home phone separates but that a community phone integrates. When asked why the Amish are afraid of the phone, a respondent said: "If you have a phone in the house and you have growing children, as they get older, why then you're going to have one child who wants one up in her bedroom and the other one who wants an extension in her bedroom and it just goes on and on and it *separates*

A telephone moves closer to an Amishman's manufacturing shop. Some businesses now have multi-line phones inside the building.

the whole family" (emphasis added). A grandfather explained: "If you have a place of business and need a phone it must be *separate* from the building, and if it's on the farm it must be *separate* from the house. It should be *shared* with the public so that others can use it. It's just not allowed in the house, where would it stop? We stress keeping things small and keeping the family *together*" (emphasis added).

Some Amishmen point out that with phones in their homes women especially would "waste a lot of time in endless chatter." A businessman described the practice as a buffer against interruptions: "If we had a telephone up there in the shop I would just be bothered all the time. I just don't want any up there. It needs to be separate from the building." Such logic—an Amish version of taking the receiver off the hook or pushing the ring switch to "off"—is a way of holding technology at bay. The inconvenience of walking a half-mile to use a phone or taking messages from an answering service is a daily reminder that membership in an ethnic community exacts a price—a reminder that things that are too handy and too convenient lead to sloth and pride.

The Amish do not consider the phone a moral evil that will lead to eternal damnation. Their question is "If we 'give in' on the phone, what will be next?" In this sense, it symbolizes worldliness. The Amish have a good grasp of the social consequences of the phone for family life—gossip, individuation (multiple phones), and continual interruptions. Its ring and frequent interruptions would impose a mechanistic definition of time on family life—an intrusion that would "spoil" the natural flow of family rhythms. The Amish think that phone use pulls families apart because it results in family members attending meetings, scheduling appointments, and spending less time together. Phones allow unwanted visitors to intrude into the privacy of one's home at any moment. The phone is indeed a modern intrusion, an instrument that threatens to impose a technological structure on the flow of spontaneous face-to-face relations in Amish life.

The phone deal that the Amish negotiated is an ingenious solution to their dilemma. They have agreed to exclude it from homes, while allowing its use in community shanties and in or near shops and barns. The bargain incorporates key understandings in the fine print: (1) It upholds their historic opposition to the phone, thus keeping faith with tradition. They can say, "As always, we don't approve of home phones." (2) It saves face with the splinter group of 1910 who live side by side with the Amish today. Banning the home phone demonstrates that the Amish have not drifted into the worldliness of the liberal churches. (3) It preserves the natural rhythms of face-to-face interaction in home and family. (4) It controls technology. The Amish keep the phone at a distance and use it only when necessary. In this way, they are its master rather than its servant. (5) It encourages cooperation through the use of community phones. (6) It symbolizes key Amish values: separation from the world, establishing limits, shunning convenience, preserving family solidarity, and respecting past wisdom. (7) It permits the development of small industries that are critical for the economic viability of the Amish community.

The phone agreement is a way to absorb change and uphold tradition and to appease both the traditionalists who strenuously object to its use and the entrepreneurs who need it for economic survival. It is a deal that allows the Amish to have their cake and eat it too—preserving tradition while bending to economic pressures. The agreement provides a common symbolic front, for both traditional and progressive Amish can say: "We don't permit home phones." And it leaves plenty of room backstage to improvise according to the local bishop's discretion.

The Riddle of Electricity

Electricity is conspicuously absent from Amish homesteads. Newer Amish homes, with contemporary decor, have pleasant kitchens and modern bathrooms. But electrical appliances—microwaves, VCRs, radios, air conditioners, hair dryers, dishwashers, toasters, mixers, blenders, can openers, electric knives—are all missing. Bottled gas is used to heat water and to operate modern stoves and refrigerators. Homes, barns, and shops are lit with gas-pressured lanterns hung from ceilings, mounted on walls, or built on mobile wooden cabinets that enclose the gas tanks.

The Amish use electricity in several ways. Flashing red lights on the back of buggies warn approaching traffic. Electric fences keep cattle in pastures. The milk in Amish bulk tanks is stirred by electric motors. The elderly read by small, battery-operated lamps. Electric welding machines abound on Amish farms. Carpentry crews use electric power saws. The solution to the riddle of electricity is found in tradition, intergroup relations, economic pressure, and conscious decisions to avoid worldly entrapments. A brief review of electrical usage in the larger society sets the stage for the Amish story.

The Edison Electric Company began operations in Lancaster City in 1886. Arc lights soon illuminated streets, and some six thousand incandescent bulbs were eventually burning in homes and businesses. From 1890 to 1900, hotels and businesses used electric motors for power. Electric trolley cars began replacing horse-drawn "buses."[20] But, for the most part, electricity was not used beyond the city in these early years. In the first two decades of the new century, power lines gradually crept into the countryside along main roads. Some outlying towns began operating their own power plants, but many rural areas still relied on the kerosene lamp and lantern. In 1924, only 10 percent of Pennsylvania farms had current for lights and appliances. By 1930, there were ten thousand private electric plants on farms, but most Pennsylvania farmers still worked by lantern light.[21]

Four types of electrical service had emerged by the thirties. First, cities and boroughs had independent generating plants. Second, many farms and businesses in rural areas operated small electrical systems called Delco or Genco plants. These private plants provided electricity from batteries charged by a generator turned by a gasoline engine. They powered lights and small motors. Third, farms and houses along main roads hooked up to public power lines as they gradually became available. Fourth, many remote areas remained in the dark. By 1946, however, 80 percent of Pennsylvania farms used electricity.

Coping with Electricity

Although the Amish hedged on using electricity from public utility lines, they had readily accepted batteries by the turn of the century. Batteries were used to start gasoline engines, which powered washing machines, water pumps, and feed grinders. Flashlights were also acceptable. Batteries were self-contained and unconnected to the outside world. They were handy but not "too handy" and posed no threat to the Amish community. However, the church soon began to frown upon the use of light bulbs. Using his gasoline engine for power, Amishman Issac Glick rigged up a generator with an electric light in about 1910. He used the light to check the fertility of eggs in his hatchery business. The church, without a firm policy on electricity, did not censure Glick's light. In about 1914, Glick's sons used batteries to hook up a light in their barn. One son stated: "The church 'got wind of it' and Father was brought to task in a church council meeting. After that, Daddy didn't want us to use the light." However, other Amish farmers were lighting their horse stables with bulbs connected to batteries without incurring the church's wrath. Thus, prior to World War I, the Amish attitude toward electricity was in flux.

The menacing shadow of the 1910 division hovered over the Amish once again as they coped with the growing use of electricity. Indeed, the split in 1910 made it easier for the Amish to deal with the electricity issue. The progressive Peachey church welcomed the new electrical innovations. Its members installed small Delco plants and generated their own electricity for lights and motors. An Amish minister described the electrical taboo: "An order was established that was not changed until the bulk milk tanks came in the late sixties. The Peachey church had it [electricity], and that just about ruled it out for us." The readiness of the liberal group to welcome electrical lights influenced the Amish decision (as the telephone had a few years earlier).[22]

As it became clear that the Peachey church would accept electricity, the Old Order Amish position began to gel. Three incidents in about 1919 hardened the Amish policy. A tinsmith known as "Tinker" Dan Beiler ran some of his power tools with a gasoline engine. A curious and inventive Amishman, he rigged up a light bulb whose brilliance flickered with the speed of his generator. Community folks— Amish and non-Amish alike—often stopped in to see the contraption. One observer said: "He didn't really need the light for his tinsmith business. He was a tinkerer, and he liked to tinker with the light." Bishop Ben Beiler, an influential Amish bishop, was not amused. He did not mind if "Tinker" Dan tinkered with his tin, but tinkering with a light bulb was taking things too far. The bishop's "no" was firm. Unwilling to yield, "Tinker" Dan soon packed up his light and moved to Virginia.

About the same time, Ike Stoltzfus, who lived a few miles down the road, bought a Genco electric plant for his greenhouse business. An electric water pump provided steady pressure for watering his vegetable plants. According to one account, Bishop Beiler "just clamped down on him without taking it up with the church. Ike didn't know it was wrong, but the bishop, in his mind, thinks this member here was always kicking over the traces and his attitude isn't too good toward the church and we just can't tolerate this. So they gave Ike several weeks to get rid of it." Unlike "Tinker" Dan, Ike got rid of it! Another Amishman, Mike Stoltzfus, used electrical power tools for repairs in his carriage shop. According to one informant, Bishop Beiler said: "This may not be. He was just not going to have any of this stupidity." So Mike got rid of his electric power tools. A former member said Bishop Beiler "was very influential on this electric question, in setting the direction, definitely. With another bishop it might have gone a different direction. It probably would have. At least the people would have been able to help make the decision. He was pretty much making the decisions and not taking them to a vote in the congregation." In any event, the Amish taboo on electricity solidified.

Although the Peachey church's embrace of electricity and Bishop Beiler's influence were instrumental in shaping the taboo, other factors were also involved. Electricity provided a direct connection to the outside world, and to practical rural people electricity was mysterious. Where did it come from? Where would it lead? The uncertainty and fear were articulated at the time by an Amish farmer: "It seems to me that after people get everything hooked up to electricity, then it will all go on fire and the end of the world's going to come." For a group trying to remain separate from an evil world, it made no sense to literally tie one's house to the larger world, and to fall prey to dependency on outside power.

Fearing an unholy alliance with an evil world, steering a careful course away from the Peachey group, and bearing the imprint of a strict bishop, an electric "policy" became inscribed into the Amish Ordnung at the outset of the roaring twenties. One member recalled: "The church worked against it when electric first came and set a tradition and it just stayed a tradition up to today." The tradition that crystallized in 1919 permitted the continued use of electricity from 12-volt batteries. Higher voltage electricity, tapped off public power lines or generated privately by a Delco plant, was forbidden. Electric light bulbs were not permitted. As before, batteries could be used to start motors and power flashlights. So, in essence, the 1919 decision was not a new decree; it was merely an attempt to uphold customary practice, to set a limit, until the Amish could see where the new electrical trends might lead. The distinction, however, between 12-volt direct current (DC) stored in batteries and 110-volt alternating current (AC) pulled from public lines became critical over the years, as standard electrical equipment became dependent on 110-volt current.[23]

Reflecting on the church's decision to limit the use of electricity, a member recently said: "Electric would lead to worldliness. What would come along with electric? All the things that we don't need. With our diesel engines today we have more control of things. If you have an electric line coming in then you'd want a full line of appliances on it. The Amish are human too, you know." Another person noted: "It's not so much the electric that we're against, it's all the things that came with it—all the modern conveniences, television, computers. If we get electric lights then where will we stop? The wheel [of change] would really start spinning then." "Electric is just not allowed," said one member, "because it's too worldly. Air power is better because it's privately owned." And according to one bishop, using electricity would simply mean "hooking up with the world too much."

In 1919, Bishop Beiler had no inkling that an avalanche of electrical appliances would sweep across society during the next seventy years. These new gadgets were automatically eliminated from Amish life because of the taboo on 110-volt current. The social reasons for banning electricity by a sectarian group that wants to remain separate from worldly influence are more obvious and compelling today than ever. Eliminating electricity was an effective means of keeping the world at bay—literally and symbolically. The electric ban conveniently preempted debate over each new electrical gadget that appeared during the course of the century.

The Generator Deal

Amish farm equipment changed rapidly in the sixties, as horse-drawn machinery became more difficult to buy. To replace worn-out equipment, Amish machine shops began converting tractor-drawn machinery to horse-drawn in a backward technological step. Electrical welders were an important tool in this conversion process. Welders were also needed on the farm to repair broken machinery. Portable electric generators, powered by gasoline engines, could produce the powerful electricity needed for welders. Amish farmers and mechanics gradually began using portable generators and welders—a clear break from the 12-volt tradition. Given the wholesome purpose of maintaining and adapting farm machinery for horses, the bishops looked the other way. But farmers and mechanics who began using electric generators for welders were tempted by their handy source of current.

Testing the rules of the church, some farmers began plugging home freezers and other electrical motors into their generators. Some even hung light bulbs in their cow barns. Frightened of where this trend might lead, ordained leaders condemned the generator in a special series of ministers' meetings in the early sixties, with one exception—it could still be used to operate electric welders to repair farm machinery. Asked about the use of generators for welders, a farmer said: "Our bishops are sometimes pretty hard-pressed. They don't know where to draw the line. Now the welder's a piece of machinery that was allowed. They said it is something that we can have, it is almost necessary to keep our equipment running and that sort of thing." Allowing the high-voltage generators to be used for welders enabled Amish farmers to convert tractor-drawn to horse-drawn equipment, and in this way maintain the use of horses in the fields. It was better to adapt the taboo on high-voltage electricity than to lose the horse altogether.

The Milk Tank Bargain

The electricity issue returned in 1968. Milk companies began requiring dairy farmers to store and chill milk in large stainless steel tanks instead of in the customary milk cans. Bulk storage tanks, powered by electricity, each hold a ton or more of milk. Amish farmers had already been chilling their milk cans in mechanical coolers powered by diesel engines for some years. The bulk tank edict placed church leaders in a quandary. The dairy industry was booming in the sixties. Amish herds of a dozen cows were doubled and sometimes even tripled. Milk prices were good. The diversified farming of the past was giving way to specialized dairy farming. Amish farmers were using mechanical milkers. The monthly milk check was fast becoming the prime source of income for many families. To improve sanitation and reduce hauling costs, milk companies insisted that milk be stored in bulk tanks. In 1968, Amish farmers received a series of letters spelling out the stark ultimatum: install bulk tanks or lose your milk market. Amish leaders were caught in a dilemma. If they banned the tanks, many members might lose their prime source of income, some would be forced to quit farming altogether, and others would sell their milk for cheese and take a financial loss. Rejecting the bulk tank might encourage young farmers to leave the church or force them to take factory jobs. The family farm would be in jeopardy.

An Amish farmer summarized the situation: "The milk companies said we had to get bulk tanks or lose our milk market. Milk was our most important income and so we tried to keep it. The bishops had a hard line to draw so that farmers could make a living off the family farm, but yet not get too big and go in debt or go for government financing. We didn't want electric or to have to tap into public lines." If the bishops took a hard line on bulk tanks, they might disgruntle enough members to trigger a new division—something they did not need so soon after the 1966 schism. And yet the bishops could not capitulate to modernity by overturning tradition and using public power lines. They could not rescind their recent taboo on electric generators. If they did, history and the Lord himself would never forgive them, and how would they ever control the use of electricity, with all its complications?

Although the milk companies were taking a hard line, they needed milk from Amish farmers and thus were willing to negotiate. In a series of three delicate meetings, a settlement was chiseled out

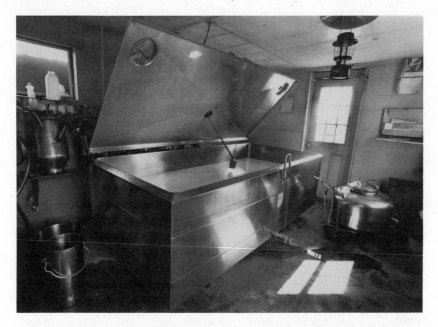

A 12-volt motor stirs the milk in this bulk tank, but a lantern illuminates the milk house. The Sputnick, lower right, is used instead of buckets to take milk from the cows to the tank.

between the stewards of tradition and the agents of modernity. Five senior bishops and four milk inspectors negotiated the deal in an Amish farmhouse. The senior milk inspector, who spoke the Amish dialect, called the meeting. He said in retrospect: "We had a long battle with them but we didn't want to lose them."

The milk inspectors and the moral inspectors dickered over a variety of issues. First, how would the tanks be powered? That was easy. The Amish were already using small industrial diesel engines to operate mechanical coolers for their milk cans. The refrigeration units on the bulk tanks could also be operated by a diesel engine. Running the diesel twice a day, at milking time, would provide power for the vacuum milking machines as well as the bulk tank refrigeration unit. This was acceptable to the milk inspectors as long as the diesel was separated from the milk house. Second, the dairy inspectors insisted that the milk be stirred by an agitator five minutes per hour to prevent cream from rising to the top, inviting bacterial growth. Additionally, the inspectors demanded that the agitator be operated by an automatic switch. Such a mechanism required 110-volt electricity—a requirement that placed the negotiators at loggerheads.

There were two problems for the Amish. First, the word *auto-*

matic sounded too modern, too convenient, too fast—downright worldly. Second, an automatic agitator required 110-volt electricity. Small generators could be installed on the diesel motors to provide 110-volt current for the agitator. However, the generator had been restricted to welders just a few years earlier. It required swallowing a great deal of pride to overturn a decision that had already been engraved in the Ordnung. Moreover, having a generator in every Amish diesel shed would open the door to other temptations. Ingenious farmers might start plugging a host of other gadgets—radios, televisions, fans, cow clippers—into their generators.

The milk inspectors would not budge on the automatic agitator. Was there no escape from this dilemma—no way to prevent an economic disaster and also maintain faith with tradition? Could the agitator be powered by a special 12-volt motor rigged up to a battery? The Amish reluctantly agreed. They would swallow their historical pride and live with the automatic starter only if it was powered by a 12-volt battery. And so a deal was forged. The bishops would accept bulk tanks as long as the refrigeration units were powered by diesel engines. They would also permit generators to be used strictly for charging the 12-volt batteries.

There was one more snag. The milk companies planned to haul the milk in large tank trucks every other day. Thus they would collect Amish milk on every other Sunday. In the past, the Amish did not ship milk on "the Lord's day." An automatic, electric starter was one thing, but shipping milk on Sunday was an unthinkable profanity. The Amish "no" was adamant! It was the milk companies' turn to concede, and they did. When asked if the milk companies considered dropping the Amish because of Sunday pickups, the head inspector said: "We never took it that far because we needed the milk. When you need it, you can't bargain too much. You can bargain but you can't put too much pressure on." So at great inconvenience, with the added cost of overtime pay and extra miles, bulk tank trucks arrive at Amish farms on Saturdays, or a few minutes after Sunday midnight.

The tank deal of 1969 was an ingenious settlement for the Amish as well as the milk inspectors. The Amish had preserved their most critical source of farm income—milk. Young men could stay on the farm. The family farm would survive, and yet the Amish had not succumbed to using 110-volt electricity from public power lines. They did accept generators and automatic starters, but they were using 12-volt current from batteries, which conformed to tradition. They had not been cajoled into profaning the Lord's day with Sunday milk pickups. Both religious tradition and economic vitality had been preserved. Moreover, Bishop Ben Beiler, so influential in shaping the 1919 electrical decision, had died some fifteen years earlier, so the approval of electric generators would not ridicule him.

The milk companies were pleased. The Amish were complying with federal and state inspection standards. The companies could not haul the milk on Sunday, a costly inconvenience, but that was not as serious as losing all of the Amish milk. Minor details of the tank deal varied by individual milk inspectors, milk companies, and local bishops. A few bishops were unhappy with the modern trend. Some farmers quit dairy farming, and others chose to move away rather than have a shiny stainless steel contraption sitting in their milk house. Still others shipped their milk to a cheese plant at a severe price cut. But most Amish farmers quickly installed bulk tanks, stabilized their economic base, and thus preserved the family farm. The basic arrangement continues today. Small generators, run by diesel, recharge 12-volt batteries, which power the bulk tank agitators.

Despite these efforts to stay on the farm, land was becoming scarce and expensive. Some Amish had to find work off the farm. Carpentry was a traditional and safe choice, but carpentry crews also needed power tools if they were to remain competitive. Thus portable generators were also permitted for mobile carpentry crews to operate electric tools at construction sites. Carpenters, working at construction sites with electricity, were allowed to tap into the public line. On the farm, however, the generator did create new temptations. One farmer said: "If you got in a pinch it might be necessary to use electric to clip cows or debeak chickens, as long as no one happened to be watching." Other farmers found it convenient to "get in a pinch" in other ways, and some ran their hay elevators and other small motors with 110-volt current from the generators. But "the bishops have really tightened up on these devious uses of the generator in the last five years," according to a young farmer. In cases of special need, the regulation is relaxed. A family with an asthmatic child needed 110-volt electricity to provide oxygen. They were happily granted an exception to use a generator.

Current Understandings

The present "understanding" of the Ordnung on electrical usage is threefold. First, battery-supplied 12-volt current is acceptable for a variety of uses: fence chargers, cow trainers, agitators on bulk milk tanks, reading lights for the elderly, and small motors to operate equipment in shops. According to one member, 12-volt motors are taken out of junked cars and used to power small motors around the farm and shop. Second, generators are permitted for welders, bulk tanks, and power tools for mobile construction crews. Generators may also be used to recharge batteries for a variety of uses. Third, electricity from public lines and home-generated 110-volt current for uses other than welders and carpentry tools are forbidden. In several cases, computers, appliances, and motors using 110-volt alternating current were operated directly from generators, but these had to be "put away." In a few cases, 110-volt electric cash registers and typewriters are powered by generators, but this practice varies widely by bishop district. As in many other issues, a distinction is made between *use* and *ownership*. Amish farmers renting a farm from a non-Amish neighbor are permitted to use electric lights in the barn and house. However, the wiring is torn out if Amish purchase the property.

The distinction between direct current stored in 12-volt batteries and 110-volt alternating current tapped from public utility lines is absurd to Moderns. When the Amish church distinguished between batteries and higher voltage electricity in 1919, they were merely stopping at a safe place. They had no idea of the long-term implications of the distinction they were drawing, but, in the wisdom of their ignorance, the ban on high-voltage current turned out to be a useful distinction. To a young Amish farmer, it makes sense to draw the line at 12-volt direct current: "The way I understand it, you are really limited, you know, with 12-volt direct current. You can't go and put in a TV or something like that because you don't have enough current, unless you hook up dozens and dozens of batteries. If you have alternating current, your 110 handy, wherever you are, there is no limit to what you can do. You can get yourself a hair dryer, if you want to. You really don't have anything to keep you from doing it, either. Because if you can have a coffeepot, who says you can't have a hair dryer?" So, over the years, limiting electrical use to 12-volt current became a practical way of arresting and controlling social change.

Amish Electricity

Despite good milk markets, financial survival in the face of shrinking farmland forced a shift to new occupations in the seventies. The transition off the farm created another dilemma for the church. Cottage industries sprang up, but they required power tools to be competitive. Diesel engines could operate large drill presses and saws from their power shaft, but 110-volt electricity was needed to operate a multitude of other tools, such as lathes, jig saws, grinders, and metal punches. The church doggedly forbid shops to hook up to public utility lines or to generate their own 110-volt electricity. Fortunately, hydraulic and air power enabled the Amish to escape this quandary with dignity and respect. Amish mechanics discovered that the electrical motors on virtually any piece of shop equipment could be replaced with hydraulic or air motors. Hydraulic and air pumps, powered by a diesel engine, could force oil or air under high pressure through hoses to power the motors on grinders, drills, and saws. Today, Amish shops run on Amish electricity—hydraulic and air pressure.

An Amish shop owner said: "We can do anything with air and hydraulic that you can do with electricity—except operate electronic equipment." Thus the latest saws, grinders, lathes, drills, sanders, and metal presses, powered by air or hydraulic pressure, stand in Amish carpentry and machine shops. Once again, tradition triumphed. This new technology allowed the Amish to modernize while retaining their historic ban of public power lines and 110-volt current. Amish shops have all the power they need to operate modern equipment and remain competitive. It is a deal that simultaneously preserves tradition and permits progress. As long as radios, televisions, and computers will not run on air or hydraulic pressure, the new technology is a safe option. Many Amish farmers also use such pressure, generated by diesel engines, to pump water, operate small machinery, run washing machines, power sewing machines, and sometimes power cake mixers. Hydraulic water pumps are gradually replacing windmills on some farms. An unwritten understanding of Amish culture says: "If you can do it with air or oil, you may do it." Thus, "Amish electricity" has facilitated vigorous economic growth without losing symbolic separation from mass society.

Electrical Deviance

Since 1975, another small deal has been quietly taking shape in the dim corners of Amish shops and barns. Electronic devices, such as typewriters, radios, and cash registers, cannot run on air or hydraulic pressure. They require 110-volt electric current. A loophole was discovered in the Amish system which respects church traditions but almost mocks them at the same time. It offers the promise of a rather delicate deal—one that may still fall through.

The electrical demon returned once again, in the form of an inverter. This small electrical gadget—the size of a car battery—can convert, or invert, 12-volt current into 110-volt current. What a temptation! Diesels in barns or shops typically run small generators to recharge 12-volt batteries—all within the scope of tradition, as altered by the milk tank decision. With inverters, the current from 12-volt batteries can be used to make "homemade" 110-volt electricity to power typewriters, cash registers, cow clippers, and small appliances. The trail of electricity thus goes from diesel to generator, to 12-volt battery, to inverter, and finally to a typical 110-volt appliance, bulb, or motor. Depending on its size, an inverter may have one to three outlets and cost from $60 to $200.

The inverter—a fascinating circumvention—symbolizes the deli-

Diesel engines power air and hydraulic pumps, generators, and machinery on Amish farms and in their shops. The Pequea battery is manufactured by an Amish shop.

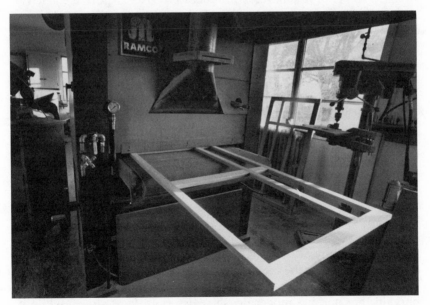

An automated sander and other tools are powered by hydraulic pressure from a diesel engine in a carpentry shop.

cate tension between tradition and modernity. A bishop can see that a 12-volt battery provides the electricity for the inverter, which is certainly within the spirit of the 1919 Ordnung. Yet the inverter, in turn, is producing "homemade" 110-volt current, which can run electronic equipment. These ingenious devices are increasingly used to power cash registers in Amish stores. Inverters are also used to operate soldering guns, digital scales, and other gadgets that cannot be powered by air or hydraulic pressure. Toasters, tape recorders, typewriters, and light bulbs can also be plugged into them. However, the inverter depends on a 12-volt battery, which severely limits the number of appliances that can be attached, and the battery must be recharged. In Amish culture such limits are welcomed.

Inverters are on probation; they are neither approved nor forbidden. An Amish businessman described them this way: "Listen, regulations [Ordnung] today say that the generator can be used for welding purposes only and the bulk tank. You know as well as I do that people are human, and there are so many ways that you can use an inverter off the batteries these days. Fifteen years ago we didn't know what an inverter was. Now they are coming out with—they can do—hundreds of things nowadays with them, but they're really not allowed." Asked what the difference is between electricity coming directly from the generator or coming from an inverter via a battery, he replied: "It's more acceptable from a battery, but it does the same thing in the end. A generator produces electricity, pure electricity, and really, I guess an inverter after the battery also produces electricity but it is in a different sense, in a different form. If we were to allow generators across the board, then we would have our own electricity right off and then everything, everything, deep freezers, lights, and the whole bit."

The use of inverters varies widely by church district and the disposition of the local bishop. Sometimes inverters are used discreetly, without the knowledge of church leaders. On this issue, there is a good deal of polite looking the other way. If handled quietly and for good purposes, inverters will likely be tolerated, because they respect the tradition shaped by Bishop Ben Beiler in 1919. Yet he would "likely roll over in his grave" if he knew that electric cash registers and typewriters were connected to the 12-volt batteries he approved. If the inverters are used to operate computers, televisions, and popcorn poppers, the bishops will surely be forced to confront the issue. And, like so many other things in the past, the inverters may have to be "put away." For the moment, at least, they remain the most ingenious recent bargain that the Amish have struck with modernity, a bargain that permits modern cash registers in their stores, while it also protects the integrity of tradition. Such compromises confound

Table 7-1 Patterns of Telephone and Electrical Use

Forbidden

Telephones in homes	Radios	Tape recorders
110-volt electricity	Computers	Video players
110-volt appliances	Electric lights	Televisions

Ambiguous

Telephones in shops	Electric typewriters	Photocopy machines
Inverters		

Acceptable

Community telephones	Electric generators[a]	Hearing aids
Flashlights	12-volt reading lights	Calculators
12-volt batteries	Electric cash registers	Digital scales
12-volt motors	Electric fences	Electric cow trainers
Electric welders		

[a]Generator use is restricted and somewhat ambiguous.

those Moderns who appreciate neither the importance of tradition nor the fragile base of a peaceful community.

Electrical Wisdom

The present regulations and the compromises emerging from Amish history point to several conclusions regarding electricity: (1) The taboo on electricity was a literal way of separating from the world and maintaining self-sufficiency—an independence that is still preserved today. For instance, the Amish are less threatened by power shortages caused by storm, disaster, or war. (2) The taboo on electricity also created a symbolic separation from the world, a daily reminder that "we are different." Such symbolic separation is valuable when religious persecution no longer separates. (3) The rejection of electricity provides a symbolic bonding that unites the community. (4) The Amish policy on electricity implies that the social impact of its use is so sweeping that community wisdom, not individual fancy, must govern its use. In other words, individuals cannot be trusted with such powerful technology. (5) The 1919 rejection of high-voltage electricity conveniently delayed social change. The taboo eliminated electrical applicances and machinery as they appeared in the twentieth century. (6) By eliminating rancorous debate over each new technological item, the Amish were able to preserve communal harmony. The bulk tank and welder are exceptions, but the big decision on electricity preempted the small debates over hair dryers, shavers, coffeepots, and so forth. (7) The proscription against electricity effectively quarantined the Amish from outside electronic media, including radios, televisions, record players, tape recorders, and VCRs. Curtailing

An electronic cash register in an Amish retail store illuminated by lantern light.

such influences is crucial for the preservation of Amish values. (8) The concessions on electricity have been guided primarily by economic concerns. While benefitting the whole community, the tradeoffs have largely facilitated the work of men more than that of women. (9) Sacrificing electrical conveniences is a daily reminder of being different—a reminder that individual desires must yield to larger community goals.

Inside the Amish world, the riddles of technology make obvious sense. Permitting the telephone and electricity in some settings and not in others is simply a commonsense solution to the everyday problems posed by industrialization. Using air and hydraulic pressure to power modern shops while forbidding 110-volt electricity is a reasonable way to permit economic growth and to control other forms of modernization dependent upon electricity. One thing is certain: although the Amish may not enjoy all the conveniences of modern life, they are in control of their technology and intuitively grasp its long-term social impact. They have learned to use it for building community and are not afraid to tame its destructive side.

8

Harnessing the Power of Progress

The first thing people do when they leave the Amish church is get a car.
—Amish leader

The Devil's Machine

The car epitomizes worldliness in the Amish mind. Car ownership is one of the few violations of the Ordnung which triggers automatic expulsion. "Well, anybody that gets a car just isn't Amish, that's all," said an Amishwoman. Describing early attitudes toward cars, an Amishman said: "Our leaders never looked at them." Other members widely agree that the car "didn't make no issue among us." Yet today the Amish ride in cars and often hire them on a daily basis. How can they conscientiously embrace a double standard—forbidding ownership while permitting use? That question lurks beneath the car riddle.

On 14 February 1900, a battery-operated car appeared on the streets of Lancaster for the first time.[1] Four years later, a six-year-old Amish boy who accompanied his father to Lancaster to sell vegetables saw nine cars in one day. In those days, cars were a rich man's hobby, frivolous playthings. The National Automobile Company organized itself in 1907 in Lancaster and advertised motoring as "the king of sports and the queen of amusements."[2] For the Amish, who disdained both sports and amusements, such slogans turned the car into a profane symbol. They viewed the early cars as luxurious, too handy, too modern—worldly toys of the rich.

Henry Ford's Model T, first produced in 1908, popularized the car for the masses after 1914. Although only 7 percent of Pennsylvania farmers had a car in 1914, 72 percent of them were driving the "devil's machine" by 1921.[3] Progressive Mennonites, along with the rest of the world, were buying new cars. An Amish leader remembers that Mennonite boys drove their cars to fairs, farm shows, and other worldly amusements. The liberal Peachey church, which had splintered off from the Amish in 1910, had few qualms about using electricity, telephones, or tractors, but even it was not seduced by the car until 1928. The Amish resolve, however, held firm over the years. The Amish were not about to stray after their Mennonite cousins or their wayward stepchildren.

A number of practical considerations made it easy for the Amish to avoid the car. Between 1900 and 1910, 150 miles of electric trolley lines were strung from Lancaster City to outlying towns. Although wary of these urban intrusions, the Amish rode the trolleys. Public trains were also used for long-distance trips to midwestern Amish settlements. Furthermore, early cars were impractical. They were often in the garage more than on the road. Over the winter they were jacked up on blocks, because the rutted roads were impassable. As late as 1930, only 22 percent of Pennsylvania farmers lived by a paved road, and the theme of the 1931 gubernatorial campaign was "Take the farmers out of the mud."[4]

The Car Taboo

The Amish taboo on car *ownership* intensified as cars became widely accepted—likely about 1915.[5] *Use* of the car, however, varied by church district in the early years but increased rapidly after 1950. Some Amish declared they would never "crawl into a car," and they never did. Others rode with neighbors. Some bishops permitted car travel when members were invited by a neighbor, but forbade hiring a car or driver. Other districts made a distinction between business use and pleasure, but sometimes even the former was curtailed. In 1928, two Amish farmers, caught with a broken corn planter in the midst of planting season, hired a trucker to haul a new planter from a dealer some fifty miles away. The farmers rode along in the truck. Gossip spread about the "unnecessary trip," and they were required to confess their transgression at the next church service. Other Amish, however, used the services of a neighbor's car regularly for business trips.

Although there is little evidence of the Amish owning cars, some did drive on the sly. About 1915, an Amishman "practiced" driving his hired man's Model T Ford behind the barn. Unfamiliar with the steering, he lost control, drove over the front shafts of his own buggy, and smashed them to bits. In the thirties, an Amishman used a pickup truck to make deliveries for a feed mill. But a bishop noted: "Before 1930, we hardly rode in cars. We had no businesses, we could drive to all the Amish places by horse. The community was all close together."

The Amish fear of the car was not a naîve one, for the car revolutionized rural life. By 1933, a presidential commission concluded that no other invention with such far-reaching importance diffused so quickly through the national culture, transforming even habits of thought and language.[6] Another historian contended that no other mechanical invention in history influenced the rural farmer more than the car.[7] Leaving no phase of rural life untouched, it facilitated interchange between urban and rural residents. Removing the obstacles of isolation and provincialism, the car widened the intellectual and social horizon of farm families. Its arrival was cheered by many at the time as an enormous boost to the farmer's success.[8] In the eyes of the Amish, however, the car endangered their ethnic community.

The very name of this new invention spelled trouble for the Amish. The car encouraged *auto*matic *mobil*ity. It freed individuals to travel autonomously, independently, whenever and wherever they pleased. For Americans frustrated by the end of the western frontier, the new promise of automatic mobility was a great antidote. Auto travel symbolized the spirit of American individualism and independence—freeing people from train and trolley schedules, breaking the confines of geography, and smashing the provincialism of rural life. The individual, liberated from geography, could travel and explore at will. But to a traditional people who preferred manual and stationary things, automatic mobility was a menace. Automatic things signaled a loss of control, and mobility was a threat for the Amish, who preferred to remain separate from the industrial world. The car—invented, manufactured, and distributed in the city—brought "city slickers" out to secluded rural areas on pleasure-seeking excursions. The car was also a separator. Individuals could now drive away from home—far away. Youth could drive away to urban worlds of vice. Adults could drive away for business. The car would pull the local community apart. A personalized version of mass transit, the car was perfect for a complicated, individuated, and mobile society. But for a stable, simple, local people who cherished community dependency and separation from the world, the car was a peril.

The car threatened to separate the community in other ways. If only wealthy members could afford it, the car would bring inequality. Proud individuals would use the car to show off their status, power, and wealth—all of which mocked the spirit of Gelassenheit. Cars would speed things up dramatically, disrupting the slow pace of Amish living. The car contradicted the core of Amish life. It was the symbol of modernity *par excellence*, for it entailed freedom, acceleration, power, technology, mobility, and autonomy. Indeed, it was a modern child, pieced together on a mechanical, rational, and highly specialized assembly line. In all of these ways, the car symbolized individualism and separation. Individuals driving cars would be out of control, mobile, independent, and free-floating.

There was little hesitation in the Amish "no" to car ownership. Yet the car did bring many advantages. So, over time, the Amish agreed to some concessions. They would ride in cars but only for emergencies and in special circumstances. They would not own them, for then things would surely get out of control. This firm line between *use* and *ownership* or, as the Amish would say, between use and abuse, often strikes Moderns as outright hypocrisy. But, from the Amish perspective, it is a practical solution that keeps the car at bay, controls its negative side effects, and yet uses it to build community solidarity.[9]

Amish Taxis

The use of motor vehicles by the Amish has liberalized over the decades. "Use of the car," said one grandfather, "is something that the church has slipped on." A bishop pointed to the collapse of the trolley system and poor rural bus service as reasons for increasing car usage. Distinctions were made between business and pleasure, need and luxury, emergency and convenience. But, in all these concessions, the taboo on ownership held firm. The use of cars expanded after 1940. The opening of a daughter colony in Lebanon County, some fifty miles northwest of Lancaster, provided an occasion to sanction the hiring of drivers. Church leaders mark this turning point as the time when hiring drivers became accepted and blessed by the church.

The first Amish taxi service came into existence in the early fifties, when a non-Amish neighbor began earning a living "hauling" Amish to funerals, sales, family gatherings, distant settlements, and hospitals. Meanwhile, rebellious youth were secretly experimenting with cars. Adults also began hiring drivers on Sunday for questionable pleasure trips. Church leaders, in the mid-fifties, fearing things might get out of hand, agreed to ban the hiring of drivers on Sunday except for dire emergencies. Present policy still prohibits hiring Sunday drivers except in special circumstances, such as visiting family members in the hospital. Many bishops even frown on accepting free rides on Sunday. The horse and buggy—core symbols of Amish identity—must, at least, be hitched up on the sacred day of worship. This ritualistic abstention from car usage on Sundays is important in reaffirming the Amish moral order and preventing the erosion of the car taboo. The Ordnung specifies that members may not own or operate a motor vehicle, hold a driver's license, or lend money to someone for the purchase of a car. Drivers may be hired when necessary. The definition of necessity is, of course, a slippery one. Members sometimes accuse one another of hiring drivers for unnecessary trips.

Today Amish taxis, operated by the non-Amish and members of

other plain churches, transport Amish to auctions, job sites, funerals, weddings, and family gatherings. Many of these taxi arrangements developed over the years as acts of neighborly kindness. Dozens of taxi operations are full-time and part-time businesses. In 1977, the Pennsylvania Public Utilities Commission (PUC) cracked down on non-Amish taxi owners who were charging fees for their service without holding a common carrier license. An abrupt crackdown on five drivers at an Amish funeral angered both the Amish and non-Amish communities. Responding to pressure from bus companies who could not compete with the informal taxis, a PUC spokesman justified the enforcement: "We've seen this thing grow like a cancer. At least a hundred people must be doing this illegally and we are going to try and cut it out. It's a thorn in our side."[10] After fourteen months of hearings and negotiations, the PUC agreed to issue taxi permits to about forty drivers who transported the Amish. The special permits allow the drivers to charge fees for their service as long as they only transport people whose beliefs and religious convictions prevent them from owning or operating a vehicle.[11]

Amish concessions to car *use* were prompted by several factors: the collapse of the rural trolley system, new settlements in other counties, geographical expansion in Lancaster County, and the development of Amish businesses. The establishment of new colonies in several other counties of Pennsylvania in the late sixties and the seventies and the proliferation of Amish industries since 1970 have increased motor travel. Carpentry crews need transportation to construction sites. Cabinetmakers sometimes travel to nearby states to install "Amish kitchens." Amish manufacturing establishments must find ways to transport their products.

Many Amish businesses have employees who provide a car or truck for company use. The employee owns the vehicle and the proprietor pays mileage. The employee may be an unbaptized son of the manager or, more frequently, a member of another plain group that permits automobiles. The mileage rate pays for the vehicle's initial cost and maintenance, and it may provide a marginal profit. Amish businessmen often have a hauling agreement with other non-Amish neighbors or commercial truckers. In some cases, shop owners have made "sweetheart" loans to employees, enabling them to purchase vehicles for company use. Most bishops have strictly forbidden such "under the table" deals, because they fear such deals amount to de facto ownership, which will eventually lead to actual ownership.

The Car Deal

The solution to the Amish car riddle is hidden beneath the public agreement negotiated with modernity. In brief, the motor vehicle policy prohibits holding a driver's license and owning, driving, and financing a vehicle. With the exception of Sundays and obvious frivolities, hiring drivers and riding in vehicles are permitted. A fascinating settlement, the bargain balances the tug of traditional values with the press of economic survival. The compromise controls the detrimental effects of the car yet allows its use for business and for strengthening community ties.

The deal acknowledges that the car cannot be entrusted to the individual. If ownership were permitted, the church would lose control of car use. Ownership would intensify the pace and complexity of Amish living. Parents and youth alike would spend more time away from home at meetings and worldly amusements. Car ownership, in the long run, would not only erode the social base of the small face-to-face community but also destroy the local church district—the cornerstone of Amish social organization. The horse holds the local community together; the car would eventually fragment and scatter it.

Hiring a taxi is inconvenient, because arrangements must be made, and drivers paid. Amish taxis provide transportation, but not automatic mobility. One yields to the schedule, itinerary, fees, and mood of the driver. One Amishman explained: "When we need a driver we call the ones who are less expensive or who we enjoy riding with. Oftentimes we must call as many as a half dozen before we can find one who is not busy. When we want to go on a long trip, there are quite a few things to consider, such as: Does he drive carefully; does he gladly go where we want to go; does he allow us to give our small children something to eat such as pretzels or crackers to keep them quiet during the long drive; is he a pleasant, courteous driver who charges a decent fee."[12] In forging the car deal, the Amish gave up autonomy and independence—attractive values to the modern owner/driver.

There are benefits to this compromise. By permitting the use of cars, the Amish are able to travel to distant places and conduct business in a kind of door-to-door limousine service without the typical costs of investment, purchase, maintenance, or even driving fatigue. In this way, the Amish have retained the virtues of simplicity, as well as the convenience of modernity. It is a way of using modern technology without being enslaved by it, without allowing it to destroy community. Taxi use is essential to the fiscal survival of Amish industries. Moreover, it links families and friends who are separated by geography.

Group travel by van also fosters community. Modern auto drivers, often alone, come and go as they please. Group traveling reduces the cost of a taxi, and the Amish are not adverse to a good bargain. So, as with other things, they travel together. Vanloads of traveling Amish are, in essence, portable social networks. Chatter and gossip keep the Amish world view alive on the daily jaunts to work and on visits to relatives in distant settlements. They are traveling at high speeds, but doing it together with like-minded others in the context of community.

Pneumatic tires, initially associated with the car, came to symbolize freedom and mobility and hence worldliness. Thus, over the years the Amish have rejected pneumatic tires on farm equipment. Hard rubber tires and pneumatic tires are permitted on small hand-held items, such as wheelbarrows, tricycles, wagons, and feed carts. The preference for steel and hard rubber wheels developed as a way to avoid pneumatic tires, which increase mobility and might eventually lead to the car.

Controlled use of the car is a way of keeping faith with tradition while giving enough freedom to maneuver in the larger society. The Amish believe that by turning the use of cars over to individuals, they would quicken the pace of their life, erase geographical limits, weaken social control, and eventually ruin their community. Their rejection of automatic mobility also encourages people to work near home, which is a crucial ploy in keeping the family together. Thus the Amish took the car, the charm of modernity, on their terms—a deal that allowed them to control and use it to enhance their community. It was an astute contract but one that baffles many Moderns, who overlook the fine print.

The Sod Packers

Tractors are standard equipment on Amish farms these days. But tractors remain near the barn and are rarely used in the fields. Horses and mules pull plows and other machinery across the fertile soil. Why don't the Amish use tractors in the fields, where they are obviously needed? What sort of logic underlies the tractor riddle?

Banning the car was an easy decision for the Amish. The tractor, however, was a different story. Tractors support agriculture—they enhance productivity, ease work, increase efficiency, and speed up planting and harvest. An attractive product from the merchants of progress, the tractor could not be easily ignored like the car. It tantalized and enticed the Amish community in the twenties, forties, and again in the sixties. Although there is little evidence, if any, that members of the Amish church drove cars, they were indeed driving tractors, not near their barns, but in their fields as well. But that is getting ahead of our riddle.

By the late 1880s large steam engines operated threshing machines on many Lancaster County farms. Small gasoline engines were widely used by the turn of the century to saw wood, grind feed, pump water, and power washing machines. Like their neighbors, the Amish owned and operated steam and gasoline engines. Horses were commonly used by Amish and non-Amish alike to pull farm machinery in the fields.

In 1906, International Harvester built a single-cylinder tractor. By 1910, a farmer on the eastern edge of Lancaster County purchased one of these clumsy contraptions.[13] Boasting the power of twenty horses, some of the early tractors weighed six tons. Because of labor shortages and the food demands of World War I, improved tractors became more common after 1918. But a general, all-purpose tractor was not on the market until the mid-twenties. The first tractors were awkward and heavy monstrosities, ill-suited for the modest farms of eastern Pennsylvania. Their wide steel wheels packed the soil, and they were difficult to maneuver in small fields. But, surprisingly, the Amish began using them.

In the early twenties, there were probably a dozen or more Amish farmers experimenting with these sod packers in their fields.[14] According to oral tradition, Moses King took his newly purchased tractor out in the field and began harrowing. The dealer who had sold the tractor did not explain how to stop it, so King simply drove it in circles until it ran out of gas. On several occasions, tractors were overturned by inexperienced Amish drivers. In about 1920, Ike Zook used his noisy tractor to plow. His neighbor Deacon Jonas Beiler, irked by the clanging noise, thought it was ridiculous to use such a thing in the field. So according to tradition, Deacon Beiler tied his horses to a post, walked across the road, and told Zook: "Now you have to get rid of this stupid thing, I'm offended by it." Deacon Beiler was not only the deacon in Zook's congregation but also the brother of stern Bishop Ben Beiler. Zook was "called on the carpet" and asked to make a confession in church. But Zook liked his tractor, so he left the Amish and joined the Peachey church, whose members were using tractors in the field without any qualms.

About the same time, two Amish ministers visiting Amish settlements in the Midwest discovered that tractors were not being used, even on large Amish farms. The ministers returned to Lancaster and concluded that if tractors were not needed on the big farms of the Midwest, sod packers certainly were not needed on the small farms of the East. The tractor experiment continued in the Lancaster area until 1923, when tractors were finally banned from Amish fields.

The Tractor Recall

Several factors tightened the Amish tractor policy. First, the wayward Peachey church permitted tractors in the field, a sure sign of decadence. If these upstarts who were talking on telephones and replacing their lanterns with light bulbs were also using the tractor, it surely must be worldly. Second, the early tractors were quite expensive and impractical. The use of horses was clearly advantageous. Although horses required feeding, they were easier to turn in the field, cheaper to buy, and did not pack the soil. Moreover, they provided free fertilizer. Third, Amish church leaders had already allowed a host of new farm equipment, including mechanical manure spreaders, hay loaders, tobacco planters, and silos, in the first two decades of the twentieth century. The Amish were often the first ones in a community to buy the new inventions as they came on the market.[15] Wasn't the use of tractors going just a bit too far? Where might this all lead? Fourth, Bishop Ben Beiler believed that the tractor seemed dangerously close to the car, which was already taboo. A nephew remembers the bishop saying he was afraid "that the tractor would lead to the car." Tractors did not have rubber tires yet, but they were self-propelled, autonomous, independently mobile—suspiciously similar to the car. So the tractors were recalled from the fields in about 1923.

Discussions about tractors quieted down in the late twenties. During the Depression, horse feed was cheap and tractors were too expensive for many farmers. By the late thirties and early forties, however, new, general-purpose tractors with rubber tires became available. They were handy for cultivating crops even in small fields. Such tractors were appearing on virtually every non-Amish farm in the early forties. Between 1940 and 1950, the number of workhorses on county farms plummeted in half from twenty-one thousand to ten thousand. Several Amish farmers who despised the deal their fathers had signed in the twenties could not resist the lure of these improved tractors for field work. Clearly superior to horses, the new tractors were versatile, lighter, and cheaper.

The bishops could no longer condemn tractors as impractical. But, in the judgment of the old bishops, the 1923 distinction between barn and field use was a wise bargain and they decided to stand firm. So, in the early forties, tractors were again recalled from Amish fields. Young farmers were soon on their knees in front of the church promising to "put their tractors away" and vowing to stay in touch with nature, tradition, community, and God.

The issue was not entirely settled, however. In the late fifties and early sixties, a wide array of new tractor-drawn machinery was coming on the market. The new equipment—hay mowers, hay crushers, grain combines, hay balers, and corn harvesters—required a powerful engine and was rather heavy for horses to pull. Horse-drawn machinery was becoming scarce as non-Amish farmers shifted to tractors. So the tractor became tempting once again. Trying to strike a balance between tradition and modernization, some ingenious Amish mechanics built a power unit nicknamed an "Amish tractor."

The power unit, a gasoline engine mounted on a four-wheel cart,

On a rare occasion, a tractor is used in the field to operate an irrigation pump, but not to pull farm machinery. Horses continue to do that work.

could be hooked up to various modern farm implements. It functioned, in essence, as a homemade tractor. The power unit was pulled, of course, by the symbolic horses, for, as one farmer said in jest, "we needed the horses to steer it." Moreover, the ingenious young farmers were staying within a senior bishop's rule of thumb— "If you can pull it with horses, you can have it." But the old sage probably never imagined that horses would pull such modern, powerful, and shiny machines—forage harvesters, combines, and haybines. The younger bishops were sure that the power unit was only a small step away from a tractor. Furthermore, the mocking laughter of Mennonite neighbors was embarrassing.

The bishops were not fooled by this new contraption and held the old line: no tractors in the field. The line has remained taut ever since. But feelings about the Amish tractor and the new farm machinery were so intense that a splinter group of progressive Amish known as New Orders broke from the main body in 1966.

The Tractor Riddle

Why did the Amish not outlaw the tractor completely? Why permit this worldly contraption to sit around the barn? Why play with temptation? When recently asked that question, a bishop said: "I don't know. I can't answer that. I still think if we don't want to go with the world altogether, why we better use horses instead of going along with the modern way." Although using a tractor in the field simply feels "too worldly" to the bishop, there were good reasons for drawing the line that way in 1923.

Gasoline engines were widely used on Amish farms by World War I. Feed silos, thirty feet high, jutted up by Amish barns. Some form of power was needed to blow the chopped silage up to the top of the silos in order to fill them. The gasoline engine and the steam engine were used for such high-power demands around the barn—grinding, threshing, and blowing silage. Several Amishmen owned steam-powered threshing rigs and harvested wheat for neighboring farmers. In fact, Bishop Beiler's own brother had a steam engine for his threshing rig. To outlaw tractors around the barn would have been a step backward, one that surely would have ignited a political ruckus in the church. In essence, limiting tractors to heavy power work around the barn amounted to freezing history on the farm, drawing a line that simply conformed to customary practice before 1923. Such a policy allowed the silage to blow and the wheat to be threshed so that things could go on much as they had before.

The ban on field tractors and other self-propelled equipment which crystallized in about 1923 remains firm today. The fear that tractors will lead to cars is the most frequently cited reason for not using them in the field. Amishmen tell numerous stories of progressive churches in other localities which permitted tractors in the field. "Before you know it, they put rubber tires on the tractors and next thing they are driving them to town for groceries. And as the next generation grows up they can't understand the difference between using a tractor for business trips to town and a car. And so they get a car."[16] The division of 1966 reaffirmed the Amish wisdom on barring tractors from the field. According to some informants, even bishops in the splinter group drive tractors to the store for groceries.

If tractors had been manufactured before cars, might the Amish be driving them in their fields today? Possibly. But there are other compelling reasons for banning tractors from the fields. They displace not only horses but also farm laborers. In contrast to Moderns, who seek to save labor at every turn, the Amish have always welcomed work as the heartbeat of their community. The church was anchored on the farm, where work, like a magnet, pulled everyone together. A tractor might save labor, but in Amish eyes that spelled trouble. For eventually, with all these labor-saving gadgets, there might not be enough work to go around for all the children. Leisure, the devil's workshop, would run rampant. Worse yet, the loss of home work would lead to factory work. So in these ways, a major labor-saving device, such as the tractor, would not only threaten the family but also the church.

The use of the tractor conspired against community in other ways as well. In the first two decades of the twentieth century, local farmers, Amish and non-Amish alike, worked closely together, especially at planting and harvest times. It was hard, manual work. But it was good work—communal work—as the community pitted itself against the forces of nature. Self-propelled tractors, like cars, would enable individuals to work fast and independently. The tractor and its accessories have indeed, over time, destroyed the neighborhood work crews that in bygone days joined together to "put in" the hay or thresh the wheat. The tractor was a great labor saver but it was a sure loser for a people who valued collective work.

Insisting on horses and mules in the field was also a way of perpetuating a horse subculture. Family members would continue to learn about the care and feeding of horses. Related industries such as blacksmith work and harness making would survive to support the horse culture—an infrastructure that was essential if the Amish were to keep the horse and buggy on the road. Pulling the horses off the field would diminish the horse culture. If the Amish maintained just one driving horse for road travel, the horse culture as well as its supporting industries would be endangered. Such a scenario would make it too easy to get rid of the driving horse. Thus, keeping horses in the field helped indirectly to keep them on the road.

The line drawn between barn power and field power in 1923 appears today as a perplexing riddle, but it was a sensible historical deal. With tractor power at the barn, silos could be filled, grain ground, and wheat threshed as always. By permitting tractors around the barn, the church avoided an economic setback and a political brawl. Furthermore, it provided some breathing space, a time out to observe the new contraptions more carefully. This workable bargain has served the Amish well over time. As new power needs developed around the barn, the tractor was handy. Today modern steel-wheeled tractors power large feed grinders, spin ventilating fans at poultry houses, run manure pumps, blow silage, operate hydraulic systems, and turn irrigation pumps on Amish farms. They provide power for all sorts of equipment operated from their power takeoff shaft, belt pulley, or hydraulic system. Tractors are also used to pull stumps out of fence rows and milk trucks out of snowdrifts. While horses continue to protect Amish identity in the field, tractors at the barn keep Amish farmers competitive.

There are some restrictions, however, even around the barn. Steel wheels are mandatory. This restriction also applies to other machinery, such as wagons, corn pickers, and balers. Hand-held items, such as small wagons, wheelbarrows, and toys, can roll on rubber, because they are not likely to lead to a car. A front-end forklift on a tractor to hoist heavy items up to a second floor is acceptable as a necessity. However, a front-end manure loader would lessen the work of family members and is off-limits. In some church districts, small Caterpillar-like tractors push and load manure inside barns. In other districts, they are strictly forbidden. Permitting tractors at the barn has aided the growth of Amish businesses, because many shops use small forklift tractors to load and unload goods.

Some Old Order Mennonite groups use steel-wheeled tractors in their fields. Thus, the use of horses in the field also reinforces Amish identity and protects ethnic boundaries. Preventing tractors from replacing horses in the fields marked a major turning point in Amish history. It maintained the pace of the past and offered daily evidence that the Amish had not capitulated to modernity. The tractor would not *separate* them from the soil, from their past, from their identity, or from their families. Thus, the horse in the field became a cogent symbol of Amish identity.

Mechanized Farming

Several other Amish riddles were taking shape in the turmoil of the early sixties. In Amish fields today, horses and mules pull modern farm implements. This unusual union of tradition and modernity gelled in the perilous years before the 1966 division. Up until the fifties, the Amish used traditional horse-drawn equipment to harvest their crops. Grain binders and grass mowers, for example, were powered or "ground-driven" by their own wheels.

In the fifties numerous factors converged to create strong pressures for change. Farming was becoming more specialized. Dairy farming became the leading type of agriculture. Amish who began farming with eight cows in the thirties expanded their herds to twenty-four or even thirty-six cows. The use of commercial fertilizer and alfalfa produced three to four crops of hay per year. Like other farmers, the Amish had traditionally stored hay loose in the haymows of their barns. The expanding dairy herds and larger hay crops created storage problems. Farmers had to either limit their herds, build larger barns, or find new ways to store hay. The engineers of progress had been tinkering with a solution. Hay balers, pulled by tractors through the field, were able to pack the loose hay into rectangular bales that were easy to load, haul, and stack in the barn. The tightly compressed bales alleviated the storage problem. After World War II, hay balers became popular among American farmers.

Some non-Amish farmers began baling hay for the Amish in the early fifties. And by 1955, several Amish farmers had purchased their own hay balers. Pulled by horses, the balers were powered by a gasoline engine installed at the factory. It seemed like an innocent turn of events, but it was a revolution of sorts, for it was the first widespread use of gasoline engines in Amish fields.[17] Surprisingly, church leaders said little about it. The economic forces propelling the dairy industry and the hay storage problem had forced the bishops' hand. The baler did conform to a favorite dictum: "If you can pull it with horses, you can have it." But it was a major labor-saving device, which could also contribute to idleness.

Amish oral historians report that the hay baler stirred little agitation in the church. One leader reflected: "It surprises me that the baler slipped through." By 1960, the baler had slipped onto many Amish farms, and, when the bishops drew up a list of taboo equipment in the early sixties, it was conspicuously missing.[18] Shunning the baler would have been foolish for both political and financial reasons. Some limits, however, have been placed on the baler. Labor-saving bale throwers, which automatically toss bales onto wagons behind the baler, are forbidden. And steel wheels, of course, are placed on the balers.

Other issues were also incubating in the early sixties. Manufacturers of farm equipment were producing large, heavy machinery designed for powerful tractors. Horse-drawn machinery was becoming scarce. The Amish began buying old-fashioned machinery in other parts of the country, but this pool soon began to dry up. Commercial fertilizers, hybrid seed, and improved methods of cultivation produced bumper crops, which were difficult to cut and harvest with antiquated equipment. Finding it hard to acquire horse-drawn machinery, knowing the baler had slipped into use, and feeling the pressure for increased productivity, some bold Amish farmers began using modern corn harvesters and wheat combines. In the past, the Amish had used "ground-driven" corn binders and grain binders pulled by horses to cut their corn and wheat. The new corn harvesters chopped green corn in the field and blew it into a trailing wagon. The green silage was then hauled to the barn and blown into silos for storage. The corn harvester was a boon to the dairy farmer, because chopped corn silage was a prime source of dairy feed. The combine—a modern threshing machine—cut and threshed wheat in one operation in the field.

A husband and wife baling hay in 1987. Since the fifties the Amish have used engine-powered balers to pack the hay for efficient handling and storage. Automatic bale throwers, however, are not permitted for loading the wagons.

Meeting in 1960, the Amish bishops singled out the harvester and combine as two inventions that they would not tolerate. Several factors likely explain the ban on corn harvesters and combines. First, the second generation of harvesters and combines on nearby non-Amish farms were self-propelled units.[19] The modern corn harvesters and wheat combines, already in use on some Amish farms, might eventually lead to self-propelled units, which were uncomfortably similar to cars and field tractors. Second, the lenient bishops had already "looked the other way" when the hay baler slipped in. Why, they reasoned, let another labor-saving device slip through? They had to draw the line somewhere, in order to govern the expansionist impulses of the dairy farmers. Unlike the baler, the corn harvester did not improve storage; it just saved labor and time, and that was no excuse for tolerance. Third, as dairy operations flourished, wheat and tobacco farming declined.[20] The combines used for harvesting wheat were not critical for the survival of dairy farmers. The few acres of wheat farmed by the Amish could still be cut with old-fashioned, ground-driven grain binders and threshed at the barn in the old-fashioned way. Although the bishops would tolerate the hay baler, the economic and political pressures were not strong enough to persuade them to accept corn harvesters and combines.

Farm Machinery Riddles

A new development in the fall of 1960 virtually sealed the fate of the modern corn harvester. An inventive Amish farmer mounted a gasoline engine on a corn binder designed to be pulled and powered by a tractor. Thus he was able to use his horses to pull the advanced tractor binder. Until this time the Amish had used ground-driven binders to cut green corn for silage. The inventive farmer explained: "We put engines on the corn binders because there weren't enough ground-driven binders around anymore and to keep away from the combines and harvesters." Amish craftsmen soon began making replacement parts for the corn binders, which were no longer manufactured. It was a watershed in the evolution of Amish technology, which took the Amish a step beyond simple ground-driven machinery. Mounting engines on their machinery enabled them to use equipment designed for tractors without giving up the horse and eliminated the need for large self-propelled models. Rather than being dominated by modern farm technology, they had used it for their purposes. Today the green corn stalks are still cut by an old-fashioned corn binder pulled by horses but powered by a state-of-the-art gasoline engine. The engine-powered binder silenced Amish pleas for a modern corn harvester.

Mounting engines on corn binders was another bargain that delicately balanced a variety of factors, for it (1) kept modern harvesters off Amish fields, (2) retained the symbolic horse, (3) provided plenty of work for farm hands, (4) permitted silage harvesting to continue in the basic tradition of the past, (5) eliminated the difficulty of buying scarce ground-driven binders, (6) created new jobs for Amish mechanics who manufactured replacement parts, (7) provided extra power to cut the larger varieties of hybrid corn, (8) enabled dairy farmers to remain financially competitive, and (9) opened a way for the bishops to escape from their political quandary.

In essence, the bishops negotiated a deal that has lasted for nearly three decades. For all practical purposes, it reads: "You may have modern hay balers and you may mount gasoline engines on farm equipment as long as you pull it with horses, but you may not have modern harvesters, combines, or other self-propelled equipment." The farmer who mounted the first engine on the corn binder described the technological watershed innocently: "I just mounted it [the engine] on to see if it would work. There was no meeting with the

An engine-powered corn binder cuts green corn stalks and ties them in bundles. They are then hauled to the barn and chopped into silage, as seen below.

Modern tractors with steel wheels are used for high-power needs at the barn, but rarely in the fields. This tractor is operating a machine that chops and blows green corn stalks to the top of a forty-foot silo.

ministers and bishops. It didn't make no ruckus." But it was a historic compromise that cleared the way for gasoline engines to be installed on other farm equipment—the hay crimper (1960), corn picker (1965), grass mower (1966), and the roto beater and sprayer in recent years. The riddle of pulling modern implements with horses is indeed a compromise between modernity and tradition. It is a way of keeping the horse in the field, the family on the farm, and simultaneously tapping new power sources that can harvest the robust crops and keep the dairymen in business.

The Breach of 1966

Despite two world wars, the Depression, and unbelievable social change, things had been relatively quiet among the Amish in the fifty years after the 1910 division. Although they had struggled with a variety of modernizing pressures, none of these struggles induced a schism. The serenity broke in the late fifties and early sixties and resulted in the second cleavage of the twentieth century. In the late fif-

Table 8-1 Patterns of Farm Equipment Use

Acceptable Modern Equipment

Tractors for power at the barn	Liquid manure pumps	Roto beaters
	Corn planters	Mechanical milkers
Forklifts on tractors	Hay mowers	Hay elevators
Hay balers	Hay crimpers	Concrete silos
Corn pickers	Hay rakes	Feed grinders
Bulk milk tanks		

Amish Manufactured or Modified Equipment

Sprayers	Corn binder[a]	Installation of engines on implements
Grain bins	Manure spreaders	
Wagons	Hay rakes	Installation of steel wheels on all equipment
Plows	Hay tedders	
Corn planters	Hay turners	Batteries
Harrows	Forage cutter/blowers	Lanterns

Unacceptable Farm Equipment

Self-propelled implements	Rubber tires	Automatic bale throwers
	Barn cleaners	Blue (Harvestore) silos
Combines	Milk pipe lines	
Forage harvesters	Automated chicken houses	Front-end manure loaders
Haybine mower-conditioners	Silo unloaders	

[a]Corn binders are modified but not manufactured by the Amish. Some parts for the binder are manufactured in Amish shops.

ties, Pennsylvania farmers were rapidly adopting mechanized field equipment, modern milking machines, and barn cleaners. Banks encouraged Amish farmers to enlarge their operations and increase productivity. Thus dairy herds were expanding.

In the late fifties, Amish farmers in several church districts began using modern machinery in the fields—pulling wheat combines, haybines, and corn harvesters with horses. Others installed mechanical barn cleaners to clean manure out of their barns. Before the days of the bulk tank discussions, a few enterprising farmers had even hooked electric generators to their diesel engines and used their homemade 110-volt electricity for light bulbs in their barns, home freezers, and appliances.

In 1960, the bishops met and identified six worldly items—combines, forage harvesters, barn cleaners, power units ("Amish tractors"), electric generators, and deep freezers—that they wanted "put away" before they got completely out of hand. Outlawing these items, which had been slipping onto Amish farms, was easier said than done. A number of bishops had difficulty enforcing the decrees, and others were reluctant to act because some of their members had used the six items for several years. The bishops agreed to permit generators to be used strictly for welders, but they would not budge on the other issues.

In the fall of 1962, twenty bishops assembled and agreed once again to prohibit these worldly items. In December 1962, a special all-day meeting of 140 ordained ministers, deacons, and bishops was called to discuss the volatile issues. The bishops gave persuasive talks on the need to "hold the line" on the six items and urged the ministers to help "clean them out." Most of the ordained men supported the eradication effort, but leaders in several districts, obviously hedging, gave qualified responses to the bishops' requests. The hesitant ministers were in a quandary—caught between the requests of senior bishops and the enormous financial and emotional price awaiting them back home if they forced their members to get rid of the six conveniences.[21] Another special ministers' meeting in July 1964 also failed to resolve the impasse.

During the spring and summer of 1966, about one hundred families severed ties with the Old Order Amish and began worshiping separately. These New Order Amish formed two church districts and by 1967 added a third one.[22] The New Order Amish accepted the controversial items and also used tractors in their fields and electricity in their homes. They placed rubber tires on their tractors, which they used on the road for errands and shopping. Since 1966, disagreements over the use of tobacco, cars, and other conveniences have fragmented the New Order Amish, leaving at least six different factions today.

Constructive Deviance

The delicate social fabric of the Old Order Amish has not been rent since 1966—an amazing feat in the face of the subsequent social changes. Ridding themselves of the progressives in 1966 fortified the Amish taboo on combines, harvesters, barn cleaners, power units, electric generators, and deep freezers. These items remain forbidden by the Ordnung, with the provision that generators can be used for welders, bulk tanks, and battery chargers.

Why would barn cleaners and home freezers appear on the bishops' taboo list? How has the community coped with these restrictions since 1966? As the dairy herds expanded in the fifties and sixties, barn cleaners became popular. Small paddles, pulled by motor-driven chains, cleaned the manure from gutters in dairy barns and saved an enormous amount of hand labor. The barn cleaners concerned the bishops in three ways: they required electricity; they would eliminate daily hard work and leave Amish boys idle; and they were a license for expansion. Farmers who had already doubled their herds from twelve to twenty-four cows would soon be expanding their herds again if they no longer had to clean up after their cows by fork. Forbidding barn cleaners was a way of putting a lid on the burgeoning dairy business. Consequently, they were placed on the bishops' taboo list.

In the seventies, high milk prices and easy credit tempted Amish farmers again. To the dismay of some leaders, many herds were doubled, with up to forty-eight cows—still a modest number in contrast to the one hundred cows of their non-Amish neighbors. Because no one enjoys the sloppy work of cleaning up after four dozen cows, Amish farmers devised two detours around the bishops' taboo on barn cleaners. Some clean their barns by scraping the manure through the gutters with a cable contraption pulled by a mule. More recently, liquid manure pits have been installed by digging "basements" underneath Amish barns at considerable expense. Used first under Amish chicken houses, these liquid manure pits hold the slop as it drains out of the gutters by gravity. The manure is pumped from the pit into a tank spreader, which scatters it over fields. An Amish minister reflecting on the barn cleaner taboo in light of twenty-five years of history said that the leaders "made a big mistake with the barn cleaner, they should have never tried to stop it, because these pits and stuff are so expensive." Rather than losing face and reneging on their 1960 decree, leaders have looked the other way as Amish farmers devised new ways to clean their barns. While their use was devious in some respects, these new barn-cleaning methods pay respect to traditional authority, and, at the same time, ease the burden of work that accompanies a larger herd. It is a gentleman's stand-off. The farmers have respected the letter of the law by not installing the forbidden mechanical cleaners, and the bishops have respected the dirty work of farming by not clamping down on the new cleaning methods, which pay polite deference to tradition.

In order to limit herd size, Amish leaders placed an additional restriction on dairy farmers which was not included in the articles of 1960. Amish farmers had been using mechanical milking machines for many years, but they carried the milk to the milk house in buckets. In the sixties and seventies many non-Amish farmers replaced their milk buckets with labor-saving glass pipe lines. Pumped through the pipe lines, the milk flowed directly from the cows to an adjacent milk house, thus entirely eliminating buckets. By outlawing these popular pipe lines, church leaders hoped to stifle expansion and preserve work for Amish boys. Furthermore, shiny glass pipes in Amish barns seemed a bit too modern. They looked worldly and certainly out of character with Amish modesty. Today Amish farmers either carry milk in buckets or use a small mobile tank to transport it to an adjacent milk house.

The bishops' rejection of the six items, with the exception of the household freezer, in the early sixties is seen by thoughtful Amish leaders as a sincere attempt to arrest social change, limit the size of farm operations, and keep the family on the farm. Describing those pivotal decisions, a farmer said: "I can't give enough credit to our leaders for keeping us back from large equipment, tractors, combines, and harvesters. They stressed not having big equipment and said that if we allow big equipment we'll go into debt and need more land to pay it off and it will break up the family farm."

Home freezers and electrical generators were also recalled from use in the early sixties. Restricted to welders, the generator was later permitted for bulk tanks. In the fifties the home freezer offered a great boost to preserving garden produce for large Amish families. But a freezer required electricity. Some freezers were first operated by electricity from the generators used on farms before the 1960 ban.

Table 8-2 Technological Restrictions

1910	Telephone installation in homes	1966	Power units (tractors)
1915	Automobile ownership	1966	Electric generators
1919	Electricity from public utility lines	1966	Barn cleaners
1923	Use of tractors for field work	1966	Deep freezers
1940	Central heating in homes	1970s	Milk pipe lines
1950s	Power lawn mowers	1970s	Silo unloaders
1966	Grain combines and forage harvesters	1986	Computers

Note: These are approximate dates for, in many cases, a decision developed over several years. The restrictions continue today.

Table 8-3 Technological Adaptations

1930s Washing machines with gasoline motors	1970s Modern bathrooms
	1970s Flashing lights on buggies
1940s Propane gas stoves	1970s Modern gas appliances
1940s Hiring cars and trucks	1970s Air and hydraulic power
1950s Mechanical milking machines	1970s Chain saws and weed cutters
1950s Community telephones	1970s Manufacturing equipment
1950s Hay balers	1970s Calculators
1960s Diesel power units	1980s Modern kitchens
1960s Generators for welders	1980s Electric inverters
1960s Engines on farm machinery	1980s Electric cash registers
1970s Bulk milk tanks	1980s Telephones in shops

Note: Many of these changes occurred over one or two decades. The dates indicate the approximate time of their widespread use.

Despite their obvious benefits to homemakers, freezers required a permanent supply of electricity. Allowing freezers in homes meant that other household appliances might also be plugged into electrical outlets. It would become an uncontrollable situation that surely would lead to televisions, radios, and all sorts of other evil intrusions. So the freezer was banned, not because the Amish view it as intrinsically evil but because of the other worldly devices that would most certainly follow it into Amish homes.

Today most Amish families have access to a freezer. Many rent small storage freezers located in fruit markets or stores. Other families, including those of ministers, own freezers located in a non-Amish neighbor's garage or basement. The Amish family makes a contribution to the electrical costs or often barters services or garden produce in exchange for the neighbor's hospitality. The riddle of keeping freezers at nearby non-Amish homes appears hypocritical to the outsider. Rather than two-faced deviance, freezer use is but another compromise. It permits the use of a modern appliance that helps preserve food, which in turn supports the extended family system. At the same time, this arrangement bars other electrical gadgets from Amish homes. Use of the freezer undergirds the Amish commitment to large families and self-sufficiency. Freezing home-grown foods assures a permanent place for the garden and its wholesome work. But to use the freezer as a wedge to bring electricity into Amish homes would have certainly, over time, invited the use of other appliances, including radios and televisions. And so the freezers are wisely placed in non-Amish homes. The freezer riddle is a way of keeping technology at a distance while using it to preserve the family garden and self-sufficiency. Gas freezers, which have recently become available, can be found in a few Amish homes. For the most part, however, they are

Power lawn mowers were prohibited in the fifties. Lawn mowers are pushed by hand or sometimes pulled by horse. Since 1966 motors have been used on field mowers to cut grass for hay. With the exception of electric wiring, newer Amish homes look quite similar to non-Amish ones.

frowned on because of the freezer taboo engraved in the Ordnung in 1960.

The turbulent early sixties, which led up to the division of 1966, were a benchmark in Amish history. It was a time when key understandings became inscribed in the Ordnung. Horses would stay in the field. Symbols of Amish identity, they would set the pace of things and curb expansionist tendencies. Self-propelled harvesters, combines, and haybines were outlawed, probably forever. Modern farm machinery, such as mowers, balers, sprayers, corn pickers, all powered by engines, would be tolerated if pulled by horses. So the Amish farmers who baffle Moderns by pulling hay balers through the fields with mules are not foolish. They are simply yielding to a reasonable compromise with modernity which respects tradition, curtails expansion, provides labor, protects ethnic identity, and permits just enough technology to let them survive financially. It has become a good bargain— one that harnesses the power of progress in creative ways for the welfare of the ethnic community.

9

The Transformation of Amish Work

The lunch pail is the greatest threat to our way of life.
—Amish bishop

The Legacy of the Soil

In the latter part of the twentieth century, the Amish experienced two major transformations that had the potential to destroy or bolster their destiny as a people. Sweeping changes in the broader society forced them to grapple with two simple but not innocuous questions: Who will educate our children? How will we earn a living? The answers could, over the years, determine their cultural fate. Public school consolidation and scarce farmland placed these questions on the bargaining table. The Amish would have preferred the serenity of the past, but the forces of progress were relentless. The Amish were not about to relinquish the education of their children. Schooling, the Amish said, was nonnegotiable.

The question of work, however, was different. The Amish refused to bargain until faced with a last-minute deadline, but then they agreed to strike a deal. Ironically, they had refused to budge on public education for fear that it would lead them off the farm. Yet a few years later, a bleak economic scenario persuaded them to hedge on their commitment to farming. Why were they willing to abandon the soil after plowing it for almost three hundred years? What factors led to this historic agreement, which some doomsayers predicted would lead to their cultural demise?[1]

The Amish have always been a people of the land. Ever since intense persecution in Europe pushed them into rural isolation, they have been tillers of the soil, and good ones. The land has nurtured their common life. They have been stewards of the soil—plowing, harrowing, fertilizing, and cultivating it. The springtime fragrance of freshly plowed ground energizes them. They pulverize the soil in their fists to test its moisture level. Whereas all soils look like dirt to city folks, the Amish have an eye for good soil. The rich limestone soil of Lancaster County, like a magnetic force, holds their community together and ties them to their history. They have tenaciously clung to the soil and have purchased more acreage at every opportunity. A leader wrote: "A longstanding tradition is that a consistent Amish family will be on the farm or attached close to the soil, and a prospective father will provide a farm for his boys."[2] In a typical family with three sons, a father hoped to purchase farms for the two sons who could not remain on the homestead.[3]

"Agriculture," according to one leader, "is a religious tenet, a branch of Christian duty." The divine injunction to Adam in Genesis "to till the ground from which he came" provides a religious mandate for farming.[4] The Amish believe that the Bible instructs them to earn their living by the sweat of their brow. Over the years, the soil has assumed a spiritual meaning; it is not to be sold and exploited at will. As the caretakers of God's garden, the Amish believe they are to cultivate it carefully, for it is their sustenance. Good soil became a sacred symbol in their culture which was believed to hold the secret to their longevity—the mystery that explained the riddle of their success as a people. Tilling the soil induced sacramental meanings, for it ushered them into the presence of God. The Amish carefully worked the soil, which in turn nourished them physically and spiritually. "I don't know what will happen if we get away from the soil," a young Amish farmer said. "I can see where it's not a very good thing. You get away from working with the soil and you get away from nature and then you are getting away from the Lord's handiwork."

Another Amishman argues that the Amish were unable to establish a stable and permanent community life in North America until they began farming the rich soils of Lancaster County, where they could "live together, worship together, and work together."[5] A businessman explained that "good soil makes a strong church" but worried that a paradox lies below the soil's surface. "The best soil," he said, "holds the best people and makes them a faster people and they become prosperous and that prosperity is not good for the church and so it gets you coming in the back door." He believes that the vitality of the Amish community depends on the quality of the local soil. But he fears that the prosperity germinating in the land will, in the long run, ruin the church with luxury.

Although the Amish delight in working it, the soil is not an end in itself; it is the seedbed for Amish families. A persistent theme, extolled by virtually all Amish elders, praises the farm as the best place to raise a family. Even the owners of booming Amish industries repeat the litany of praise for the family farm. Despite their obvious pride in their thriving enterprises, businessmen worry about the fate of their grandchildren, who will not grow up on farms. The farm provided a habitat for raising sturdy families. Parents and children worked together. Daily chores taught children the value of personal responsibility. More importantly, they learned the virtue of hard work, a value credited with keeping them out of trouble. Parents were always nearby—directing, supervising, advising, or reprimanding. As a family, they were pitted against the forces of nature—a challenge that forged a strong sense of identity and cohesion. Moreover, the demands of farm work kept young people at home and limited their interaction with the outside world. Thus, the family farm was the cradle of Amish socialization—a cradle that until recently held the very essence of their way of life.

A Demographic Squeeze

Although farming has always been the foremost occupation, early Amish settlers also worked as millers, tanners, brewers, quarry operators, and veterinarians. But according to one Amishman, the number of Amish in nonfarm jobs dwindled by 1830 and remained scant for a century. Even during the Depression the Amish resorted to nonfarm jobs only when they were unable to operate a farm.[6] A few Amish have always been employed in traditional crafts and farm-related occupations, such as blacksmith work, carpentry, painting, watch repair, and furniture making.

Nonfarm work evolved in three phases after the Depression. In the first phase, as cars gained widespread acceptance and horse travel declined, the Amish developed their own carriage and harness shops and began shoeing their own horses. In the second phase, Amish shops began repairing horse-drawn machinery as tractor farming gained in popularity among non-Amish farmers. In the early sixties they also started converting tractor equipment for horse-drawn use. The third phase sprang up in the seventies, as farmland dwindled and land prices skyrocketed.

Rapid changes in farm technology had already ruptured Amish society in the schism of 1966. The bishops were able to restrict changes in farm technology, but they soon found themselves in a more serious quandary—they could not farm without land. In the late sixties and early seventies, the Amish were caught in a demographic squeeze. Their birth rate was high, and their population had doubled between 1940 and 1960. In the early part of the century large families had provided a hedge against fatal diseases and attrition to other groups. Improved medicines, which the Amish began using, resulted in a plummet in infant mortality rates. Moreover, the expanding community had already purchased much of the salable farmland in eastern Lancaster County. In fact, one public official reported that between 1920 and 1940 the Amish had bought every farm near the center of their settlement which had been put up for auction except one, which was sold on a Sunday.[7] The pressure peaked in a year in the late sixties when eighty young couples started housekeeping and only ten farms were sold on the open market.[8]

The Amish were not the only people desiring land. Lancaster County was the fastest growing metropolitan area in Pennsylvania between 1960 and 1970. Suburbs began nibbling away at prime farmland. The number of tourists jumped from approximately 1.5 million in 1963 to nearly 4 million by 1974. Tourist sites and their accompanying motels and restaurants also required land. Lancaster County was an enticing area for industry, because of its dependable, anti-union labor force as well as its proximity to eastern seaboard markets. Some thirty-six new industries entered the county between 1960 and 1970.[9] They, of course, needed land and attracted employees, who required housing. All of these factors increased the squeeze on farmland. The cheap land of the Depression years had turned into gold in only a few decades. In 1940, in the heart of their settlement, the Amish were paying between $300 and $400 per acre for farmland.[10] By the

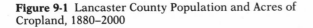

Figure 9-1 Lancaster County Population and Acres of Cropland, 1880–2000

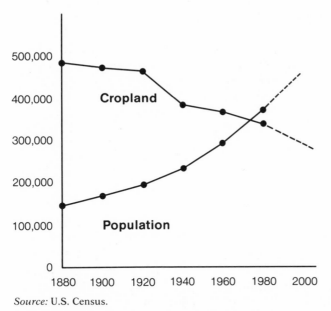

Source: U.S. Census.

Note: Estimates for 2000 are based on current trends.

early seventies, farmland had escalated to $2,000 per acre, and it more than doubled again before peaking in 1981, at an average of $4,550. So the sixty-acre farm that sold for $21,000 in 1940 had skyrocketed in cost to $273,000 by 1981. In 1984, an Amishman bought a fifty-four-acre farm in the center of the settlement for $7,593 per acre, totalling $410,022. Land prices dipped in the mid-eighties with the depressed national farm economy; however, farmland in the heart of the Amish settlement still averaged $5,200 per acre, compared to $1,450 in the state and $596 in the nation.[11] Farmland preservation stirred heated public debate in the county throughout the eighties. Because of their desire to remain separate from government programs, the Amish have refused to participate in a public program designed to preserve farmland in Lancaster County. Yet, ironically, they are doing more than any other group to preserve farmland because they rarely sell their farms for development.

The recession and exorbitant interest rates of the late seventies prevented many Amish couples from buying a farm. Some who began farming were forced to sell out—a rare occurrence for the Amish, who historically had good credit ratings with local banks. In cases of financial difficulty, the church typically appoints several trustees to supervise a farming operation and salvage it if possible. When all else fails, the church-appointed trustees supervise the sale of the farm.

The Lunch Pail Threat

Without a high school diploma, the Amish could not pursue professional jobs. If they did leave the farm, their training restricted them to manual labor. By 1960, some Amish were already working in shops, warehouses, and even factories. Higher wages made nonfarm work so attractive that some even rented out their farms in order to take on "outside" jobs. Church leaders were alarmed. A bishop contended that "the lunch pail is the greatest threat to our way of life." Working in factories was not only frowned upon, it was actually a test of church membership in the forties. In the school controversy of the late thirties, the Amish repeatedly promised state legislators to keep their youth on the farm. Church members were excommunicated in that era if their jobs were not in a rural area or closely associated with farming.[12]

When the Amish left the farm in the seventies because of diminishing farmland, a bishop worried: "Leave this one generation grow up off the farm, and their sons won't want to farm." In 1975 another bishop articulated his fears this way: "Past experiences have proven that it is not best for the Amish people to leave the farm. If they get away from the farm they soon get away from the church, at least after the first generation."[13] The lunch pail threat had intensified in the six-

A suburban development encroaches on an Amish farm.

ties, when mobile-home factories were built on the edge of the Amish community in hopes of employing hardworking, anti-union Amish and Mennonites. By the early seventies, over one hundred Amishmen were carrying their lunch pails to several mobile-home plants, accounting for 5 percent of the total work force. By the mid-seventies, the economic recession resulted in the closing of several of the trailer factories, with quiet applause from Amish leaders. Other factories cut their work force drastically, retaining only a handful of Amish employees. Such economic uncertainty increased the Amish suspicion of factory work.[14]

Why did the factory system, symbolized by the lunch pail, frighten the Amish? First, they believed that removing the father from the family during the day would weaken his influence over the children. Amish youth would not see their father working and would lose a significant role model for Amish values. Furthermore, the father could not supervise his children from a factory. His absence from home placed an additional burden on the wife, not only for child rearing but also for meeting and dealing with strangers. Second, the factory might subvert the father's own values. Worldly culture, conveyed by non-Amish employees, would undoubtedly tarnish even the most faithful member who spent five days a week in a foreign setting. Third, factory employment threatened community solidarity in other ways. Personnel policies, timecards, and production schedules would make it difficult to take time off for community events, such as funerals and weddings, as well as barn raisings and other mutual-aid activities. Fourth, factories provided fringe benefits, such as health insurance, retirement funds, and life insurance—menaces to a community that thrives on mutual dependency. With such perks, who would need the support of an ethnic community? The factory, in short, would fragment the family and eventually destroy the community. The lunch pail was a serious threat in the eyes of Amish elders. An elderly bishop summed up the dilemma: "It's best for a Christian to be on the farm. When they carry a lunch pail and go to a factory and some places it's not too good, men and women working together and so on, and we'd rather have them on the farm but the land just doesn't reach around anymore."

Compared to the stormy school crisis of the fifties, the occupational quandary of the seventies was a quiet battle with little publicity or government interference. But the subtle, long-term consequences of Amish work were no less crucial to their survival. Amish sages knew intuitively that factory work could be dangerous to Amish identity. Even some experts predicted that "without the agricultural setting it is doubtful if the Old Order Amish could survive."[15] Nevertheless, they could hardly stretch their land any further. They had to make a living somehow. Was there no way out of this dilemma? The Supreme Court could not bail them out this time. They would have to find their own way out of this ordeal. Given the harsh economic and demographic facts facing them at the bargaining table, the Amish—with great reluctance—were willing to talk.

Sizing Up the Options

Was there no middle ground between the stark choice of factory work or financial collapse? There were a variety of alternatives: population control, migration out of the United States, migration to other regions of the county and state, subdivision of farms, and alternative work. Population control was unthinkable. The Amish perceive birth control as reckless interference with God's will, an unforgivable attempt to play the role of God. Migration to other countries was never discussed seriously. Familial and historical bonds prevented a massive evacuation to foreign lands. However, the other alternatives were thinkable.

In the midst of the school controversy in the early forties, new colonies were established in Lebanon County, some forty miles north of Lancaster, and in St. Mary's County, Maryland. But for the next twenty-five years, Amish migration to other counties was at a standstill. In the fifties, the Amish population began to sprawl toward southern Lancaster County, where land could still be bought for $250 an acre, but by 1980 the Amish were pushing against these southern boundaries. Migration within the county provided only temporary relief from the land and population squeeze. In the mid-sixties, land

Figure 9-2 Expansion in Lancaster County, 1880–1985

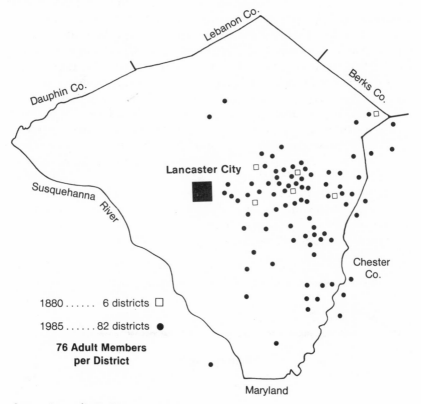

Source: Appendix B, *Directory* (1965, 1973, 1980).

Note: From 1945 to 1985 the settlement increased from twenty-two to eighty-two districts.

pressures as well as internal unrest prompted some families to start new settlements in other counties of the state.[16] Land in the new areas could often be purchased at one-fourth the cost of that in Lancaster. Nearly a dozen new settlements were spawned by the Lancaster Amish, until high interest rates made land purchases prohibitive, even in outlying counties. The outward migration abated in the early eighties, but by then roughly 15 percent of the Lancaster settlement had moved to other counties of the state.[17] The Amish migrations were not enough to offset the population pressures and land prices that were still rising at home.

Subdividing farms provided a second solution. A farm of seventy acres, divided in half, could support two families. Larger farms were sometimes divided into three sections. A new house and barn were often erected on each section. A subdivision was frequently accompanied by a shift to specialized farming that required less land. Large chicken houses or hog operations were built on smaller plots, so the family could still cling to the farm, or at least a corner of it. The outward migration and the subdivision of farms kept the Amish family on the land and perpetuated their home-centered culture in continuity with past tradition. But these adaptations were not enough.

Population growth continued because young people were staying with the church. Market demands and inflation doubled the cost of farmland in Lancaster County between 1973 and 1978.[18] Moreover, escalating interest rates made the cost of purchasing a new farm virtually prohibitive for a young couple. Interest payments alone on a sixty-acre farm could exceed $30,000 a year. The Amish doggedly pursued their quest for farmland. Yet at times they were no match for powerful real-estate developers. In 1985, for example, an Amishman was the next-to-last bidder on a fifty-five-acre farm, which was sold to a developer for over $7,000 an acre, eighteen times its 1940 value.

Increased land prices elsewhere and high interest rates have de-

Figure 9-3 New Settlements in Pennsylvania Originating from Lancaster

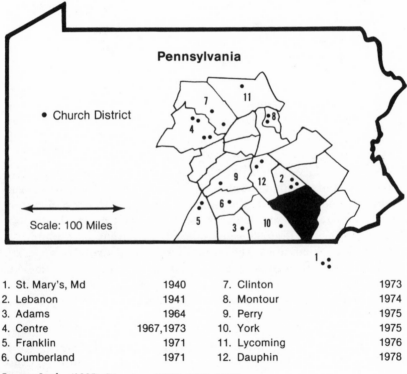

1. St. Mary's, Md	1940	7. Clinton	1973
2. Lebanon	1941	8. Montour	1974
3. Adams	1964	9. Perry	1975
4. Centre	1967,1973	10. York	1975
5. Franklin	1971	11. Lycoming	1976
6. Cumberland	1971	12. Dauphin	1978

Source: Luthy (1985), *Directory* (1973, 1979, 1980).

creased outward migration to other counties to a mere dribble. The last new settlement was founded in 1978.[19] The friendly options had been exhausted. Finally, the Amish were forced to negotiate the nature of their work. By 1980, it was clear that they had decided to enter nonfarm occupations. It was not a formal decision by any means, but the signals were clear—the Amish would leave the farm rather than migrate. By the late eighties, they were pressuring township supervisors for commercial zoning in the hub of their settlement. Represented by a planning consultant, the Amish pressed for expanded commercial rights on their historic farmland—a sure sign that they had decided to shift occupations rather than flee.

Preserving Home Work

Although nonfarm occupations increased simultaneously with migration and the subdivision of farms in the sixties, they flourished in the late seventies and the eighties. Nonfarm employment became the chief strategy for coping with scarce land and the population surge. The establishment of farm repair shops in the early sixties inaugurated the Amish shop movement. Small businesses in the Lancaster area expanded rapidly, and by 1977 more than 130 were listed in a directory of Amish shops. A national survey of Amish shops estimated that 400 had sprung up in a seven-year period (1970–77), with 50 starting in 1977.[20] Since that time, several hundred have proliferated in the Lancaster settlement. An Amishman described the surge of shops as "a sharp turn towards home, that is back to an Anabaptist culture. Many of these shops are erected on the farm or adjacent to it. They provide the off-farm worker a job at home with or near his family, self-dependent, self-supporting, making, repairing, or selling a product that he knows is useful, one which he has a right to be proud of."[21]

Although the Amish were willing to negotiate the type of work they would perform, they refused to budge on the conditions of work. First, they wanted to work at home or as near it as possible. Second, they wanted to control the nature and quality of their work. Third, they insisted that the work, whenever possible, be performed in the context of a supportive ethnic environment. Finally, they wanted work to remain within the confines of the moral order of Amish culture (for example, television repair was unacceptable).

Rejecting the lure of factory jobs, the Amish reluctantly agreed to leave the farm if they could retain control over their work. Today, although 30 percent of married Amishmen are not farming, many of their jobs indirectly support the farm economy.[22] The proportion of nonfarm jobs varies greatly among church districts. In the heart of the settlement, with high population density, scarce land, and commercial access, nonfarm jobs climb to over 60 percent. In more rural

Small shops and businesses are often built on the edge of a farm. This shop makes lawn furniture that is sold in several states.

areas, on the community's fringe, they dip to 15 percent.

The location of Amish work is cross-tabulated by sex and marital status in table 9-1. Perhaps the most striking fact is that though fewer Amishmen plow fields these days, 74 percent of the married men are, nonetheless, working at home. Among single men, the number employed at home drops to 50 percent. A large proportion of those not employed at home work nearby, often in a shop within a mile or so of home. There are, of course, carpentry crews that travel long distances to construction sites, but the overwhelming majority of the married men work at or near home. So, despite a transformation, Amish work has not vanished from home.

Even more impressive, in light of modern trends, married Amishwomen still work at home. It is rare to find a married Amishwoman with a full-time job outside her home. Many of them have sideline jobs—such as quilting, baking, craftwork, and sewing—but these are usually based at home. Quilting is nearly full-time work for many Amishwomen.[23] Women and children often tend small roadside stands on their property, where they sell produce, baked goods, and crafts to tourists and non-Amish neighbors. Some married women hold part-time jobs cooking in restaurants or tending market stands

Table 9-1 Location of Occupation by Sex and Marital Status

	Single		Married	
	Female (%)	Male (%)	Female (%)	Male (%)
Full-time Work at Home	41	50	100	74
Full-time Work Away	59	50	0	26

several days a week on a seasonal basis. The married Amish "career woman" simply does not exist.

Among single females, 59 percent of those with a full-time job work away from home. Young women hoping to save money before marriage or older single women make up this percentage. One older single woman harnesses her horse on Sunday mornings to travel to church. On Monday she walks across the road to a small real-estate office, where she works as a receptionist. She operates the office computer, which in a split second can display real-estate listings throughout the county. The more typical pattern is for single women to work as cooks in restaurants, domestics in motels, bakers in bakeshops, salesclerks in Amish stores and market stands, or teachers in Amish schools. Others do part-time cleaning for non-Amish neighbors.

The Context of Amish Work

Table 9-2 charts the relationship between age and other dimensions of work performed by married Amishmen. The major occupations spanning the age spectrum are farming, carpentry, and machine shop work. Approximately 44 percent of the males who work away from home are employed in carpentry—in a shop or with a mobile construction crew. Those under thirty-five are, surprisingly, more likely to be farming than are their elders. Farmers often retire at a young age to allow a son to take over the farm. After retirement, a grandfather or grandmother may set up a small shop on the farm to provide supplemental income. Whenever possible, a father "gets out of the way" so that a son can raise his family on the farm, until the process repeats itself in the next generation. Among those under thirty-five who work at home, 91 percent are farmers.

Perhaps even more important than the location of work is its social context. Married Amishmen who work away from home might carry lunch pails, but not to factory jobs—28 percent are self-employed and 48 percent work for an Amish employer. Thus, over 75 percent of those who work away from home are employed in an Amish environment. "Where," asked an Amish businessman rhetorically, "is

Table 9-2   Occupational Characteristics of Married Males by Age

	35 and Under N = 64 (%)	36 and Older N = 66 (%)	Total N = 130 (%)
Occupation			
Farming	67	62	64
Carpentry	13	14	13
Machine Shop	9	9	9
Miscellaneous	11	15	14
Full-time Employment			
At Home	72	76	74
Away from Home	28	24	26
Occupation at Home			
Farming	91	79	85
Other	9	21	15
Occupation Away			
Carpentry	44	47	44
Machine Shop	28	13	21
Other	28	40	35
Employed Away			
Self-employed	33	21	28
Amish employer	47	50	48
Non-Amish employer	20	29	24

the best place for these Amish boys to work if they can't all farm? In a big factory or tobacco warehouse in Lancaster city or in a shop with an Amish boss and other Amish employees?"

Those who are not self-employed or working for fellow Amish are often part of an Amish work crew employed by a Mennonite or other plain-dressing employer. Still others, employed by non-Amish employers, typically work side-by-side with fellow ethnics. The Amish rarely work outside of ethnic networks.[24] In the final analysis, 75 percent of Amish married men work at home, and those who do work away from home are usually enveloped by an ethnic web, which defuses the lunch pail threat. Non-Amish employers are usually local people, sympathetic to Amish values, who willingly adapt to community concerns in exchange for conscientious work. Some Amish work in a more secular setting, but the number is minuscule. At best, not more than 6 percent of married men work in a non-Amish milieu. Even among the younger married men, less than 3 percent work in factories.[25]

Given the crescendo of nonfarm jobs in recent years, it is surprising to find few differences between age groups in table 9-2. Men under age thirty-six are more likely to be employed away from home, to work in machine shops, or to be self-employed than older men. However, younger married men are less likely than their elders to work for a non-Amish employer. The data suggest that the younger generation is more likely to become entrepreneurs than to head for the modern factory. Thus, while nonfarm jobs have increased dramatically in some church districts, the Amish have not relinquished control over the conditions of their work. They were willing to dicker with modernity over the type of work, but they were not about to negotiate its location, control, or ethnic setting.

Business Enterprises

When asked what you cannot buy these days from an Amish shop, an old sage wryly remarked: "About the only thing we don't have is an undertaker." While not quite true, his quip symbolizes the mushrooming infrastructure of Amish-owned services. The Amish own shops that sell dry goods, furniture, shoes, and wholesale foods such as cereals, and they also work as plumbers, painters, and even self-trained accountants. However, the Amish do not have lawyers, doctors, dentists, or veterinarians in their ranks. The explosion of nonagricultural jobs has ushered in a new era of Amish history. Instead of depending on outsiders for the bulk of their services, they have developed the capacity to supply many of their own services and products within the ethnic community. A streak of modernity lies beneath this ethnic umbrella, for some functions that were previously lodged at home are now performed by a specialist, to be sure, but an Amish one. This network of shops provides jobs, financial revenues, and a buffer zone with the larger culture.

Amish enterprises vary in size, location, and function. The three major types are small cottage industries at home, larger manufacturing establishments, and mobile work crews. Home-based operations, often located on farms, are housed in tobacco sheds or other farm buildings refitted for the new task. Bakeshops, craft shops, machine shops, hardware stores, health food shops, and flower shops are a few of the hundreds that are often annexed to a barn or house. In some cases, new buildings are constructed for the enterprise. Many home-based shops cater to tourists, the Amish, and non-Amish neighbors. These shops, like the old mom-and-pop grocery stores of bygone America, are family operations. One young father, for example, operates a washing machine shop in an oversized garage on his farm. He buys used washing machines and replaces their electric motors with solid-state ignition, gasoline engines imported from Japan. The refurbished washing machines are sold to Amish customers. The shop also repairs washing machines. Several adults, an uncle, cousin, or sister, may assist the nuclear family as part- or full-time employees. Children help or hinder the operation, as the case may be. These cottage industries, lodged at home, range from one-person operations to those employing half a dozen people. One thing is certain: work in these settings is securely under the family's control. "What we're trying to do really," said one proprietor, "is keep the family together."[26]

Larger shops or manufacturing concerns are established in newly erected buildings on the edge of a farm, or on a plot with a house. These formal shops, with as many as fifteen employees, function as established entities in the larger business community. Blacksmith shops, and welding shops that manufacture horse-drawn equipment, cater primarily to the Amish. Other businesses, such as cabinet shops and hydraulic shops, serve both Amish and non-Amish customers. Many retail outlets—harness, hardware, paint, household appliance, and food stores—also sell to both groups. Other entrepreneurs build silos, small storage barns, doghouses, lawn furniture, and mailboxes, which are sold across the eastern seaboard to non-Amish customers. Some metal fabrication shops thrive on subcontracts with larger non-Amish businesses, as well as with other Amish manufacturers.

The larger manufacturing shops are efficient and modern. At first glance, hanging gas lanterns provide the only clue to their Amish ownership. Air and hydraulic power operate modern machinery. Amish mechanics have learned to adapt electrically powered machinery to air and hydraulic pressure to meet virtually all their power demands. Diesel engines power the air and hydraulic pumps. Even burglar alarms are powered by air. One Amishman argued that air pressure is superior to electricity and that "some shops have electric systems beat hand over fist. That's all there is to it. They even have their doors rigged up to an alarm. You know, if someone breaks in at night they have air alarms all over the place that will blow a horn loud enough to scare a thief half to death." These modern Amish shops have evolved a long way from the smoke-filled blacksmith shops of yesteryear. Low overhead, minimal advertising, austere management, modest wages, quality workmanship, and sheer hard work provide many Amish shops with a strong competitive advantage in the commercial marketplace.

Mobile work crews are the third type of Amish enterprise. Amish construction crews travel to building sites in Lancaster County and other counties as well. Carpentry and construction work have always been acceptable alternatives to farm work. Today, 13 percent of married Amishmen are engaged in carpentry, which rates second to farming as the most preferred occupation. Amish construction crews, using the latest power tools operated by portable electric generators or on-site electricity, engage in subcontract and general construction of both residential and commercial buildings. Amish cabinet shops produce high-quality cabinetry, which is sometimes installed out of state. Trucks and vans provided by employees or regularly hired drivers are used to transport the Amish work crews.

As the Amish have struggled to keep their work at home and their families together, they have encountered another modern obstacle: zoning regulations. Ironically, the zoning laws that had protected their farms from developers and large industry now prevent some of them from building commercial establishments on their own farms. The proliferation of cottage industries and small manufacturing operations, often built in agricultural zones, have caused tension with public officials. In some townships, zoning officials overlooked the violations, but in other townships they closed down the Amish manufacturing plants. In the late eighties, several townships negotiated with the Amish—hoping to adapt zoning codes that would control the size of small Amish businesses in rural areas. Under pressure from the Amish, one township amended its agricultural zoning ordinances in 1988 to permit home industries if they did not exceed 2,500 square feet or employ more than four workers, including the owner. Another township has a limit of two non-family employees.[27] It was an interesting twist, because modern law and government were being used to enforce Amish values of small-scale operations and family involvement.

The Texture of Amish Business

Amish industries bear the imprint of Amish culture in several ways. They are uniformly small. It is rare for them to have more than fifteen employees. When they do, church leaders caution owners about the dangers of mushrooming size—pride, worldliness, excessive power, publicity, status—the evil trappings of large-scale operations. The larger Amish industries have annual sales that exceed $1 million, and several are multimillion-dollar operations. Discreet expansion that is not consolidated in one manufacturing site is more acceptable than a large complex of buildings, which gives the appearance of aggrandizement. Installing cabinets or building silos around the country is less auspicious, and thus more palatable, than operating a large manufacturing complex on one site which employs one hundred people. Stories are told of Amish business owners who, refusing to bend to the size limits of their culture, became proud and eventually left the church or were excommunicated. Describing one of the casualties, a businessman said: "You just have to be careful not to get proud wings and spread them like Ike Smoker did. That just won't fit. You need to keep your humility and keep your head down under the covers."

Even the larger businesses employ primarily fellow Amish. A na-

Amish crafts and lawn furniture are sold at an Amish-owned tourist stand by the side of a home.

tional survey found that only 18 percent of the Amish shops employed non-family workers on a full-time basis.[28] The non-Amish employees are frequently members of other plain churches with similar cultural values. Non-Amish employees may be hired at times for the use of their vehicles in the business or for particular technical skills. A business leader regretted hiring a non-Amish employee who "left his mark" by creating problems with his Amish employees, and since then he has not hired outsiders.

Table 9-3 lists typical Amish businesses. Products ranging from mushrooms to chain saws can be bought in Amish stores. Hundreds of Amish-made products—from finely sculptured cornhusk dolls to clumsy manure spreaders—are sold. In general, the products and services must be compatible with Amish values. Selling and repairing radios, for instance, would be off-limits, as would car, computer, or video sales. Selling new chain saws and the latest hardware tools is acceptable, because these are used routinely by the Amish themselves. Farm equipment (for example, a wagon) is sometimes manufactured by Amish shops in two versions—a steel-wheeled edition for the Amish and a rubber-tired one for the non-Amish. The taboo on electricity makes it difficult to sell refrigerated or frozen-food products. Repair work, crafts, manufacturing, and construction, as well as retailing, provide the majority of nonfarm jobs. Few Amish work in service or information roles that require formal education and extensive interaction with the outside world.

An inventive streak runs through Amish culture. A tinkering attitude, the taboo on electricity, and a bent for self-sufficiency have stimulated a variety of inventions. For example, a manufacturer developed a hay turner, which flips hay upside down and speeds its drying time in the field.[29] Drawn by a tractor, the hay turner is in high demand by non-Amish farmers. Another Amish mechanic developed a horse-drawn plow with a wheel-driven hydraulic pump that presses the blade into the soil at uniform depths. The plow automatically resets itself in the ground after hitting a rock. A young inventor designed an outdoor, frost-free watering trough for cattle. It uses the earth's natural heat to prevent freezing in the winter. Another inventor designed a wheel-driven liquid manure spreader. An Amish shop developed and manufactures its own 12-volt Pequea battery. The list goes on and on. One thing is clear. The feeble Amish repair shops of the sixties have been superseded by manufacturing facilities that, in the opinion of one leader, will soon enable the Amish to manufacture virtually all of their horse-drawn farm equipment. Using commercial manufacturing equipment, they are able to fabricate farm machinery according to their own designs. One snag worries a leading manufacturer. He fears that newer manufacturing equipment, increasingly dependent on electronic operating systems, may be difficult to convert

Table 9-3   A Sampler of Amish-operated Shops and Businesses

Air pumps and systems	Foundry	Masonry
Bakery	Furniture	Plumbing
Battery and electrical	Groceries	Printing
Beekeeping supplies	Hardware	Quilts
Bookstores	Hat manufacturing	Retail stores
Butchering	Health foods	Roadside stands
Cabinetry	Horseshoeing	Roofing and spouting
Carriage	Household appliances	Spray painting
Clock and watch repair	Hydraulic systems	Storage buildings
Construction	Lantern manufacturing	Storm windows and glass
Crafts	Leather and harness	Tin fabrication
Drygoods	Log house construction	Tombstone engraving
Engine repair	Machinery assembly	Toys
Fence installation	Machinery	Upholstery
Floor covering	manufacturing	Vegetable plants
	Machinery repair	

to air and hydraulic power—thus keeping it out of Amish reach.

The bishops, who had stubbornly insisted on horse-drawn equipment in the early sixties, inadvertently seeded a host of new jobs in Amish machine shops that build or refabricate farm equipment. In the same manner, Amish clothing, horse and buggy transportation, and the rejection of electricity have fostered occupations that serve the unique needs of Amish society. These new jobs have diminished the lure of modern factories. The riddles that baffle outsiders are not only rites of deference to tradition, they also create a panoply of jobs for many Amish families. Not all the nonfarm jobs cater to the peculiar needs of the Amish community; many serve the larger society. However, agricultural services and ethnic specialty jobs constitute a major portion of the economic structure undergirding the Amish community.

The Impact of Nonfarm Work

Instead of threatening the community, nonfarm jobs have actually bolstered its vitality in several ways. They have increased the Amish population density. Single-dwelling houses on small lots have reduced the geographical size of church districts, which in turn enhances face-to-face interaction. This not only reinforces the oral base of Amish culture but also increases the practicality of horse and buggy travel, because family and friends are nearby. By encouraging members to work in an Amish social context, the church has actually tightened its grip on them. Instead of interacting with strangers in a factory, nonfarmers spend their working hours in the midst of Amish chatter. The dialect constantly reaffirms the sectarian world view and provides a buffer against modern ideas. In this way the new occupational roles embellish community solidarity and Amish identity, and they augur well for its survival.

Day workers in Amish shops may earn from $5 to $10 per hour, and many work a forty-five-hour week. Because self-employed Amish are exempt from Social Security, many shops are set up as legal partnerships, with employees considered partners or owners. Thus unemployment tax, Social Security tax, and workmen's compensation are not paid because of the partnership arrangement. The employees, or owners in this case, are not eligible for any benefits from these government programs. Retirement benefits and hospitalization programs are generally not provided by Amish enterprises. Profits are shared with the partners or employees, but they are not necessarily distributed equally; senior partners, who carry the risk of investment, may reap a greater share.

Small-scale sole proprietorships and family-operated cottage industries provide flexible work schedules that accommodate the com-

The hay turner, invented by an Amishman, is manufactured by an Amish machine shop and sold to non-Amish farmers across the nation.

munity's predictable and unexpected needs. Requests to attend a half-dozen all-day weddings in November, welcomed with delight by the small Amish proprietor, might horrify personnel managers in modern corporations. Although they may seem numerous, the "community days" taken by Amish employees hardly exceed the sick days, personal days, and holiday time taken by typical modern employees. Small Amish industries can more easily respond to community needs for volunteer help at work "frolics," barn raisings, or disaster sites than public industries can. Although employees can participate in ethnic events, they forego high salaries and the perks of hospitalization and retirement benefits, which over time would sever their ties to the ethnic community. In all of these ways, the new cottage industries are truly Amish in character—designed to serve the needs of the community rather than those of the individual—and yet, paradoxically, the individual is also served rather well, with high levels of job satisfaction, a humane work environment, a high degree of control over the work, and ethnic pride in the product. Alienation between worker and product, and between employee and employer, typical of some modern industries, is largely absent in these small shops.

Although the rise of nonfarm work has momentarily stalled the lunch pail threat, the long-term consequences of this fundamental shift in the structure of Amish life are unknown. Small, home-based cottage industries promise few disruptions to traditional Amish values, even in the long run. The social ramifications, however, of the retailing and manufacturing businesses that exceed a half-dozen employees and boast million-dollar sales are a different story. Amish leaders, including some proprietors, are uneasy about the debilitating social effects of these ventures. Amish manufacturing establishments and construction firms follow typical business procedures in their fixed hours and policies. Like housework, farm work never ends. In planting and harvest seasons, sixteen-hour workdays are not unusual. Church leaders worry that the spare time afforded by an eight-hour workday will lead adults, and especially youth, into questionable recreational activities. A major Amish retailer voiced his anxiety: "The thing that scares me the most is the seven-to-five syndrome with evenings free. Our people, not just the young ones, have too much leisure time, and money in their pockets. In the past we were always more or less tied within a small radius of home because there were always chores. I even thought that Pop raised some weeds for us to pull."

Family size typically declines in times of industrialization because children, no longer needed for farm work, become an economic liability. A decline in family size would certainly temper Amish population growth. Traditional Amish attitudes toward work and leisure will certainly be revamped with an exodus from the farm. Furthermore, even though young fathers are working within a mile of their families, they are nevertheless away from home. Despite a supportive ethnic system, some leaders worry that this will have a detrimental effect on child rearing. Children will no longer work with, or learn occupational skills from, their fathers.

Financial concerns are an additional threat. Farm income often arrived in the monthly milk check or annual tobacco check. Even though family members attended a work "frolic" or wedding, other members returned home to milk the cows—twice every day. Dependence on daily wages and the press of production schedules in small Amish factories can obstruct community activities, even with sympathetic managers. The employee whose budget depends on daily wages may find it difficult to forgo a whole day's wage just to attend a wedding or work "frolic." Even Amish businessmen, under the stress of tight production schedules, may become reluctant to release employees for barn raisings or family reunions. The Amish have not followed the typical path of industrialization, but it remains to be seen whether they will be able to prevent the long-term effects of this occupational shift from undermining family and community stability. Furthermore, many of the regulatory concessions that the modern world made for the Amish—for instance, in schooling and Social Security—were based on the premise that they were self-employed farmers. As the Amish become successful entrepreneurs, the legislative tolerance and leniency may wane.

The New Commercial Class

The larger uncertainty, however, focuses on the growing number of business owners. Despite an eighth-grade education, entrepreneurs of the emerging commercial class are bright, literate, assertive, and, for the most part, astute managers. Some have taken special training in technical areas, such as hydraulics. Through self-motivation and experience, they have, within one generation, become proficient managers. Their stunning success in many ways validates the competency of an eighth-grade Amish education. They understand the larger social system and interact with ease on a daily basis with suppliers, business colleagues, customers, attorneys, and credit officers. They are oriented to management procedures, rational calculations of profit ratios, cost/benefit analyses, and marketing strategies. While they know well the boundaries of traditional Amish culture, they operate their businesses on rational and prudent calculations. Reflecting on the electricity taboo, the young owner of a retail store said: "There is a whole new group of young shop owners who think some of the old traditional distinctions are foolish!" The rise of this managerial class may destabilize Amish life in several ways.

First, the managers, immersed in the logic of the business world on a daily basis, may, over several generations, become disenchanted with traditional Amish values. Will they, for instance, be satisfied on Sunday mornings with the slow cadence of Amish hymns and pleas for humility when their daily work orbits around the aggressive business world? How long will they pay polite deference to the logic of tradition when it defies rational planning? Second, this emergent class represents a new, still informal, power structure in the Amish community. The business success and worldly acumen of this class earn it both respect and envy within the subculture. In some cases businessmen have been given greater freedom to modernize than farmers, causing ill will on the latter's part.[30] Business knowledge and organizational experience arm this new breed of Amish with a power base that, if organized, could pose a serious threat to the bishops' traditional clout.

Third, business owners often feel caught in the cross fire of traditional values and economic pressures. They know expansion and aggressive promotion will enhance profits, yet church leaders criticize and even excommunicate them if they expand too fast. One leader, under fire from church leaders for his booming business, voiced his frustration at being torn between business opportunity and small-scale values: "My own people look at my growth as a sign of greed—that I'm not satisfied to limit my volume. The volume bothers them. The Old Order Amish are supposed to be a people who do not engage in large business, and I'm right on the borderline right now. I'm a little over the line and maybe too large for Amish standards. My people think evil of me for being such a large businessman and I don't need any more aggravation right now." Struggling with the delicate tension between modernity and tradition, he continued: "Identity, having a people, is a very precious thing."

The owners of Amish businesses also find themselves in fiscal quandaries that force them to use the law to protect their own interests—a traditional taboo in Amish culture. The Amish use lawyers to draw up farm deeds and wills and to transfer real estate and set up articles of incorporation. However, filing lawsuits is cause for excommunication. In the spirit of nonresistance, modeled on the suffering Christ, the Amish traditionally have suffered injustice and financial loss rather than resort to legal force. Such humility defies normal business practice and makes Amish owners vulnerable to exploitation in the marketplace. "You know," said a businessman, "we are in a bind, being in business. When you deal with the business community you are at a distinct disadvantage, because there are those who would take advantage of you." Whether the growing number of businessmen will be able to retain the traditional values of nonresistance in the midst of a cutthroat business culture is unknown. Already Amish businessmen, the victims of shrewd debtors, are asking their attorneys to write threatening letters, but they have stopped short of filing lawsuits.

Fourth, many of the new commercial class are doing well financially. The consolidation of wealth in a small circle may erode social equality in Amish society. Will Amish millionaires be content to drive horses and dress in plain clothing over several generations? In the past, profits from farming were reinvested in the farming operation and used to help children become established on their own farms. Some young entrepreneurs are motivated by profit. The church, inexperienced in coping with inequalities of wealth, is uncertain how to respond. The healthy revenues from Amish business ventures typically are invested in real estate, used to underwrite farms for family members, or contributed to causes within the ethnic community, rather than invested in the stock market or devoured by conspicuous consumption. At the moment, the church deals with social inequality by discouraging the ostentatious display of wealth and by limiting the size of businesses. Businessmen and bishops alike fear that, in the long run, prosperity could ruin the church. Some church leaders view prosperity as a new form of persecution. The solution partly rests on whether the church will find ways to motivate wealthy Amish to use their resources for the community rather than for self-aggrandizement. One Amish leader worries that "with all the change, in fifty or maybe in twenty-five years the Amish in Lancaster County may only be history."

The Bargain's Fine Print

The occupational agreement that the Amish negotiated with modernity reflects the nuances of shrewd bargaining. They would not consider birth control or migration to other countries to escape the demographic squeeze. At the same time, they were not about to yield to economic forces that would strangle their fiscal vitality as a community. Instead, they would migrate to nearby counties, and they would subdivide their farms. Indeed, when push came to shove, they were even willing to give up farming. Although they did budge on the type of occupation, they refused to carry lunch pails and walk into factories in full force. They would drop their plows, but they would not negotiate the location, context, or conditions of their work. They would leave their fields, but they were not about to turn the control of their work over to the forces of modernity. Ironically, without professional degrees, the Amish, like professionals, control the terms and conditions of their work as they venture off the farm.

The transformation of work in Amish society in the last quarter of the twentieth century is indeed a negotiated settlement, for, though a third of them have walked off the farm, they have not embraced modern work. Nonfarm work is, by and large, local, family-centered, small-scale, and nestled in ethnic networks. The Amish have retained personal craftsmanship and job satisfaction, as well as a high degree of identity with, and control over, their products. Moreover, they also control the time, speed, and other conditions of their work. The imprint of the large corporation, typified by assembly line workers alienated from their managers, products, and environments, controlled in turn by abstract policies in faraway offices, is not stamped on Amish shops. Amish work is performed in a congenial ethnic environment that reinforces sectarian values. Amish craftspeople take great pride in their personally tailored products. As small proprietors working for themselves, they control the design, production, and sale of their products. Although the work is hard and the hours are long, the small establishments provide a humane work environment that is responsive to the daily needs of employees, customers, family, and community. The Amish view work as a calling—not a rung in a professional career ladder. In all of these ways, nonfarm Amish work is not modern work.

10

Managing Public Relations

Paying for Social Security is like buying a dead horse.
—Amish businessman

The Riddles of Separation

Groups that hope to resist modernization must regulate the interaction of their members with the outside world. This chapter explores the link between Amish society and the larger world. Amish ties with the outside world can be viewed from two perspectives: the individual and the social system. The Amish church regulates the participation of members in the larger culture. But there are also systemic bonds—contracts and patterns of economic exchange—that fuse the two social systems.

The Amish have always emphasized separation from the world. This historic belief has taken an ironic twist in the throes of modernization, producing yet another riddle. Their plain dress, rejection of higher education, large families, and horse-drawn transportation keep them further away from the world than ever before. Rapid technological change in modern society has also widened the gap. Yet the Amish are more intertwined with the larger economic system than at any previous time in their history. How is it that the cultural gap widened as the economic systems merged? A second riddle also lies beneath the knots linking the two systems. As Amish dependency on the larger society increased, a mutual dependency emerged. Today the Amish not only lean on the larger social system but it, in turn, leans on them. How did the larger society come to rely on the Amish?

The Paradox of Separation

An Amish farmer uses the telephone in his tobacco cellar to call the veterinarian about his sick cow, to order fertilizer for his fields, or to check the weather service forecast before making hay. Amish housewives cook with Teflon pans, buy butane gas for their stoves, use disposable diapers, clean with detergents, and buy permanent-press fabrics. Some households depend on income from the sale of quilts, produce, crafts, and baked goods to non-Amish. An Amish businessman depends on commercial suppliers for his raw materials, the latest machine technology to manufacture his products, and the modern transportation system to deliver them. In all of these ways, the Amish are dependent on the larger social system. Without these economic ties to the outside world, Amish culture in its present form would collapse.

As the Amish modernized their farming, created their own industries, and accepted a more contemporary lifestyle, their dependency on the larger society increased. Although considerable money is loaned among the Amish within their community, they also borrow from commercial banks. As interest rates rise and fall, Amish fortunes fluctuate. As milk and hog prices dip, Amish profits fall. The sales of Amish businesses vacillate with the costs of transportation, raw materials, diesel fuel, and competing products. The price of Amish buggies rises with the price of fiberglass and other raw materials. The welfare of the Amish community rides on the market forces of the larger economy.

The Amish also use the services of professionals—physicians, dentists, optometrists, real-estate agents, accountants, lawyers, morticians, bankers—as well as those of banks, hospitals, stores. They do not rely on professionals as heavily as Moderns do, but, nonetheless, they could barely function as a community without the assistance of these experts. Furthermore, the vitality of Amish society is indebted to the technological achievements of the scientific age. Antibiotics and other medicines have cut their infant mortality rates and increased the longevity of their elderly, which, of course, have resulted in their increased population. Artificial insemination of dairy cows, hybrid seeds, chemical fertilizers, scientifically prepared cattle rations, veterinary medicines, pesticides, and the careful management of flocks and herds have all boosted Amish agricultural output. The use of the latest welding, fabricating, carpentry, and manufacturing equipment allows Amish businesses to compete successfully in the dominant society. In all of these areas, Amish success hinges on the scientific advancements of the larger society. They do not live in a closed social system but are indeed entangled in the economic network of the larger social system.

Ironically, as the systemic links tightened, the cultural gap widened. Amish sages agree that the gulf between their life and that of their non-Amish neighbors is wider today than ever. An Amishman described the growing separation between the two cultures: "Oh yes, there's a stronger separation today, oh yes, oh certainly, and it's growing faster all the time. Even though we are drifting fast, and faster, and getting out more, it seems that the margin between us and our English neighbors is getting wider. The margin today is wider than it was in the thirties and forties, oh my goodness, yes!"

What factors have stretched the social distance between the Amish and the surrounding culture? In the first half of the century, the Amish often worked closely with their rural neighbors and shared a similar cultural outlook. The century's massive changes separated rural farmers from their Amish neighbors as tractors, cars, televisions, and consolidated schools found their place in rural life. The consolidation of public schools, in particular, is cited by some Amish as increasing the cultural gap. Until mid-century, Amish youth attended public schools, where they developed friendships with neighborhood children. Many of these friendships continued into adulthood and brought mutual understanding. With the rise of Amish schools in the sixties, a new generation of Amish grew up without the influence of non-Amish teachers and with few non-Amish friends. These developments have widened the cultural gap.

The proliferation of Amish enterprises has also increased this gap. Today's Amish can purchase most of their everyday supplies and services from Amish proprietors. A grandmother explained: "When I was little we had to go to English stores for everything, to have our implements repaired, for groceries, for dry goods, for everything. There were no Amish stores or shops then. But now we can buy everything we need in Amish stores—even these little calculators, we can get in an Amish store. Groceries, hardware, underwear, mittens—you name it—we can buy it in an Amish store." The surge of Amish stores and shops has curbed interaction with non-Amish merchants and channeled day-to-day transactions inside ethnic networks. There are momentary ventures into the larger world to visit a doctor, an attorney, or an accountant, but most daily interaction flows within the Amish community.

The growing reliance on electronic technology in American society has also widened the cultural gap. Despite creative uses of hydraulic power by the Amish, the rejection of electricity has held electronic technology out of their reach. The absence of television and other media shields the Amish from the influences of mass culture. Although Amish society is changing, the pace of social change in the larger society is even faster, thus increasing the cultural gulf over the years.

The Amish are friendly and have many relationships with their non-Amish neighbors. Amish businessmen deal with a variety of non-Amish clients, suppliers, and professionals. But the relationships, though pleasant and cordial, have limits. They rarely lead to romantic involvements, intimate sharing, or legal partnerships. The church's ability to regulate attire, control participation in secular organizations, and maintain the dialect has reinforced Amish separation from the world. Over the years, the cultural distance between the two worlds has increased. As the worlds pulled apart, the economic ties tightened—all of which produced the riddle of a separate people who are entangled with the modern economy.

Social Participation

Amish participation in outside organizations is selective, informal, and locally oriented. The Amish usually do not hold public office, or join public organizations such as Rotary clubs, country clubs, swimming pool associations, Boy Scout clubs, 4-H clubs, Little League softball teams, the Red Cross. Membership in professional organizations is also taboo. Amish farmers are discouraged from joining the Dairy Herd Improvement Association. Those who do join are careful not to have their achievements publicized. In some communities, the Amish are members of volunteer fire companies, because these service organizations often protect their properties. In the heart of the settlement, a fire company holds an annual benefit auction with sales topping $400,000. The auction is largely planned and staffed by the Amish. It is a prime example of a pleasant partnership between the Amish and their neighbors.

In the first half of the century, Amish fathers frequently served as board members of one-room public schools. This practice, of course, ended when such schools were closed by consolidation. Before World War I, an Amishman, in a rare instance, even served as postmaster in a rural village.[1] Holding a federal job or public office is generally taboo, because it involves an "unequal yoking" with the larger world. Despite their avoidance of public offices and political organizations, the Amish are good neighbors who readily assist their non-Amish friends in time of disaster, fire, or illness. They participate informally in community benefit auctions, garage sales, and historical celebrations. In one case, an Amishman was appointed to a township planning commission, but such public involvement is frowned upon. Amish businessmen consult with township supervisors as concerns arise. When zoning regulations restricted industries on family farms, a group of Amishmen hired a planning consultant to help them design a new zoning code for the township supervisors. Occasionally, special township meetings are held to deal with issues concerning the Amish—zoning, road wear from horseshoes, immunization of children, and so forth. An increase in polio cases among the Amish in 1979 threatened a public epidemic. An outbreak of measles posed a similar risk in 1988. In both instances, Amish leaders cooperated with health officials by encouraging mass immunization. In such ways, they seek to be good neighbors.

The Amish participate selectively in other community affairs. Attendance at fairs, amusement parks, carnivals, dances, and theater is prohibited for church members. However, some Amish youth may indulge in these worldly activities before baptism. Occasionally adults and more frequently youth travel to the beach or attend a professional baseball game or tennis tournament. Before baptism, some youth play on a local softball team and even wear a uniform. Church members, of course, do not join such teams. Families occasionally travel to the Philadelphia Zoo or go to a state park for a day of recreation. Amish participation in community affairs tends to be local, selective, and informal. Moreover, they seek to avoid publicity and public confrontations at all costs.

Government Ties

The Amish are law-abiding citizens. Church leaders strongly encourage members to obey civil laws. Yet when civil law and religious conscience collide, the Amish are not afraid to "take a stand" and call their members to "obey God rather than men." They support civil government but have always kept a healthy distance from it. Self-reliance, community autonomy, and the church's responsibility for the social welfare of its own members are persistent themes in Amish teaching which have made them wary of government.

The Amish view of civil government is ambiguous. On the one hand, they believe the Bible teaches that government is ordained by God. On the other hand, the government epitomizes worldly culture, for it is the formal and legal apparatus of the world. The European persecutors of Amish ancestors were often government officials. Government embodies the force of law. When push comes to shove, governments engage in warfare and use capital punishment and raw coercion to impose their will; these methods are contrary to the gentle spirit of Gelassenheit. Moreover, because the Amish church regulates the conduct of its members, it has little need for governmental controls.

The Amish have a long history of caring for their own members and thus have little use for public welfare programs, Medicaid, Medicare, and agricultural support programs. To allow their members to tap into these federal programs would, in the long run, erode the base of Amish mutual aid. Such an erosion would ultimately limit the church's influence. The Amish are adamantly opposed to government "handouts." Why, they ask, should they be forced to participate in government welfare programs such as Social Security and Medicare when they have cared for their own people for three centuries—long before such programs were even conceptualized?

The Amish *do* pay their taxes, contrary to popular misconceptions. They believe the Bible teaches Christians to pay taxes and to respect government. They pay state and federal income taxes, county taxes, sales taxes, real-estate transfer taxes, and local school taxes. In fact, they pay school taxes twice—Amish school taxes as well as public school ones. They, of course, pay few gasoline taxes. The only tax from which they are exempt is Social Security.

With the exception of serving on local school boards, the Amish position on holding public office has been a rather firm "no" for several reasons. First, running for office is viewed as arrogant, out of character with Gelassenheit. Second, holding government office would mean participation in the most worldly of organizations—an embarrassing violation of the principle of separation from the world. Finally, a public official would need to support the use of legal force to settle public disputes, an act that mocks nonresistance. In short, seeking, holding, and promoting a political office simply contradicts Gelassenheit. This nonpolitical posture has not wavered under the press of modernization.

The Amish attitude toward voting is more tolerant. The church has not formally prohibited voting for public officials. Surprisingly, voting is left up to individual choice. Amish who do vote tend to be younger businessmen who are involved in community affairs. The Amish are more likely to cast a ballot in local elections than in national presidential ones. One minister said that he stopped voting after he was ordained to the ministry. It is safe to assume that the Amish voting rate is lower than the national average. After a recent discussion of voting and jury duty, the Amish National Steering Committee discouraged both activities. The committee concluded that "if we are concerned in this line let us turn to God in prayer that HIS will be done."[2] While voting has been a matter of individual choice, serving on juries has always been strongly discouraged.

The Amish church has strictly forbidden participation in military service. In fact, entering military service would promptly bring excommunication. In the Amish view, the instructions of Jesus to love one's enemies and to live a nonresistant life are simply incompatible with the soldier's role. The purposes, attitudes, and techniques of military service utterly violate the essence of Gelassenheit. Obedience to biblical teaching always transcends civil duty.

During World War II, many Amish conscientious objectors received agricultural deferments and were able to continue working on the family farm. Others, ineligible for a deferment, were assigned to work on a large farm in Maryland supervised by the Amish under the auspices of the Selective Service. As the draft continued in the sixties,

General Lewis B. Hershey, director of Selective Service, negotiates alternatives to military service with an Amish leader in Lancaster County in 1941. Three Old Order Mennonites listen to the discussion.

some who were ineligible for farm deferments contributed two years of alternative service in public hospitals. Working in a secular environment created serious problems, as explained by an Amish spokesman: "Many boys went with good intentions, but having so much idle time they became involved with amusements, with the nurses, or in other ways were led astray."[3] When it came time for them to return home, many no longer wanted to remain with the church, or could not join the church because they had married a wife of a different faith. To alleviate this threat, the Amish negotiated an agreement with the Selective Service. Those ineligible for deferments on their own farms could be assigned to farms under the supervision of the Amish National Steering Committee. In fact, it was this problem that led to the creation of the committee in 1966. The end of the draft in 1973 eliminated the problem of military service. Amish leaders continue to stay in contact with Selective Service officials in the hope that, if national conscription returns, they will once again be able to assign youth to farms supervised by the committee. The church encourages young men to register with the Selective Service on their eighteenth birthday.

Social Security

Although the Amish pay local, state, and federal taxes, they have conscientiously refused to pay into the Social Security program or to tap any of its benefits. The Amish view it as a national insurance program rather than as a tax. Indeed, when the federal program began in 1935 it was called Old Age and Survivors Insurance. The Amish have objected to public insurance programs for several reasons. First, they believe that the church is responsible for the welfare of its own members. The Amish record on this score is commendable. Widows, orphans, the retarded, and the handicapped are cared for by extended families and the church. In cases of extreme financial difficulty, the needy are assisted by the church's alms fund. The elderly retire at home under the care of their children. Sometimes families take turns caring for senile members or others requiring special attention. Rather than institutionalizing dependent people, the Amish have used church resources to provide care in extended family networks. To turn these responsibilities over to the state would, in their mind, abdicate a fundamental tenet of faith—the care of one's brothers and sisters in the church.

Second, insurance programs—especially life insurance plans—are viewed as gambling ventures that seek to plan and protect one's fortune rather than yielding it to God's will. Insurance programs defy the stance of Gelassenheit—of waiting and submitting to divine destiny—because they guarantee a favorable financial outcome. Participation in such programs also entails economic involvement with and reliance on the world—a violation of the biblical injunction of separation. Finally, Amish involvement in public insurance programs would destroy dependency on the church and erode its centrality in the lives of members. Mutual-aid programs provided by the community would be severely undercut.

The Amish plea for exemption from Social Security was voiced by an Amish spokesman in hearings before the Ways and Means Committee of the U.S. House of Representatives in 1983: "The Amish are only human and not as perfect as our non-Amish neighbors would take us to be, and not near as perfect as we would like to be, and we would not wish to be a burden to our government or men in authority or to be a hindrance to anyone. We desire no financial assistance from our state or federal government in any way. But again, we would humbly plea that we be allowed to take care of our own, in our own way, through alms and brotherly love as has always been our custom and has been sufficient to this day."[4]

When the Social Security program began, it created little problem for the Amish because the self-employed were exempt. The loophole closed in 1955, when the self-employed, including farmers, were required to participate. The government, in the Amish view, had overstepped its bounds by forcing them to pay into, and receive benefits from, a federal insurance program. By May 1955, Amish representatives from across the nation, led by a Lancaster bishop, presented a petition asking for exemption to federal officials and members of Congress. The petition, signed by nearly fourteen thousand Old Order members, baffled Washington bureaucrats. This was the first time in the twenty-year history of Social Security that citizens were begging *not* to receive benefits. The Amish argued that, if this generation of their people began paying into the program, it would be hard to keep their sons and daughters from collecting benefits, and in a generation or so the Amish would be hooked on the system.

For the next several years, the Amish argued their case before congressional committees, but the legislators were hesitant to open the door for special exemptions, fearing it might dismantle the system. Finally, in 1958, the Internal Revenue Service (IRS) began filing liens on farm animals and other Amish assets in Ohio.[5] IRS enforcement varied by state and region. Frightened by the crackdown, some Amish farmers began making payments but others still refused. In 1958, IRS agents in the Midwest began confiscating and selling Amish-owned horses. Such seizures continued intermittently. In 1961, agents seized three horses from an Amishman in western Pennsylvania while he was working in the field. By the time legislative relief arrived in 1965, there were an estimated fifteen hundred delinquent Amish accounts and three thousand liens on Amish properties.[6] National publicity and public outcry supporting the Amish brought the issue to a stalemate.[7]

Over a dozen bills seeking to exempt the Amish from Social Security were sponsored by legislators from heavily populated Amish states in the early sixties. A Social Security exemption was passed by Congress and signed into law by President Lyndon B. Johnson on 30 July 1965, as an appendage to the bill that established the national Medicare program. An Amish negotiator said Lancaster Bishop David Fisher told House Ways and Means Chairman Wilbur Mills that "we take care of our own people and if we start paying in, the next generation will collect and we don't want no government handouts." Mills replied that "there's nothing wrong with that." So Mills, according to this observer, "just hung an exemption rider on the Medicare bill and it sailed right through the Congress."

The exemption approved in 1965 applied only to the self-employed. A special IRS form (4029) was developed for religious groups conscientiously opposed to paying for Social Security. Today, within

Amish Social Security lends aid when a neighbor is ill.

six months after baptism, young Amish complete the exemption form, which is then signed by their bishop. After filing the exemption, they receive an "exemption number"—in essence, a Social Security number. Signers of the form agree to "waive all rights to any social security payment or benefit." Thus the Amish today receive no Social Security checks for welfare, retirement, disability, Medicaid, or Medicare. In some cases, heads of large families with low incomes have inadvertently received "unearned income" checks from the government, but Amish leaders urge members to return them. Changes in the federal tax code in 1987 required wage earners to obtain a Social Security number for each dependent child over five years of age. The Amish objected to this and negotiated an agreement with the IRS that waived the requirement.

Boycotting Government "Handouts"

The Social Security exemption, approved for the Amish in 1965, has functioned smoothly for the self-employed. However, in the seventies this restriction created legal problems for the Amish as they began moving into nonfarm occupations. A variety of employment patterns have developed as the Amish have coped with the self-employment restriction: (1) Amish who work for non-Amish employers have Social Security deducted routinely from their paychecks even though they will never receive Social Security payments. (2) Amish employers pay the Social Security tax for their non-Amish employees. (3) Amish businesses pay Social Security premiums for their Amish employees even though they will never benefit from the program. "It's like paying for a dead horse," said a businessman. A retired Amish shop owner said: "I paid thousands of dollars for Social Security taxes for myself and my employees and don't expect to get a penny of it back." (4) A large number of Amish businesses are organized as legal partnerships. The employees—owners or partners in this case—are considered self-employed and thus are exempt from Social Security payments, workmen's compensation, and unemployment insurance. (5) A group of Amishmen may work together as a carpentry crew. They keep their own records, however, and collect their pay separately in order to qualify for the self-employment exemption. (6) Instead of wages, some farm workers receive a percentage of the milk check or tobacco crop to qualify as self-employed partners in farming operations. (7) In some cases, an Amish business is organized as both a corporation and a partnership. The senior partners incorporate for liability reasons. The corporation contracts with outside parties to perform work but subcontracts the labor to the Amish partnership.

With business arrangements pressing the legal definition of self-employment and with more Amish working in nonfarm jobs, the Amish have tried to expand the Social Security exemption to all members regardless of employment status. Several legislators from heavily populated Amish areas have sponsored bills aimed at removing the self-employment restriction.[8]

In a 1982 test case, the Supreme Court ruled that, according to present law, Amish employers are required to pay Social Security taxes for their Amish employees. However, in the late eighties several lawmakers reintroduced legislation to expand the exemption beyond self-employed Amish. Amish leaders were hopeful that a legislative compromise could eventually be worked out.

Two other federal programs, workmen's compensation and unemployment insurance, have also created problems for Amish employers. The Amish view these, like Social Security, as government insurance programs. Self-employed workers are exempt from workmen's compensation and unemployment insurance. However, both non-Amish and Amish employers are required by law to contribute to these two programs. Amish teachers were caught in a dilemma with these programs, as employees of Amish school boards. In 1978, Pennsylvania legislators unanimously passed a bill exempting Amish teachers from workmen's compensation. The IRS considers Amish teachers self-employed, because they teach without direct supervision, thus freeing them of paying unemployment insurance.

Over the years, numerous federal programs aimed at stabilizing prices of agricultural products have tampered with supply and demand. The Amish have consistently refused to participate in agricultural subsidy programs. They have refused to sell their cows to federal buyout programs and to accept payment for letting farmland sit idle. They have adamantly opposed government "handouts," from Social Security to agricultural subsidies. This repudiation has baffled government bureaucrats. The Amish feared that members who were heavily insured and living on government "handouts" would have little interest in giving and receiving mutual aid. The Amish rejection of Social Security and other government subsidies was necessary to preserve two cherished ideals: community self-reliance and the religious belief that church members are obliged to provide for the economic welfare of their brothers and sisters.

Using the Law

The Amish want to be law-abiding citizens but are reluctant to use the legal system to protect their rights. Lawyers are readily used by the Amish to prepare wills, establish business partnerships, and handle real-estate transactions, but using the law to protect one's personal or business rights contradicts the humility of Gelassenheit. Filing a lawsuit is cause for excommunication. The Amish are taught to bear abuse and suffer insult rather than engage in legal confrontation. But as more Amish move into business, use of the law becomes ever more tempting. In some instances, non-Amish customers have bilked Amish businessmen, knowing they would not likely sue. Using implicit threat, some Amish business owners have asked their attorneys to write letters to debtors asking for payment of delinquent bills. In other cases, under the advice of their attorneys, Amish have asked dubious clients to sign a "confessed judgment," which is then filed in the courthouse if products or services are not paid in full. The confessed judgment places a lien against the debtor's property. Asking a client to sign such a judgment is an implicit threat, but an Amish person will rarely execute such a note or testify at enforcement hearings.

In other situations, Amish businessmen have asked district magistrates to initiate bad debt collections. The Amish person is named as plaintiff, but this is not publicized. If the defendants want to defend themselves at a public hearing, the Amish rarely appear but ask their attorneys to resolve it for them privately. Careful not to file an actual lawsuit, some Amish businessmen increasingly use the services of attorneys to resolve disputes quietly, out of the public limelight. Greater participation in the business world will increase the tension between historic Amish values and the hard-nosed realities of the marketplace.

The *Witness* Controversy

In the spring of 1984, the Amish found themselves in a peculiar public relations quandary. They learned, to their astonishment, that

Amish life would be depicted in a major Hollywood film, *Witness*, which Paramount Pictures planned to shoot on location in Lancaster. The Pennsylvania Bureau of Motion Picture and TV Development, eager for the national publicity and tourist revenues promised by a major film, had solicited Paramount to do an Amish picture.[9]

The story features a Philadelphia detective (Harrison Ford) who finds refuge with an Amish family. Endangered by a criminal investigation, Ford lives with the Amish family and falls in love with an Amish widow (Kelly McGillis). The drama ends with a violent shoot-out on an Amish farm. The violence of a cop thriller framed by the pastoral scenes of Amish countryside created a dramatic clash of images.

As the film was being shot in the early summer of 1984, the Amish began to protest for several reasons. First, they had always opposed television, films, and photography. They resented being portrayed in a medium that they had historically condemned. Second, they have typically shunned publicity, and a commercial film would publicize Amish images on screens around the world. Third, *Hollywood*, perhaps more than any other word, symbolized worldliness in the Amish mind—a "den of iniquity" that imprints sex and violence on the minds of viewers around the world. Thus to have Hollywood, the symbol of moral vice, make a film of the Amish and catapult them into international publicity was a triple insult. Finally, the Amish knew that they were being exploited commercially by the tourist industry. Writing in protest of the film to Pennsylvania Governor Richard L. Thornburgh, an Amishwoman said: "We Amish feel we are serving as a tool to lure tourists to Lancaster County."

As the filming got under way, Amish bishops warned members not to work for or cooperate with the Paramount production crews. "We can't stop them," said one Amishman, "but we don't have to help them. We don't want it. It doesn't belong here." In a conciliatory overture, director Peter Weir promised not to use Amish persons in the cast. However, the Amish soon discovered that Kelly McGillis had spent several days in disguise in an Amish home. Upon identification, she was asked to leave. This breach of trust added insult to injury. An irritated Amish grandmother said: "Now, that was an intrusion. I thought that was pretty bad. We wouldn't do that to them [the public] and they wouldn't want us to either. They'd hike us out the door faster than we ever came in." Although the Amish stayed aloof from the filming, they felt betrayed by government officials who eagerly assisted Paramount Pictures. And as the Amish suspected, the monetary rewards were lucrative. The filming alone pumped several million dollars into the local economy.

Unable to overlook the insult, three bishops and another Amish leader took their protest to Lieutenant Governor William W. Scranton

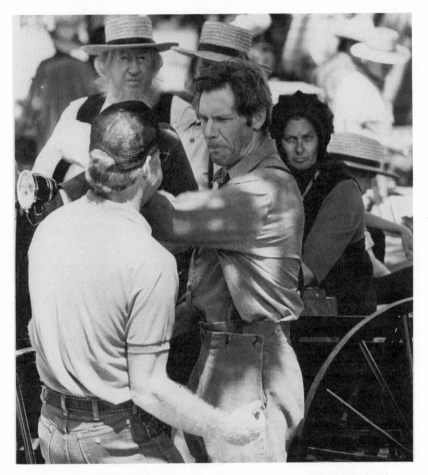

Harrison Ford defends the Amish with fists during on-site filming of *Witness*. This was an objectionable scene to the Amish because Ford, dressed in ethnic garb, was fighting.

in the state capital. The delegation argued that the Amish had been used and misrepresented because actors had been dressed as Amish and were engaged in physical fights and shown making nasty remarks. Said one leader: "If our principles were to fight, I feel we could go to court and get an injunction on the basis of misrepresenting the Amish, but this is not our way." Using the ultimate bargaining chip, one bishop mentioned the possibility of the Amish moving out of the area if they could not maintain their lifestyle and sense of privacy. After hearing their pleas, Lieutenant Governor Scranton promised to talk to Governor Thornburgh and Secretary of Commerce James Pickard.

A second meeting involved Secretary of Commerce Pickard as well as the Lancaster County commissioners and the director of the Pennsylvania Dutch Visitors' Bureau. The Amish again explained their aversion to being used as objects in a film. The county commissioners supported the Amish plight. The chairman, James Huber, said: "I fear that continued invasions of their privacy and violation of their religious principles would encourage them to leave Pennsylvania so they can be free of harassment."

In a third meeting, the Amish negotiated the broad outlines of an agreement with Secretary of Commerce Pickard and the director of the Pennsylvania Bureau of Motion Picture and TV Development. The agreement was formalized in a letter from Secretary of Commerce Pickard on 12 September 1984. It was sent to the Amish with copies to state and county officials. In brief, the settlement stipulated that the state:

> Will not promote Pennsylvania Amish as subjects for feature films or television productions.
>
> Will not promote any script that uses the Amish and/or its culture as subject matter.
>
> Will refuse to deal with film companies that attempt to film the Amish without their consent or to trespass on their property.
>
> Will inform potential producers of the Amish community's strong opposition to having photographs taken and having its culture represented in any theatrical production.[10]

By the time the agreement was finalized, filming was finished and *Witness* was well on its way to completion. The agreement placated both parties. The state was pleased because no restrictions were placed on *Witness*, which would soon be stirring the curiosity of millions about Pennsylvania's Amish. And though the state promised not to solicit producers to film the Amish, the secretary of commerce told reporters that "really, nothing would change if *Witness* were coming in tomorrow as a new production . . . other than making it clear that the Amish community does not wish to be intruded upon." The state commerce department, he noted, would again offer the same sort of support that it offers other films.

"We were quite happy with the agreement," an Amish leader said. "We felt it was as far as the secretary of commerce could possibly go, legally." A bishop concluded: "We think we got what we asked for." Negotiating the agreement gave the Amish an opportunity to vent their frustration with the whole ordeal and inform state officials that there were limits to Gelassenheit—they would not merely pray while being trampled upon by Hollywood greed. Although the state did not want to shut the door on future Amish films, it also did not want to provoke an Amish migration.

The local Pennsylvania Dutch Visitors' Bureau maintained a discreet distance from *Witness*. According to its director, Harry Flick, Jr., the bureau was not involved in soliciting Paramount Pictures, and its representatives did not attend a highly publicized premiere of *Witness* in Lancaster City in February 1985. The bureau supported the agreement reached with the Amish. After release of the film, bureau brochures began inviting tourists to Lancaster County, "as seen in the critically acclaimed movie *Witness.*"[11] *Witness* was doing well. It grossed $37.7 million at the box office in its first six weeks and even knocked another Paramount film, *Beverly Hills Cop*, out of the week's top box office slot. Meanwhile, things were also going well in Lancaster County. By the end of the first six-week run of *Witness*, tourism had climbed 13 percent, even before the summer tourist season was in full swing.

The Ironies of Tourism

The rise of tourism in Lancaster County brought several ironic twists in Amish public relations. The European forebears of the Amish had been violently persecuted and exterminated because they dared to be different. Paradoxically, the Amish defiance of modern culture has brought them not persecution, but admiration and respect—enough to underwrite a massive tourist industry. The course of history has converted them from despised heretics into esteemed objects of modern curiosity. Moreover, the world, which the Amish have tried so hard to keep at a distance, is now reaching out to them. Oddly enough, the more separate and unusual they seem, the more attractive they are to Moderns. Surprisingly, the tourism that appears to threaten their solitude and privacy may actually help to bolster their cultural identity. Ironically, the tourism that exacerbates the problem of shrinking farmland and nudges them off the farm has strengthened their ties to their Lancaster home by providing a ready market for Amish crafts. Finally, the larger culture, from which the Amish have sought to be independent, has now come to depend on them. These and other riddles permeate tourism.

Tourism in Lancaster County began in the late thirties, after the Depression. An Amish historian dates the origin of Amish tourism as 1937, with the publication of an Amish tourist booklet and the East Lampeter Township school dispute, which received national press coverage.[12] An Amish farmer dates the mushrooming of tourism as the public celebration in 1954 of the two hundredth birthday of Intercourse, a village in the heart of the Amish settlement. "Mix together the word *Intercourse* and some Amish buggies," he said, "and you're bound to attract some tourists." Still others attribute the rise of tourism to the national press coverage of the Amish school controversy in the early fifties. In any event, by 1965 nearly 2 million tourists were trekking annually to Lancaster County to catch a glimpse of the Amish. Today, about 5 million tourists visit Lancaster County annually—some 350 visitors for each Amish person. The tourists spend over $400 million—$29,000 per Amish person.

The nearly six hundred members of the Pennsylvania Dutch Visitors' Bureau operate a variety of tourist sites throughout the county, including many attractions unrelated to the Amish. However, the charm of the plain people, especially the Amish, is the cultural magnet of tourism. The importance of the Amish for tourism is documented by several factors. The tourist sites are concentrated in the county's eastern part, near the Amish settlement. Tourist promotions—brochures, billboards, videos, and newspaper ads—highlight Amish images, especially the horse and buggy silhouette. The popularity of "Amish" sites, tours, trinkets, food, and crafts underscores the primacy of Amish symbolism in the tourist culture. Without the Amish, Lancaster's tourism would probably not have soared to its present peak, and, if the Amish suddenly vanished, it would certainly decline. If the Amish lure half of the tourists, to use a conservative estimate, they are annually attracting $200 million into the local economy as well as creating thousands of jobs. This economic fact has given the Amish a hefty bargaining chip in their negotiations with modernity.

When a human culture becomes the focus of a tourist industry, special problems arise. Some tourists hope to gain firsthand knowledge of the "natives" by talking with them. The goal of the natives, the Amish in this case, is to avoid the bothersome interruptions that treat them as museum objects. The tourist enterprise can be viewed as a dramatic encounter with both front stage and backstage dimensions. Tourists welcome opportunities to venture backstage and meet the Amish in their real homes. Commercial tourist attractions provide a front stage portrayal of Amish life which simulates an encounter by offering tours of refurbished Amish farms. Guided tours in the countryside are one attempt to move closer backstage. Busloads of tourists meander through the Amish countryside—the equivalent of a wild game preserve—ever on the lookout for a glimpse of genuine Amish life.

Tourist sites play several crucial roles. They provide a buffer zone that protects the Amish from tourists. Tour guides and simulated attractions occupy the tourists' time and keep them a respectable distance from the Amish. Several million tourists roaming at will would shatter the Amish community. Tourist sites and guides provide

An Amish family shares the hospitality of food and home with a tour group ca. 1960.

structured restraints that permit Amish life to continue in a normal fashion backstage. For the most part, tourists and their bus drivers follow established routes and stop at spots designated on tourist maps. Following the script and using the props organize the tourist experience into a predictable drama. The appearance of an Amish person may temporarily disrupt things. But, in general, the structured patterns of tourism—the guides and sites—serve as a curtain that insulates the Amish from what would otherwise be a chaotic intrusion on their life.

The front stage operations provide tourists with descriptive information and a succinct overview of Amish life, which would be difficult to obtain even from an Amish person. Most tours and establishments offer an educational setting where questions can be asked without fear of embarrassment or insult. Finally, the tourist sites fuel

A tour bus filled with college students leaves an Amish homestead ca. 1960.

the local economy with new revenues and jobs. In these ways, the front stage tourist enterprises bring Amish and tourists close to each other but avoid face-to-face encounters.

The formal attractions, however, have two drawbacks. Discerning tourists realize that they are being duped—that the representations of Amish life are not authentic, but merely front stage replicas. Thus the mystique of the backstage lingers. What would it be like to walk inside a real Amish home and talk to a real Amish person? The Amish are also shortchanged. The commercial tourist enterprises are operated at a profit by non-Amish entrepreneurs. A boon for the local economy, these enterprises bring handsome profits to outsiders but are of meager benefit to the Amish.

In the eighties, the Amish and the tourists quietly negotiated a new form of encounter—the native stand. Craft and produce stands operated by the Amish sprouted up by the hundreds along country roads throughout the Amish heartland. These sites allow tourists to peek behind the curtain and get a glimpse of backstage life. While buying a product, they can talk with a real Amish person on Amish property. The tourist is treated to a close-up view of genuine Amish clothing and can buy authentic Amish food or crafts. In exchange, the tourist stand enables the Amish to reap some financial benefit from the tourist industry. As a scarcity of farmland nudges more and more Amish off the farm, the tourist trade provides supplemental income for many families. These miniature tourist sites, with their signs announcing No Sunday Sales and No Photographs, are Amish-owned and -operated. In these brief exchanges, the Amish are able to regulate the type and scope of interaction—effectively keeping tourists at arm's length. The small native stands are a symbolic and literal middle ground—at the end of the lane—where tourist and Amish can safely interact at a polite distance. The stands also allow the Amish a first-hand look at the gaudy and frivolous dress of pleasure-seeking tourists. The proliferation of the small sites symbolizes yet another negotiated compromise between the Amish and modernity. The Amish have allowed the tourists to come one step closer to backstage Amish life, but the Amish are clearly in charge of this buffer zone—controlling its hours, personnel, location, and decor. In this sense, even the Amish produce stand is a front stage operation and the tourist who hoped to get backstage is duped again.

The Consequences of Tourism

In many ways, tourism is a nuisance to the Amish. Cars and buses clog main roads, forcing some Amish families to revise their weekly shopping patterns during the peak of the tourist season. As many as fifty buses a day stop at back road sites marked on tourist maps. Tourists who wish to photograph children sometimes bribe them. The clicking cameras, gawking strangers, and congested roadways are bothersome.

Other aspects of tourism border on economic and cultural exploitation. The Amish realize that the bulk of tourist revenue fills the pockets of non-Amish entrepreneurs. "We are serving as a tool," said one Amishwoman, "to lure tourists to Lancaster County. Personally, I do not feel any resentment against tourists, but these tourist places are what's working against us. We are not living our peculiar way to attract attention. We merely want to live pure, Christian lives according to our religion and church standards and want to be left alone, like any human beings. We are opposed to having our souls marketed by having our sacred beliefs and traditions stolen from us and then distributed to tourists, and sometimes having them mocked." An Amish farmer said: "Some tourist places set up the most ridiculous stories about Amish craftsmanship, Amish dress, Amish cooking, and the

Amish ways of life."[13] To see one's religious symbols—bonnet, buggy, beard—taken by outsiders and sold as plastic dolls, plastered on billboards, erected as statues, and fashioned into trinkets of all sorts is a commercial assault on a religious culture. Insensitive entrepreneurs who have snatched sacred Amish symbols and converted them into profitable products have exploited the Amish soul.

The Amish insulate themselves from tourism in several ways. Some tourists, according to the Amish, are sincere, friendly, and courteous. But tourism, in general, symbolizes worldly pleasure to the Amish. Tourists kill time, seek entertainment, and waste money— which contradict basic Amish virtues. "The tourist attractions," said one minister, "have converted our Amish land into a leisure lust playground."[14] Others see tourism as a new form of persecution, a modern form of tribulation that must be endured with patience. "Tourism," suggested a minister, "is a test of our faith to see if we are as strong as our forefathers." The Amish also use humor to defuse the tourism menace. Jokes about the stunts and foolish questions of tourists abound. Such humor diminishes the threat of tourists by trivializing their role and influence. By defining tourism in these negative ways, the Amish reduce its credibility. Some Amish, of course, develop lasting friendships with tourists, but most Amish maintain a healthy social distance from tourists by converting them into a negative or humorous reference group.

Permanent relationships with tourists could erode Amish/non-Amish boundaries, but tourists are relatively harmless, because they eventually return home. Sometimes bothersome, they are at least temporary. They offer fleeting moments of interaction—highly regulated and staged in public settings—which hardly endanger Amish life. Prolonged, close relationships with non-Amish neighbors are more likely to lead Amish individuals astray.

Does tourism endanger Amish life? An Amish minister said: "We are caught in the jaws of tourism . . . and if the heat gets too high we better get out . . . if it is our lot to move, we will."[15] Despite occasional threats of migration, the evidence is to the contrary. The Lancaster settlement established its last new colony in 1978. Since then, tourism has flourished and the Amish community in Lancaster has remained and grown in spite of it. Ironically, tourism may inadvertently energize Amish life in several ways. An older Amish person noted that with the rise of tourism, "we are no longer looked down on." An Amish leader remarked: "We get loads of praise for our way of life." To many Amish, the fact that tourists from around the world come to see and learn of their ways suggests they have discovered some wholesome ways of living. Reluctant to admit to pride, there is a quiet satisfaction in knowing that their culture is worthy of such respect. Tourism has bolstered Amish self-esteem.

In a worst-case scenario, the rise of Amish-owned tourist shops, over time, might lead to an ironic dependency if the Amish became social parasites living off tourism. Such a paradoxical situation might force the Amish to maintain a unique lifestyle in order to attract tourists for the economic welfare of the Amish community. At the present, tourism underscores the cultural separation of the Amish. Tourists may be bothersome, but they do reinforce Amish separation from the rest of the world. Although the Amish complain of feeling "like monkeys in a zoo," the imagery does focus the sharp difference between monkeys and zoo visitors. In this way, tourism galvanizes the cultural gap between the two worlds and helps define Amish identity.

Tourism creates expectations for Amish behavior. The symbolism on tourist billboards reinforces the boundaries of Amish culture even in the minds of the Amish themselves. Knowing that tourists come to see a people driving horses and living without electricity strengthens the expectation for such behavior. Amish behavior, in part, fulfills the expectations created by the tourist industry. Such external expectations likely fortify rather than weaken actual Amish practice. To discard the buggy, for instance, would not only break Amish tradition but also shatter powerful expectations placed upon them by the outside world.

In these ways, tourism, rather than endangering Amish culture, may inadvertently fortify it. There is little if any empirical evidence that links tourism directly to a breakdown of Amish culture. Tourism may indeed strengthen Amish life. In any event, the economic value of the Amish as a tourist attraction has greatly enhanced their bargaining power in the modern age. Organized curiosity in the form of tourism may be their staunchest ally in new confrontations with the state. Indeed, there have been few public clashes with government officials since the mid-sixties, when tourism thrust the Amish into the public spotlight. In fact, local, state, and federal governments have made striking concessions to the Amish, from overlooking road damage from horses to the Supreme Court vindication of their school system.

In the fall of 1987, the Pennsylvania Department of Transportation proposed six possible routes for a limited-access highway through Lancaster County. The new highway was planned to relieve traffic congestion caused by tourism and development growth. The most direct and least expensive of the proposed routes cut through acres of prime farmland in the historic heart of the Amish settlement. Over one thousand Amish residents attended a public meeting to review the highway plans. Several public groups went on record against the routes that would slice up Amish farmland, for, in the words of a county commissioner, "they would kill the goose that laid the golden egg." After several public meetings and numerous statements by a variety of organizations for and against the proposed highway plans, the swirling controversy abated when Pennsylvania Governor Robert P. Casey intervened. In January 1988, he declared: "We will not build a new highway in any corridor that will bisect the Amish farming community or cause major disruption to the Amish lifestyle."[16] Apart from its other rewards, tourist fame has provided the Amish with new leverage in their negotiations with modernity.

The Amish occasionally threaten to migrate if things get too bad. And public officials worry about the muffled threats, for an Amish evacuation would be catastrophic for the thriving tourist industry. All of this brings us full cycle in the riddle of Amish public relations. Like it or not, the Amish are heavily dependent on modern society for their survival. But it is not a one-way affair. Lancaster County's image, identity, and tourism also depend on the Amish. It is a symbiotic relationship and, for better or worse, the county's dependency on the Amish has given them an equal hand in many of the bargaining sessions.

11

Regulating Social Change

We try to keep the brakes on social change, you know, a little bit.
—Amish craftsman

Amish Changes

Amish society is not a nineteenth-century relic; it is dynamic and evolving. Consider some of the household changes since 1940. Amish women no longer wash clothes in hand-operated machines. They use wringer washing machines powered by air, hydraulic, or gasoline engines. Gas refrigerators have replaced iceboxes, indoor flush toilets have replaced outdoor privies, hydraulic water pumps have replaced hand pumps, and gas water heaters have replaced fires under iron kettles. Modern bathtubs have superseded old metal tubs. Kerosene lanterns have given way to gas lights. Wood-fired cookstoves have yielded to modern gas ranges. Hardwood floors and permanent-shine vinyl have replaced linoleum and rag carpets. Spray starch, detergents, paper towels, instant pudding, and instant coffee have eased household chores. Permanent-press fabrics have lifted the burden of incessant ironing. Although canning still predominates, some foods are preserved by freezing. Air-powered sewing machines are beginning to replace treadle machines. The list goes on and on, but, despite all these changes, electric appliances, central heating, telephones, and electronic media have not entered Amish homes.

Things have changed outside the house as well. In Amish shops, hand tools have given way to air and hydraulic power equipment, but the shops remain unhooked to public utility lines. Amish farmers no longer milk their cows by hand, but the milk squeezed by the mechanical milkers is not pumped directly to bulk tanks through glass pipe lines. Automatic-reset, riding plows have replaced old-fashioned, walk-behind plows. But horses still pull the newer hydraulic plows.

Modern hay balers towed by horses have superseded old-fashioned hay loaders. But the sophisticated balers, running on steel wheels, cannot carry automatic bale loaders. Weeds and insects are sprayed by horse-drawn sprayers. Hybrid corn is grown with chemical fertilizers but cut and picked by horse-drawn equipment. New occupations have increased the need for hiring cars and trucks.

These examples and dozens of others illustrate two facts: the Lancaster Amish have changed dramatically in the twentieth century, but they have regulated the change within prescribed limits. The Amish have avoided divisions within their church since 1966 despite rapid technological change, accelerated by the shift to nonfarm work. In the same years, the population of the settlement has doubled in size, making it even more difficult to control change in any uniform fashion. Somehow Amish society has been pliable enough to absorb the changes in stride. The riddle of social change is perplexing. Why do some aspects of Amish life change in stride while others remain untouched by modernization? By what formula are some new innovations accepted into the culture and others rejected?[1]

Moving Cultural Fences

The Amish view social change as a matter of moving cultural fences—holding old social boundaries and setting new ones. Church members who are moving too fast are "jumping the fence" and getting too involved with the world that encircles Amish society. Cultural fences mark the boundaries of separation between the two worlds. Coping with social change involves fortifying old fences in some areas, as well as moving fences in other ones. But regardless of whether they are old or new, cultural fences must be maintained if the Amish way of life is to be preserved. No single principle or value regulates change in the Amish social system. Rather, a variety of factors impinges on a decision to accept or reject a particular practice. Decisions to move cultural fences emerge out of a dynamic and fluid social matrix. The number and importance of factors shaping a particular decision vary greatly. A diversity of lifestyles exists within and especially between church districts. There are some fifty bishops, and thus it is impossible to maintain uniform standards in all aspects of life across the settlement. This diversity, camouflaged by common symbols—horse, dress, lantern, dialect—will likely increase as the settlement grows.

The acceptance of new products and the relaxation of old standards often occur by default. One Amishman said: "Well, change just kind of happens. Sometimes it is reviewed at a ministers' meeting but then it just kind of happens by itself." Leaders rarely plan or *initiate* social changes. The establishment of Amish schools is one of the few examples of a deliberately planned change. Yet, even with that, a consensus did not arrive for at least a decade. There are, however, collective decisions to *resist* change. If a questionable practice begins to gain widespread acceptance, the bishops may take deliberate action to curtail it. The bishops understand their role as "watchmen on the walls of Zion," responsible for guarding the flock. They are on the lookout for "little foxes" of worldliness who dig under the walls of Zion and undermine the welfare of the community. The bishops are not a source of innovation; instead, their duty is to inspect impending changes and resist the detrimental ones.

Changes in Amish society come not from the top or the center of the social system, but from the periphery. They are often instigated by those living on the edge of the cultural system who try to stretch its boundaries. Often called "fence jumpers" or "fence crowders," these people push against traditional fences to see what they can get away with. Fence jumpers experiment with new gadgets—a silo unloader, a cake mixer operated by air pressure, a computer plugged into an inverter, a tape recorder, a portable weed chopper. If someone complains and church leaders make a visit, the deviant may make a confession and "put away" the questionable item. Although Amish society has changed dramatically, it has also experienced many painful steps backward when devious practices were stopped and modern conveniences put away. Tractors have been recalled from the field. Bathrooms have been torn out on bishops' orders, only to be permitted two decades later. Rubber tires have been taken off machinery; electric wires and light bulbs have been ripped out. Computers have been sold, and telephones have been disconnected.

The fence jumpers usually know what is likely to "pass inspection." If a new item—a calculator, disposable diapers, a cash register—is adopted by others and no one complains too much, eventually the practice will creep into use by default. The metaphors "walls of Zion" and "fence jumpers" vividly suggest that the community has a clear understanding of Amish cultural boundaries. Many members explore the boundaries, "crowd the fence," or "test the waters" in nearly ninety districts under the watchful eye of ordained leaders.

A preacher described the importance of keeping the fences around "the Lord's vineyard" in good repair:

> The Saviour warned against the little foxes that dig their way into the Lord's vineyard. I often think of this illustration of the Lord's vineyard and compare it with a good fence around the church of Christ, how it is like a good *Ordnung*. If the little foxes dig their way in and are not dealt with at once, or if they are allowed to remain, there is great danger that still more will come in. And finally because they are allowed to remain and are not chased out, they grow

bigger and become used to being there. They feel free, and build nests and dig themselves in and multiply, and do great injury to the grape stalks. Finally, they become tame and take over completely and finally the grape stalks wither and die. It is just the same with permitting little sins to go on till they are freely accepted as the customary thing and have taken a foothold. Wickedness takes the upper hand, and then, as the Saviour says, the love of many becomes cold.[2]

The Amish are slow to make decisions regarding the adoption of new practices. They will act quickly if a technological development is obviously off-limits—purchasing a video camera, for example. Borderline practices such as artificial insemination of cows or the use of telephones may be tolerated—put on probation—for several years while their long-term impact on the community's life and harmony is assessed. Eventually the practice may grow by default (as with artificial insemination of cows) or leaders may decide to forbid it. There is a delicate line of no return. It is one thing to ask a half-dozen people to "put away" their calculators but quite another thing to forbid them when they have been widely used for several years.

"When people are testing the lines," an Amish leader explained, "the leaders don't want to act too quick and harsh, so they just let it ride a little bit until they see what happens, or till they can get a picture of what might happen if they let it go. Then they clamp down if it's something that we don't need, that would disrupt the community, the closeness." The division of 1966 erupted when the bishops tried to eradicate several pieces of farm equipment that had been in use for ten years in several church districts. "The problem came," said one person, "when too many things were left go too many years." New products may be toyed with during a probation period, but to be effective a ban must be placed on them before they slip into widespread use. The fate of new products or practices is weighed cautiously, for, once engraved in the Ordnung, taboos are difficult to change. A rash decision may appear foolish with hindsight and force a painful loss of face in later years.

Once drawn, lines become hard to erase. The Amish believe it is better to keep a few taboos consistently than to revise a host of them with each new whim of progress. Thus it is easier to accept a new practice, never inscribed in the Ordnung, than to change an old taboo. It is difficult, for instance, to relax the taboo on power lawn mowers but relatively easy to accept new hand-held weed cutters powered by tiny gasoline engines. Side-by-side on an Amish lawn, the old-fashioned push mower and modern weed cutter appear incongruous to the outsider. Although their functions are similar, the portable weed cutter can be accepted without embarrassment, because it was never prohibited by the Ordnung.

Symbolic considerations are important in the change process. The popular adage of a senior bishop in the fifties, "If you can pull it with horses, you can have it," is highly instructive. There are two levels of meaning in this statement. On the practical level, the old bishop understood that horses keep farming operations rather small. But he was also saying, in essence, "You can use modern equipment in the field as long as you pull it with horses." The horse not only limited the size of farms but also played a symbolic role. All sorts of new farm equipment were permissible as long as they remained in the horse's shadow, for the horse marked off and protected the boundaries of Amish culture. In the same way, the unwritten rule in Amish shops, "If you can do it with air or hydraulic, you can do it," also protects cultural boundaries. Although hydraulic and air power provide symbolic boundaries, they will not be able to restrain the size of Amish shops, as the horse restrained the size of Amish farms.

The verbal explanations for accepting or rejecting new practices often mask the real reasons. Underlying reasons are often simply not articulated. The labels "too worldly," "too modern," "too liberal," or "too handy," frequently cited as reasons for rejecting something, may hide underlying factors such as economic forces, social interaction, family integration, and labor implications. One businessman made the connection between the outward label of "worldly" and the underlying reasons for rejecting tractors:

> Our people will always come out with the statement in the Bible that says be not conformed to this world. Any good Amishman will always say that the tractor's worldly, the automobile's worldly, the radio's worldly, and the telephone and electricity. But why? If we allowed tractors, we would be doing like the Mennonite people are doing, grabbing each other's farms up out there, mechanizing, and going to the bank and loaning $500,000 and worrying about later paying it off, putting three other guys out of business and sending them to town for work, away from their home. Do you follow? So we take the position, why do that? Let's put a guideline on our faith and say that it's [the tractor] not necessary; it's too worldly.

Technological advances that are rejected by the Amish are, surprisingly, not considered immoral. Owning a car, using tractors in the field, and installing a telephone in one's house are not considered evils in and of themselves. The evil lies in what a new invention might lead to. The Amish ask: "What will come next?" Will other changes be triggered by this one? How will acceptance of a new practice affect the community's welfare over the years? Describing the taboo on the telephone, an Amish craftsman said: "If we allow the telephone, that would just be a start. People would say, 'Okay, now we'll push for this and then we'll push for that. . . .' It would be a move forward that might get the wheel rolling a little faster than we can control it, if you know what I mean." A bishop noted: "I might have a car and it wouldn't hurt any, but for the oncoming generation you oughta be willing to sacrifice for them." Such selective modernization, rather than highly moralistic, is strikingly reflective, rational, and calculating—indeed quite modern!

Finally, permitted changes often have the appearance of a compromise—a willingness to edge toward progress, but not too far; a willingness to accept some new gadgets, but with certain limits. Riding scooters (halfway between walking and riding a bicycle), using modern bathrooms without electricity, riding in cars but not driving them, using public transportation but not air travel, voting but not running for office, pulling modern machinery with horses, using permanent-press fabric for traditional garb, and placing nonfarm work in a small shop are just a few examples of negotiated compromises that permit some modernization but not too much. In these instances, social change is a matter of setting new fences—but, nevertheless, setting fences.

The introduction of a new practice may follow several scenarios: (1) It may be terminated in a local district by the bishop. (2) If not extinguished at first, it may spread to several other districts. (3) A "friendly" change may gradually creep into practice by default in a large number of districts and eventually spread throughout the settlement. (4) A "hostile" change may become an "issue" and provoke debate and controversy. The ordained leaders may then decide to overlook it and allow it to slip into practice. (5) The "issue" may come before the bishops' meeting; if the bishops agree to prohibit the practice, local congregations would be asked to support the taboo. (6) If the bishops cannot reach agreement, the issue may simmer for several months or years and eventually find de facto acceptance, or it may trigger renewed debate and new attempts to forbid it. Maintaining old fences and setting new ones is a delicate process, for, as one leader said, "if we're not tolerant, we'll have more splits, but too much tolerance can wreck the whole thing too."

Cultural Regulators

The mix of factors which determines the fate of a new cultural practice or product is always in flux. The decisions are made in a dynamic matrix of social forces. It is hopeless to search for a simple cultural formula to predict the destiny of a new practice. We can identify, however, the regulators, the forces in the ever-changing cultural equations, that influence the outcome. The decision to accept or reject a practice emerges from a dynamic social process—not a static one fixed by cultural rules.

What are the regulators that govern social change in Amish life? The following propositions identify the cultural regulators that influence the decision-making process. A single factor will rarely be adequate to explain a particular outcome. Decisions to move cultural fences arise from the convergence of various social factors. The statements rest on the assumption that the influence of other cultural regulators is held constant. But in real life, of course, things are never held constant.

1. Economic impact. Changes that produce economic benefits are more acceptable than those that do not. "Making a living" takes priority over pleasure, convenience, or leisure. Thus a motor on a hay mower in the field is more acceptable than one on a lawn mower.

2. Visibility. Visible changes are less acceptable than invisible ones. Using fiberglass in the construction of buggies is easier to introduce than changing the external color of the buggy itself. Working as a cook in the kitchen of a restaurant is more acceptable than working as a waitress.

3. Relationship to Ordnung. Changes that reverse or contradict the Ordnung are less acceptable than ones unrelated to past decisions. A calculator is more likely to be accepted than musical instruments, because the Ordnung has consistently forbidden them.

4. Adaptability to Ordnung. Changes that are adaptable to previous Ordnung specifications are more acceptable than those that are not. Tools that can be converted to hydraulic power or farm machinery that can be outfitted with steel wheels are more acceptable than a television, which cannot be adapted to the Ordnung.

5. Ties to sacred symbols. Changes that threaten symbols of ethnic identity—horse, buggy, dress—are less acceptable than ones unrelated to key symbols. Using a modern tractor in a shop is more acceptable than using a tractor in the field, an obvious threat to horses. Jogging shoes are more acceptable than new hat styles because headgear for both men and women is a key identity symbol.

6. Linkage to profane symbols. Changes linked to profane symbols are less acceptable than those without such ties. Computers, whose screens appear uncomfortably similar to those of televisions, are rejected, whereas gas-fired barbecue grills are acceptable.

7. Sacred ritual. Changes that threaten sacred ritual are less acceptable than those unrelated to worship. Changing to nonfarm work is more acceptable than changing the patterns of singing, baptism, and worship.

8. Limitations. Changes with specified limits are more acceptable than open-ended ones. Hiring vehicles primarily for business on weekdays is more acceptable than hiring them anytime for any purpose.

9. Interaction with outsiders. Changes that encourage regular, systematic interaction with outsiders are less acceptable than those that foster ethnic relationships. Working as a clerk in an Amish retail store is more acceptable than serving as a hostess in a public restaurant. A business partnership involving outsiders is less acceptable than one involving church members.

10. External influence. Changes that open avenues of influence from modern life are less acceptable than those without such connections. Membership in public organizations and the use of radios, televisions, and news magazines are less acceptable than subscriptions to ethnic newspapers.

11. Family solidarity. Changes that threaten family integration are less acceptable than those that support the family unit. Forms of work and technology that separate the family are less acceptable than changes that strengthen family interaction. Bicycles are less acceptable than tricycles. Factory work is less acceptable than nonfarm work at home.

12. Ostentatious display. Decorative changes that attract attention are less acceptable than utilitarian ones. Landscaping a lawn is less acceptable than eating hot dogs. Window drapes are less acceptable than permanent-shine vinyl.

13. Size. Changes that significantly enlarge the scale of things are less acceptable than those that reinforce small social units. Tractors and high-volume business enterprises are less acceptable than permanent-press fabrics and modern bathtubs.

14. Individualism. Changes that elevate and accentuate individuals are less acceptable than those that promote social equality. Higher education, public recognition, and commercial insurance are less acceptable than calculators and instant pudding.

The Political Context of Change

Apart from the cultural values that regulate the acceptance of a new practice, there are also political considerations. In some cases, internal political factors may play as important a role as cultural ones.

1. Status of innovators. The status of the innovators—the "fence jumpers"—within the Amish community plays a key role in determining the acceptability of a new practice. If insulated ice chests, in contemporary colors, are used by respected and esteemed church members, they will likely spread rapidly throughout the community. When the innovators occupy marginal, low-status positions on the fringe of Amish society, new practices are more likely to fail or spread slowly.

2. *Leadership.* The opinion and diplomatic style of the senior bishops regulate the acceptance of major changes that come to their attention. The influence of the ranking bishop was especially important when the bishops numbered less than a dozen. If elderly bishops have a strong aversion to a practice, its acceptance may need to await their death. Thus the political mix—the prevailing sentiment of the senior bishops—may be crucial in determining the welcome received by a new practice.

3. *Rate of change.* The Amish sometimes talk of "how fast the wheel of change is spinning." "We are all moving," said one member, "some are just moving faster than others, but we're really moving in Lancaster County." The rate of change in the larger culture may determine the acceptability of a particular item for the Amish. The divisions of both 1910 and 1966 came at times of rapid technological advances in the larger society. In the midst of turbulent change, some practices may be arbitrarily rejected to simply brake the rate of change. In the early sixties the ordained leaders placed taboos on six technological innovations, after major ones such as modern hay balers and gas appliances had been accepted. It was simply a case of how much change could be absorbed in a short period of time. Furthermore, restrictions on some of the six innovations were gradually relaxed over the years. Thus, the acceptability of a particular item may hinge on whether it becomes available during an era of rapid change, as well as on the number of other new practices recently adopted.

4. *External pressure.* Legal and political pressure from the larger society has an obvious impact on Amish fence moving. Highway codes were responsible for adding electric lights, signals, red flashers, and large fluorescent triangles to Amish buggies. In another instance, pressure from public health officials encouraged massive polio vaccinations following the outbreak of several polio cases among the Amish in 1979. Dairy inspectors pressed for indoor toilets for sanitary reasons in the fifties.

5. *Cultural lag.* Imposing limits on new practices enables the Amish to maintain symbolic separation between their subculture and modern life. While change is necessary and acceptable, unrestricted change would erode the boundaries of the Amish world. Thus new practices are often accepted with certain limits to protect Amish identity and maintain at least a symbolic separation from the world. Restricted change signals that, true to their role, the Amish are still lagging behind modern society. A modern kitchen without a dishwasher, a silo without an unloader, a shop without a telephone, a telephone with an unlisted number, wallpaper without designs, and a hay baler without an automatic bale thrower are all ways of maintaining cultural separation while still permitting change. Although the Amish are pleased to lag behind modern life, they have avoided the cultural

lag that often plagues modern societies when technology leaps ahead of human values and beliefs. By holding a tight rein on technology, the Amish have kept it subservient to their values and community goals and have thus minimized cultural lag *within* their subculture.

A Bargaining Update

Throughout this book the Amish encounter with modernity has been viewed as a process of negotiation—with give and take on both sides. On some issues the Amish have surrendered to the demands of modernity, but at other times the agents of modernity have conceded to the Amish. In other instances, compromise was the order of the day as bargains were negotiated between the stewards of tradition and the proponents of progress. Finally, the Amish have also refused to place certain aspects of their life on the cultural bargaining table. Thus, four outcomes can be identified: concessions *by* the Amish, concessions *to* the Amish, compromises, and nonnegotiables.

The first outcome, concessions *by* the Amish, typifies aspects of their culture which have undergone modernization. Some concessions were *internally* induced changes that the Amish permitted by default—modern-looking homes, milking machines, washing machines, state-of-the-art tools, cash registers. Other changes came about because of *external* pressure from the outside world—legal, political, economic. Acceptance of bulk milk tanks, lights and signals on buggies, zoning regulations, school attendance through eighth grade, and the payment of Social Security for members who are not self-employed resulted from external pressures. Some concessions—indoor toilets—were prompted by a desire for convenience as well as ultimatums from milk inspectors for sanitary reasons. In any event, these adaptations represent areas in which the Amish have conceded to the pressures of modernization for a variety of reasons. The following is a sample of these concessions:

lights, signals, and reflectors on buggies

bulk milk tanks

modern farm management techniques

larger dairy herds

chemical fertilizers

insecticides and pesticides

artificial insemination of cows

nonfarm employment

power tools for manufacturing

indoor bathroom facilities

modern kitchens

contemporary house exteriors

use of professional services, including those of lawyers, physicians, accountants, and dentists

Social Security payments for employees

modern medicine

Concessions *to* the Amish are found on the other side of the bargaining table. Here the agents of modernity made allowances for the Amish by lax enforcement, exemptions, or special legislation. In these instances, the Amish were able to achieve their objectives and prevail in the bargaining sessions. The Supreme Court endorsement of Amish schooling exemplifies the most dramatic concession. Other examples include Social Security exemptions for the self-employed, the waiver of the hard hat regulation, and no Sunday milk pickups from Amish farms. These capitulations to the Amish include:

alternatives for conscientious objectors

exemption from high school attendance

waiver of school certification requirements

waiver of school building requirements

waiver of minimum wage requirements for teachers

Social Security exemption for self-employed

workmen's compensation exemption for self-employed

unemployment insurance exemption for self-employed

waiver of hard hat regulation

alteration of zoning regulations (by township)

horse travel on public roads

avoidance of Sunday milk pickup

A third outcome of the cultural bargaining sessions is the riddles—the negotiated settlements. These agreements reflect a mixture of tradition and modernity, for they typically involve some give and take on both sides. They symbolize a delicate balance between tradition and modernity. The scooter, for instance, is a compromise between walking and riding a bicycle. The distinction between the use and ownership of motor vehicles and the use of modern gas appliances reflects the delicate tension. The rise of Amish businesses, halfway between farm work and factory work, is a structural compromise. Other bargains represent an attempt to save both parties from an embarrassing loss of face—the vocational school, for example. The following is a sample of these compromises:

vocational school

selective use of telephones

modern farm equipment towed by horses

use of engines on field equipment

air and hydraulic power

hiring of cars and vans

modern gas appliances

Amish-owned tourist stands

selective use of electricity

nonfarm work based at home

permanent-press fabric for traditional garb

home freezers in a non-Amish neighbor's home

contemporary materials for carriage construction

electrical inverters

use of tractors at barns and shops

Amish-owned and -operated businesses

scooters

Finally, the nonnegotiables are aspects of traditional Amish life which have remained untarnished by modernity. These staunch features of Amish culture never appeared on the bargaining table. They have remained secluded, in their traditional form, despite the press of progress. Amish liturgy, ritual, and music, as well as the subordination of the individual to collective goals, remain intact. Limiting education, using horses, and speaking the dialect are just a few of the mainstays of Amish culture which have withstood the massive sweep of history. Such nonnegotiable features include:

worship in homes

worship service format

confession, excommunication, and shunning

traditional authority structure

lay ministers

mutual aid

limited education

horse-drawn equipment

horse and carriage

traditional dress styles

Pennsylvania German dialect

traditional sex roles

family size and importance

primacy of the church district

small and informal social units

Solving the Big Riddle

We have explored the many ways in which the Amish have coped with modernity. These excursions have solved some of the smaller riddles and unraveled clues to the big one: How did they manage to thrive in the face of modern life? Their dual strategy of *resistance* and *negotiation* has worked, for they indeed have flourished. What cultural secrets have enabled them to preserve their identity as a peculiar people for some three hundred years? They have successfully blended a variety of social ingredients in their cultural recipe. One ingredient alone cannot explain their success, and eliminating a single factor would not spoil their good fortune. Rather, a delicate mix of ingredients explains the longevity of Amish life in the twentieth century.[3] What, then, are the clues to the big riddle?

1. Recruitment. Large families and low attrition have enabled the Amish to replenish their population and thus perpetuate their community over the years. The farm economy, rejection of birth control, and acceptance of modern medicine have all contributed to large families. Vigorous childhood socialization, limited education, and controlled interaction with the outside world have held young people in the ethnic community. A slump in the birth rate or a rise in attrition would slow their spiraling growth.

2. Flexibility. The Amish have been willing to negotiate. They have made numerous technological concessions that have reaped handsome financial benefits. While holding firm to some taboos, they have not allowed religious practices to erode the economic base of their community. Their flexibility has energized the fiscal and cultural vitality of their community.

3. Gelassenheit. Despite their flexibility, the Amish have insisted on the supremacy of the group over that of the individual. Excessive individualism, which threatens to splinter the collective order, is simply not tolerated. In both childhood and adulthood, the individual remains subordinate and submissive to community discipline.

4. Ethnic organizations. The rise of Amish schools and businesses has created a chain of ethnic institutions which surrounds people throughout their life span. The interlocking organizations shelter and insulate individuals from contaminating relationships with the larger world. A structurally separate world makes Amish life believable and plausible and reconfirms it in daily interaction.

5. *Social control.* Small-scale units, ethnic symbolism, centralized authority, and ethnic organizations enable the church to exercise persuasive control over members. Behavior within the community, as well as interaction with the outside world, is regulated in harmony with cultural values. Confession rituals and the practice of shunning—powerful techniques of social control—have significantly contributed to the subculture's vitality.

6. *Small scale.* Small-scale units from congregations to farms and from herds to businesses have boosted Amish success. Small social units increase interaction, enhance social control, and maintain social equality. Moreover, they preserve the individual's identity and integration within the collective order.

7. *Managing technology.* Part of the Amish genius is the careful management of technology. They are neither enamored by it nor afraid to tame it. Able to perceive both its detrimental and productive consequences, they have tried to manage technology in ways that complement and reinforce community goals.

8. *Restricting consciousness.* By encouraging a practical education that ends with eighth grade, the Amish are, in essence, restricting consciousness. Critical, rational analysis that fosters independent thought would surely spur individualism and fragment the community. Limiting the flow of ideas and banning threatening world views through ethnic schooling is essential to preserve the Amish way of life.

9. *Symbolizing core values.* Key symbols—horse, dress, carriage, and lantern—articulate core values of simplicity, humility, submission, and separation. These everyday symbols, used over and over again, are ubiquitous reminders of the Amish world view. They objectify cultural boundaries and confer a group identity on individual members. Thoughtful care and use of these symbols has fortified the subculture.

10. *Managing social change.* Amish survival pivots on the astute management of social change. It involves a delicate balance—allowing enough change to keep members content without destroying their identity as a people. It requires selective cooperation with modernity without relinquishing cultural identity. Part of the Amish genius is the ability to allow change while ever setting new boundaries to preserve the lines of separation from the world. Pulling out old stakes without setting in new ones would surely erode Amish identity.

Faced with dramatic changes in their social environment in the twentieth century, the Amish have survived by carefully managing their cultural fences. While holding firmly to some ancient boundary markers, they have permitted discreet change in the shadows of the old markers. In other cases, they have moved old fences to keep up with the times. They have also staked out some new boundaries. Whether moving old fences or erecting new ones, the secret of the riddle lies in their insistence on fence keeping. They have discovered that good fences are important for preserving a people, and so they move fences rather than discard them.

12

The Dialogue with Modernity

Having an identity as a people is a real plus, but it's not the only way to heaven.
—Amish leader

Homeless Moderns

The authors of a recent study of individualism and community in American society worry that "individualism may have grown cancerous . . . that it may be threatening the survival of freedom itself." Is there anything we can learn, they wonder, from the wisdom of more traditional societies?[1] We have been tapping the wisdom of a traditional society as we explored the riddle of Amish culture. What have we learned about the Amish, ourselves, and modern culture?

Struggling with the Amish riddle raises questions about our own journey in the modern world. What is the price of progress? Is modernity a step forward or backward? Peter Berger has argued that modernity has left us "homeless," without a place in a coherent social order, as it dismantled the stable social structures that provided "homes" for us in preindustrial days. Rapid social change, specialization, mobility, and cultural pluralism have chipped away at our roots, our identity, and at the very core of our lives, leaving our minds "homeless" as well.[2]

The Amish remind us that the modern story is a mixed tale—one of delight and despair. Beyond dazzling technological achievements, modern life has freed us from the bondage of provincial views, restricted opportunities, enslavement to oppressive systems, and geographical entrapments. However, human liberation has been expensive. Although modern life has brought major strides in fundamental human rights and unprecedented opportunities for human fulfillment, it has also been accompanied by the blight of alienation—by an evaporation of meaning.[3] The erosion of meaning and the loss of belonging have contributed to our "homelessness"—the bleaker side of modernity, which in so many ways has liberated the human spirit.

The Amish have managed to preserve their "home" despite the march of history. They have remained untouched by the blight of homelessness. Roots, meaning, identity, and belonging remain intact in Amish life. The Amish "home" looks nostalgically serene to us, but it remains entrenched in provincialism, sexism, and dogmatism. It is certainly not a modern home—or is it?

Modern Amish

The riddle of Amish culture raises intriguing questions about the meaning of modernity. What exactly does it mean to be modern? Are the Amish modern? Our first response to that question is surely "no." However, some scholars have argued that although the Amish do not appear modern, they act in modern ways. They have fashioned their life in deliberate ways in the modern world as they selectively adopted the fruits of the industrial revolution. If the freedom to make choices is the trademark of modernity, then perhaps the Amish have indeed joined the modern world.[4] By deciding not to be modern—by rejecting the sway of progress—they have ironically acted quite modern.

The Amish have made self-conscious, collective decisions to reject computers and accept chain saws, to build their own schools, and to argue their convictions before congressional committees. They have controlled the conditions of their work, organized the equivalent of a political lobby group, and rejected car ownership.[5] In these ways and many others, they have taken charge of their destiny. They have made choices. In this sense they are modern, and quite different from traditionalists who simply take whatever fate bestows. Some Amish decisions were guided by economic concerns; others were made to uphold religious values, bolster family solidarity, sharpen separation from the world, and promote social equality.[6] In any event, the Amish as a group have made choices. They have decided just how modern they want to be.

This is not the whole story, however. When we shift from the group to the individual, things are different. An Amish individual has fewer choices than a modern one. Choices regarding dress, education, and transportation are dictated by group standards. Marriage is limited to other members of the church. Occupational choice is nil compared to the astonishing array of job opportunities in a postindustrial society. Amish society, as experienced by the individual, is quite restrictive—quite traditional. The restriction of individual freedom among the Amish is little different, however, than restraints placed on individuals by sports teams, monastic orders, or military organizations in modern society.

The Amish practice of adult baptism in which individuals voluntarily decide to join the church is indeed a rather modern idea. It is a choice, however, that entails a decision to set aside personal rights and submit to the collective order—church Ordnung. It is not an entirely free choice, because Amish socialization funnels youth toward church membership. But the Amish have acted in modern ways by making self-conscious decisions to preserve their identity as a people—decisions that often restricted individual choice. To use the bargaining metaphor—the Amish negotiators were unwilling to give up or trade away collective identity in exchange for greater individual freedom.

Are there other ways to think about modernity? If to be modern means using the latest electronic technology, if it means the unfettered pursuit of individualism, if it means the embrace of scientific research, if it means ultraconvenience, if it means the erosion of religion, if it means a disdain for tradition, if it means that life's joys are to be found in consumerism and leisure—then the Amish have surely not joined the modern world.

If, however, being modern means controlling the terms and conditions of one's work, if it means a delight in craftsmanship, if it means protecting the individual from the burden of choice, if it means taming the detrimental effects of technology, if it means safeguarding community identity, if it means caring for the unfortunate and elderly, if it means guaranteeing the individual a secure identity, if it means bestowing meaning to all of life—then perhaps the Amish have not only joined the modern world but are leading it.

Nagging Questions

Moderns are bothered by some nagging questions. By what right do Amish parents limit the education of their children, restrict occupational choice, cap opportunities for personal achievement, stifle artistic expression, and prescribe rigid sex roles? Doesn't such control squander human potential? Such restrictions are downright oppressive and sexist by modern standards. Denying Amish youth educational opportunity makes a mockery of modern justice. Would it not be only fair, Moderns wonder, if Amish children were required to attend at least several years of public high school to taste the fruits of progress? Then they would be free to pursue professional careers or return to Amish life. Such exposure would at least allow them to explore artistic and scientific careers, as well as their own potential.

The Amish are amused by such thinking, for they can flip the questions upside down. By what right, they ask, do modern parents

push their children through the turnstiles of modernity, to face incessant choices that carry heavy emotional loads? By what right do Moderns deprive their youth of the psychological security and personal
identity that come from membership in a lasting and durable group?
In fact, the Amish wonder, should not modern youth be required to
live several years in a traditional community to experience communal
life firsthand? Modern youth could then join the cultural system of
their choice. The Amish would remind us that those who do leave the
Amish faith typically fare quite well in the modern world, for they
have been taught the values of hard work, integrity, and frugality—
values that serve them well in a variety of careers. Thus, the Amish
contend that they are hardly depriving their youth—at least not any
more than modern parents.

The provincialism of Amish culture irritates the modern pench-
ant for diversity and pluralism. The cosmopolitan, well-rounded,
well-traveled person is the charm of modern culture. The intolerance
and rigidity of Amish life stifle the human spirit and nurture a myopic
world view. By what right, Moderns ask, can the Amish in the name of
Christianity oppose the liberation of the human spirit and the mind?

The Amish would likely agree that their culture is indeed local,
parochial, and sectarian. But they might ask, are Moderns as liberated as they proclaim to be? Blind adherence to some modern ideas
results in its own form of bondage. An obsession with individualism
precludes understanding and appreciating the benefits of collective
control. Rigid insistence on diversity thwarts the building of stable,
disciplined, and trustworthy communities. Intolerance for socialism,
patriarchal sex roles, traditional authority, and religious world views
not only belittles the very notion of tolerance but also betrays a provincial mentality enslaved to modern ideologies. The Amish might argue that they at least understand the modern world as well or better
than Moderns understand the Amish world and hence are less provincial. How many modern youth, the Amish might ask, are bilingual by
the end of eighth grade? The Amish would contend that in the final
analysis one must choose among ultimate values. Tolerance, diversity, and pluralism may have to yield if they threaten to spoil the
greater values of a stable community and secure personal identities.

Yet the conformity of Amish life nags Moderns. Dutiful adherence to tradition—dressing alike, driving identical carriages, meekly
following church regulations—cultivates a bland, even boring, conformity. The recipe for success in Amish culture not only cultivates a
herd mentality but also ridicules human dignity by promoting, even
applauding, thoughtless ritualism. To modern ways of thinking, the
Amish are puppets of their culture, controlled by the strings of their
religious traditions.

The Amish would likely agree. Conformity does guide much of

their conduct. They would simply remind Moderns that puppets abound outside Amish culture as well, that even in modern life individuals are puppets of their culture. Consumer fads, dress fashions, leisure trends, housing styles, and decorating crazes are all thriving. The preponderance of such conformity suggests that even modern individualists are swayed by the strings of social opinion. Moreover, the Amish might ask, which is more mindless, conformity to religious traditions or conformity to mass advertising and popular fads? Under the pretense of free choice, Moderns bow to cultural routines that endure beyond the fashions of the moment. From breakfast foods to social etiquette, vast areas of modern life are subservient to established customs. The Amish would remind us that their choice of an alternative lifestyle is not so much a matter of conforming to tradition—for that is inherent in the human experience—as a matter of deciding which traditions are worthy of respect.

Cultural Tradeoffs

Tourists are enchanted by the Amish. Social analysts hold them up as models for development, and energy experts herald their efficiency.[7] Others point to the humane character—the human face of the Amish social system. Despite these accolades from academicians, few have chosen to join them. Few outsiders have chosen to place aside technological convenience and the delights of individualism and submit themselves to the collective order of Amish life. There is a price to being Amish—a price that few outsiders have been willing to pay. It means giving up self-assertive individualism—submitting to the Ordnung, to religious tradition, to the voice of elders, and to communal wisdom. It means foregoing individual preference in many areas—dress, marriage, transportation, education. It means limited mobility, limited occupational choice, and limited possibilities for self-enhancement. It means foregoing many conveniences, restricting social friendships, avoiding many types of leisure, and turning off electronic media. It means, in short, inhabiting a different social world, where the group, rather than the individual, reigns supreme.

It is a world of restricted ideas—where scientific thinking is unacceptable—where the agenda of ideas is controlled. It is a world that in many ways is provincial, narrow, and restrictive—where free choice and individualism do not rule. It means accepting a religious world view, indeed a literalist view of the Bible. To give up, to submit, to obey, to respect limits, and to believe are the price of being Amish. For the outsider, it is a high price—a sacrifice few are willing to make. For those growing up on the inside, the price is of course lower, for it is the bestowed way of life. But in either case, it is costly.

There are benefits that come in return. The Amish offer genuine social security—not an impersonal system that sends computerized monthly checks. Their spontaneous social security springs into action in the case of fire, death, sickness, senility, or physical handicap. There is also the benefit of belonging, of being part of a people, of an extended family, of having a place in a group and knowing it will always be there. There is the security of family with dozens of aunts, uncles, and cousins surrounding one in play, work, and worship. There is the reward of identity, of knowing who one is and where one fits in regardless of personal or occupational achievements. There is the security of tradition, of knowing that things are in order, that things are the way they are supposed to be, as handed down. There is also the reward of meaning, of knowing that one's life is acceptable to God if one has lived faithfully by church teachings. There is the reward of having a permanent place—acreage, trees, a stream; a place where ancestors farmed and fished and where one's own offspring will likely do the same. There is the security of ritual, of predictable routines that tie one into the community via worship, play, family, and work. There is, in short, a stable, social "home." The cost of being Amish is high, but the benefits—identity, meaning, and belonging— are precious commodities in the midst of modern homelessness.

How does Amish society fare when we look at quality of life indicators? Here we have a social system without poverty. Widows, orphans, and the destitute are cared for by the church. The Amish are rarely imprisoned. Here is a society virtually without crime and violence. Amish youth are occasionally arrested for drunken driving and children are occasionally paddled, but incidents of violent crime and murder are conspicuously absent. Amish suicide and mental illness rates are substantially lower than those in the larger society.[8] Alcohol abuse, while present among some youth, is practically nil among the adult population. Divorce is unheard of. Individuals are not warehoused in institutions—large schools, massive factories, retirement homes, or psychiatric hospitals—but are cared for within the family.[9] Recycling goods, frugal management, a thrifty lifestyle, and a rejection of consumerism produce scant waste. Energy consumption per capita is remarkably low. Beyond exhaust fumes from diesel power plants and the contamination of streams by manure run-off, the Amish add little to environmental pollution. Personal alienation, loneliness, and meaninglessness are for the most part absent. There are, of course, some unhappy marriages, lonely people, cantankerous personalities, and family feuds. But all things considered, the quality of life indicators for Amish society as a whole are remarkably robust. The Amish have created a humane and enviable social system.

On the Other Hand

Foul play, Moderns might argue, for this is a lopsided view of the Amish story. Moderns might contend that the Amish are social parasites, who feed off the larger social system. They are only able to survive and thrive because they have found themselves in a political system that has been remarkably tolerant of their religious views. As conscientious objectors, they have not participated in the military programs that have protected the very religious freedoms that allow them to be different. Although they expect tolerance from the state for their dissident views, they show little tolerance toward dissidents in their own ranks. Indeed, Moderns might ask if the Amish are using the outside world as their human trash heap when they excommunicate troublemakers and cast them off on the rest of society. Their agricultural achievements and business profits rest firmly on the shoulders of modern science—a profession that is off bounds for their youth. They have tapped the benefits of science but have certainly not contributed to it. Modern medicine (for example, the use of penicillin) is partly responsible for their successful growth rate, but they did not contribute to its development.

Their environmental pollution rate may be commendable, but the diesel trucks that transport products to and from Amish shops add their own share of pollution to the environment. Besides, what sort of justice allows their horses to chop up roadways without paying gasoline taxes to repair them? While it is honorable that they care for their own needy, the Amish boycott of Social Security shortchanges the welfare of the destitute in the larger society. Thus, Moderns might argue, in these and other ways the Amish are freeloaders who have directly benefitted from the resources of the larger society without contributing their fair share. Without scientific achievements, higher education, the modern state, and electronic communication—all of which the Amish eschew—the quality of their life would be remarkably dismal in many ways.

An Amish Reply

The Amish would obviously concede that much of this is true—they certainly are dependent on the larger world. But this is a rather cockeyed view. Freeloaders, they would retort, hardly! By what standard are they social parasites when they pay school taxes for public schools they do not use? They pay millions of dollars in federal and state income taxes and use few federal services—even rejecting farm subsidies and other forms of government "handouts." Some of their members pay into the Social Security system though they know they will never receive any benefits in return. In these ways the Amish are subsidizing state and federal government programs. They are paying into the national coffers at the rate of everyone else while using relatively few services. They are not collecting welfare checks, sitting in penitentiaries, borrowing federal funds for college, or using Medicare for expensive heart surgery. They are not living off agricultural subsidies and Social Security checks. True, they have not contributed directly to scientific achievements, but their tax dollars have supported scientific and medical research as well as the defense budget. Moreover, they have cooperated with scientists who have used their tight-knit community to study the genetic transmission of diseases. Although they have not contributed scientists, they have contributed hundreds of subjects for medical study. Furthermore, their unique presence has fueled a huge tourist industry that profits non-Amish entrepreneurs. Freeloaders? Who is kidding whom? According to Amish calculations, the bottom line shows that they are subsidizers, rather than parasites, of the larger economic system.

Surely, their conscience has not allowed them to participate in military programs. But, they might ask, is it not valuable in the midst of a violent world to create a society where harmony, passivity, and quiet discipline are the norm rather than aggression and hostility? The embodiment of a peaceful social order may be as significant as nuclear threats in nudging the international community toward global harmony. What is so wrong, the Amish ask, with creating a social security system with a human face where the destitute and helpless are cared for in the context of extended family, neighborhood, and church? Would the world not be a better world if other groups did likewise? Besides, the Amish point out, they are quick to help when disasters—fire, storm, flood—strike far outside the boundaries of their own people. Moreover, is it not helpful to have a human model, a society that allows us to observe the social impact on people when technology is harnessed, the speed of social change is regulated, and the rush of progress is tamed?

Such a hypothetical debate between the Amish and their modern neighbors raises profound questions about the nature of human freedom, the meaning of progress, the role of the individual in the modern world, and the ties between individuals and social systems. The social benefits of Amish society appear nostalgically pleasant, indeed enviable. They are possible, however, only at the high price of personal freedom. Individual rights, privileges, and freedoms, so fundamental to modern culture, are severely curtailed in the Amish experience. The right to unlimited self-achievement, to unbridled artistic expression, to free occupational choice, to political participation, to defense of one's legal rights, to consumerism, to personal expression in dress—in short, the right to be or do whatever one wants to be or do— is limited in Amish culture. The communal social benefits come at the expense of individual freedom—the cardinal value so deeply enshrined in modern culture.

The Other Side of Freedom

There is another side to freedom.[10] Although the Amish are not *free to do* some things, they are *free from* many others. They are not free to buy the latest electrical appliances, but they are free from enormous consumer debt. They are not free to buy the latest car, but they are free from the frustrations of commuter traffic. They are not free to buy the latest convenience, but they are free to enjoy the convenience of walking across the driveway to their work. They are not free to travel on airplanes, but they are free to have lunch at home on their own schedules with their families. They are not free to pursue higher education, but they are free to control the curriculum and organization of their own schools. They are not free to buy the latest fashions, but they are free from the anxiety of what to wear and free from endless shopping trips. The Amish are not free to watch television, but they are free from commercials. The Amish are not free to pursue many occupations, but they are free from the constraints of boring jobs and bureaucratic regulations.

Although the Amish are not free to make up their face in the latest styles, they are free from the pressure to present a "perfect" face. They are not free to accept Social Security checks, but they are free from worrying about who will care for them in their old age. They are not free to pick the college of their choice, but they are free from agonizing decisions about college selection and occupational choice. They are not free to discard the traditional ritual that surrounds Amish funerals, but they are free from worrying about who will support them in the time of grief.

The cultural norms of Amish life severely circumscribe personal freedoms but also lift the burden of choice from the individual. They liberate the individual from the incessant need to decide. In Amish culture, the burden for success and failure leans on the community; in the modern world, the weight of success and failure pivots on the individual, who often lacks the support of a durable group. The Amish are not as free to make up their own mind, shape their own destiny, and follow wherever their heart may lead, but they are freer from endless trips to the therapist's office, from the emotional burden to make it on their own—to shoulder the consequences, regardless of costs.

What does all this mean for happiness? Which culture—modern or Amish—optimizes the conditions for human fulfillment and best satisfies the yearning for meaning, belonging, and identity? Happiness is a relative thing. It hinges on cultural expectations, on social values, on the gap between expectations and achievements, and on comparisons with one's social peers.

It would be wrong to assume the Amish are unhappy because their personal freedom is constricted. Indeed, one likely reason for their success as a people is their culture's ability to fulfill basic human needs of identity, belonging, and meaning in a rather profound way. Those Amish who experiment with the boundaries of their culture feel the tug of both worlds, but most members do not experience the midlife and career crises so typical of Moderns. The toll of modern individualism is high, as evinced by the number of therapists who manage identity crises, the popularity of stress management seminars, the rise of wellness centers, the soaring number of lawsuits, and the standard barometers of malaise: the rates of divorce, crime, drug abuse, fraud, suicide, and violence. Yet, despite the psychic toll, Moderns cherish the exhilaration of individualism. Few would be willing to relinquish its thrills in exchange for the tranquillity, order, and meaning offered by Amish culture. The Amish provide a social model wherein the individual's needs are fulfilled not through the delights of individualism, but in sacrifice and submission to a greater collective good. There are no promises of freewheeling self-fulfillment in Amish life, but the individual is cared for and cherished by a supportive social system—a humane and durable promise.

For "weaker" people, often discarded by the modern system, the Amish setting provides a caring environment, where no one slips through bureaucratic cracks. In the eyes of "stronger" people, the Amish system feels oppressively tight compared to the pliable fabric of modern culture. Tilted toward the rugged individualist, modern culture easily tramples on the weak. By contrast, Amish culture, tilted toward the collective welfare, easily suffocates the strong. The wisdom distilled in Amish culture suggests that some limits on individualism may, in the long run, serve the deeper needs of the individual better than an unbridled pursuit of self-gratification.

Our Common Riddle

Some riddles remain. How is it that those who have not been educated beyond the eighth grade have been able to devise such a humane social system? Without consultants or strategic planners, the Amish, in simple and down-to-earth ways, have devised a social system that not only merits the attention of tourists and scholars but also raises profound questions about the underpinnings of happiness, freedom, and meaning. Moreover, how is it that, despite the best efforts of the most learned planners and strategists, our modern world is strewn with fragmentation, alienation, and despair, as well as startling technological advances? Moderns plan incessantly yet seem out of control. The Amish, who do little, if any, strategic planning, seem firmly in command of things.

Side by side, Amish and modern culture tilt in opposite directions—one toward the community and the other toward the individual. Their comparison evokes a common riddle that engulfs the larger human community, both Amish and modern alike. Would it be possible to construct a social "home" where the need for individual expression and the need for community are suspended in creative tension? Can we envision a culture where individuals discover their true selves only as they plant their roots in the communal soil of a larger body, where self-fulfillment is achieved in the context of a social mission that transcends egotistic interests, where personal identity is firmly grounded in the identity of a larger body, where the pursuit of greed and self-aggrandizement yields to the collective welfare—the common good?

Is it possible to pursue such lofty goals without stifling initiative, without suppressing creativity, and without restricting individual freedom? Can we only have meaningful community at the expense of individual freedom; and must such freedom result in a cancerous debilitation of community? Or is it possible to forge a culture—a social habitat—where the individual and community are not pitted against each other as adversaries, but where they supplement, complement, and enrich each other? That is the common riddle that begs all of us—Amish and Moderns alike—for solution.

Such a delicate mix would not only champion the charms of community but would also empower and enable individuals to achieve their highest creative aspirations. Such a "home" would welcome the gifts of mind and body with the understanding that these unique gifts are embraced not for selfish ends in themselves but for the embellishment of the larger body, not for self-acclaim but for collective celebration, not for personal gain but for corporate enhancement. Can we find a middle ground, a social order that anchors the individual in a larger body and at the same time applauds choice and creative expression? The solution to our common riddle promises to arrest the cancerous growth of individualism and to relax the stifling restrictions of traditional life. Hidden within our common riddle is the hope of a social order, a "home" that taps both the achievements of modernity and the wisdom of Amish life.

APPENDIX A
Research Procedures

The empirical data and observations in this book describe the Amish settlement in Lancaster County, Pennsylvania. The details of social life vary in Amish settlements across the United States, making it unwise to apply the specifics of the Lancaster Amish to other communities. Although the particulars vary from settlement to settlement, the basic values and philosophy of Amish culture described in this book are applicable to other Amish settlements as well.

Various data sources were used: in-depth interviews, primary source documents, ethnographic observations, and a demographic profile of the Lancaster settlement. I conducted face-to-face interviews in 1986 and 1987 with over two dozen members of the Amish community. The informants included males and females, farmers and businessmen, housewives and teachers, married and single people, ordained leaders and lay members. They were purposively selected to tap a representative cross section of the community. Virtually all of the interviews involved two sessions; some involved as many as five sessions. A significant portion of the book's argument is based on the notes and transcripts of these interviews. Non-Amish people who relate to the Amish community as lawyers, physicians, accountants, and veterinarians were also consulted.

A stratified, two-stage cluster sample was used to obtain demographic data on a sample of 382 people living in 168 Amish households in 1986. The small number of church districts made it unwise to select a random sample of districts. The eighty-two church districts were initially stratified by their size, location, and longevity. A purposive sample of twenty districts (24 percent of all districts) was selected proportionately from each of the three strata. A systematic sample of one-fourth of the households in each of the selected districts was then taken. A household was defined as a living unit with its own kitchen facilities. Demographic data were gathered on all people eighteen years of age and older in each of the selected households. A trained

Amish informant compiled the information on the members of each household. The completion rate was 100 percent.

The Amish are hesitant to publicize minutes of meetings, organizational documents, and policy statements. In many cases, generous informants shared copies of the minutes of meetings, personal letters, and other primary sources for which I am deeply grateful. Having lived in the Lancaster area all of my life, I have long been familiar with the Amish. Furthermore, I have many friends and acquaintances in their community. These experiences have provided opportunities to observe Amish society first hand. I designed and supervised the data collection of the demographic profile of the settlement. In all of these activities, the Amish were gracious and helpful neighbors who generously shared their time and ideas with me.

APPENDIX B
Old Order Amish Population Estimates, 1880–1990, Lancaster County Settlement

Date	Districts	Less than 18 Years	18 years and Older	Total
1880	6	400	350	750
1890	6	400	350	750
1900	6	400	350	750
1910	9	600	500	1,100
1920	11	700	650	1,350
1930	15	1000	850	1,850
1940	18	1550	1400	2,950
1950	25	2200	1900	4,100
1960	35	3050	2700	5,750
1970	46	4000	3500	7,500
1980	65	5650	4950	10,600
1985	82	7150	6250	13,400
1990	95	8700	7700	16,400

Sources: The number of districts is based on data from the 1973 *Pennsylvania Amish Directory of Lancaster and Chester County Districts*, 1980 *Amish Directory of the Lancaster Co. Family*, Raber's *New American Almanac* (1986), and Amish informants. In 1931 four districts divided to make a total of fifteen, and this number is used for the 1930 calculations. The 1985 population estimates are based on a sample of every fourth household in twenty districts (see Appendix A). The 1985 average district size of 163 people was used to estimate the population from 1940 to 1990. Informant estimates of 125 people per district were used for the years prior to 1940. The 1985 ratio of those eighteen years of age and older (46.8%) to those under eighteen years of age (53.2%) was used to estimate the two age groups throughout the years. The 1990 estimates are based on current trends. Numbers are rounded off to the nearest 50.

APPENDIX C
Old Order Amish Population Estimates by Settlement Areas in North America

	North America	Pennsylvania	Lancaster
Settlements	175	40	1
Districts	661	165	82
Adults (18+)	50,500	12,606	6,250
Adults and Children	107,743	26,895	13,400

Sources: North American and Pennsylvania settlements and districts are from Luthy (1985:1–6) and Raber (1986). Lancaster estimates are described in Appendix B. North American and Pennsylvania membership estimates were calculated using the assumption of 76.4 adults (eighteen years and over) and 87.0 children under eighteen years per district, as calculated for the Lancaster settlement. The estimates could vary, as the size of church districts in other areas departs from the Lancaster norm of 76.4 adults and 87.0 children per district.

NOTES

1. The Amish Story

1. For readable introductions to the origins of the Anabaptist movement, see Dyck (1981), Klaassen (1973), and Weaver (1987). The *Mennonite Encyclopedia* (1956) covers a wide range of topics related to Anabaptist and Amish beginnings.

2. Kauffman (1975:42).

3. An overview of the suffering and persecution is provided by Dyck (1981:50–61; 1985) and Schowalter (1957). Vivid descriptions of the persecution printed at the end of the *Ausbund* (1984) have been translated from the German by Kauffman (1975). The classic account of Christian martyrdom and suffering from New Testament times to the Anabaptist persecution was compiled by Braght (1951) in 1660 in the *Martyrs Mirror*.

4. For a discussion of the historical setting and the significance of the Schleitheim Confession of Faith, more properly called the Brotherly Union of a Number of Children of God Concerning Seven Articles, see Yoder (1973:34–43).

5. Bender (1957:29–54).

6. For a record of his writings, see Simons (1956).

7. The term *Mennonite* was first used by Dutch Anabaptist followers of Menno Simons. Eventually it was assumed by other Anabaptist groups as well. It was not widely used by the Swiss Anabaptists at the time of the Amish division in 1693. See Dyck (1981:208–9) for a discussion of the evolution of the term *Mennonite*. For a brief and recent introduction to Menno Simons, see Horst (1986).

8. Séguy (1973:182).

9. Numerous letters exchanged in the controversy have been preserved. They have been translated by Mast (1950) and are discussed by Gascho (1937). Extended discussions of the Amish division can be found in Bachman (1961:27–50), Hostetler (1980:31–49), and Yoder (1987:43–58). For a succinct overview of the division, see Luthy (1971a). Hostetler (1980:42–43) provides suggestive evidence that Ammann may have been a recent convert to Anabaptism, which might explain his boldness in confronting the Old Swiss leaders.

10. Hostetler (1980:50).

11. Beiler (1983:17–18). For a discussion of Amish immigration and early settlements, see Beiler (1976a, 1983), Crowley (1978), Fisher (1987), Hostetler

(1980:50–71), MacMaster (1985:69–87), Stoltzfus (1954), E. S. Yoder (1987:60–68), and P. Yoder (1987a:286–90). A series of articles about the early Pennsylvania settlements by Amish historian Joseph F. Beiler appeared in the *Diary* in 1972 and 1974. Amish genealogist Amos L. Fisher's (1984) work provides new information on the early settlements.

12. The Dunkards, formally known as Brethren, originated in Germany in 1708. The nickname Dunkard, based on their mode of baptism by immersion, eventually gave way to German Baptist Brethren in 1871. Today they are known as the Church of the Brethren.

13. The Holmes County, Ohio, settlement is somewhat larger than the Lancaster community, but it is divided into various Amish subgroups or affiliations that do not share a common religious discipline. For an excellent ethnography of Amish life based on the larger settlements, see Hostetler's *Amish Society* (1980).

14. The Hutterites emerged as a separate branch of Anabaptism in 1528. For a discussion of their origins, see Dyck (1981:71–82) and Hostetler (1974). Today they live in communitarian groups in the western United States and in Canada.

15. Hostetler (1980:93).

16. A settlement may have one or several affiliations, and each affiliation may have one or numerous congregations. In the Lancaster Amish settlement the Old Order Amish, New Order Amish, and Beachy Amish represent three different affiliations.

17. Luthy (1985).

18. The Amish do not maintain population statistics. Estimates can be calculated by multiplying the known size of church districts in some settlements by the total number of districts as reported by Luthy (1985) and Raber (1987). Procedures for estimating the population of the Lancaster settlement are described in Appendix B. See Appendix C for North American and Pennsylvania population estimates.

19. Kraybill (1985).

20. Kraybill (1985).

21. The age, size, and location of the Lancaster settlement have made it a target of several studies and scholarly investigations. For nineteenth-century descriptions of Amish life, see Beiler (1888), Gibbons (1869), Umble (1948), and Yoder (1979a). An excellent collection of nineteenth-century primary sources has been edited by Yoder (1987a). Twentieth-century analyses include Bachman (1961), Ericksen et al. (1979), Gallagher (1981), Getz (1946), portions of Hostetler (1980), Kollmorgen (1942, 1943), Loomis (1979), and Smith (1961). Kephart (1987) and Loomis and Dyer (1976) also focus on the Lancaster settlement. Both of these studies are seriously flawed and very outdated. For a critique of Kephart, see Kraybill (1988).

22. These answers are reported in Ericksen et al. (1979). This comprehensive study of Amish fertility was conducted on the Lancaster Amish settlement. The authors report a completed family size of 6.8, which is quite similar to the 6.6 found in the 1986 survey described in Appendix A.

23. This range is reported by Hostetler (1980:106). A description of the procedures and an extensive discussion of the same findings can be found in Ericksen, Ericksen, and Hostetler (1980).

24. Although the Lancaster settlement and the total number of Amish throughout North America are growing, not all settlements have fared so well.

For a discussion of Amish settlements that failed, see Luthy (1986). He discusses one hundred settlements that failed between 1840 and 1960.

25. Numerous analytic concepts have been employed to understand the social organization of the Amish. Typical conceptualizations view the Amish as a sect (Wilson, 1970), a folk society, and a *Gemeinschaft*. Hostetler (1980) suggests that they have formed a "commonwealth" and exemplify a "high context" culture. Loomis and Dyer (1976) use a social systems model to interpret Amish society. Olshan (1981) has questioned the appropriateness of using the "folk society" model for conceptualizing Amish society. All of these conceptual frameworks highlight different aspects of Amish social organization.

26. Although it is common for scholars to assume that the Amish have withdrawn from the modern world, this is simply not the case. Hunter (1983:15) cites the Amish as an example of a community that attempts "almost total isolation," and Kephart (1987:3) makes the ludicrous comment that the Amish reject "virtually all the components of modern civilization."

27. The sociological literature on modernization is voluminous. An introduction to the sources is available in Brode (1969). My conceptualization of modernization is heavily indebted to the work of Peter L. Berger. See especially Berger (1974, 1977, and 1979) and Berger, Berger, and Kellner (1973). All of Berger's work is anchored in the sociology of knowledge framework developed with Thomas Luckmann in *The Social Construction of Reality* (1966). For two synoptic reviews of Berger's theorizing on modernity, see Wuthnow et al. (1984) and Hunter and Ainlay (1986). Hunter (1983) uses Berger's model to analyze American Evangelicals.

28. Bellah et al. (1985).

29. No new settlements have been initiated by the Lancaster community since 1978. However, individual families do occasionally move from the Lancaster area to other settlements for a variety of reasons.

30. These tactics are an expansion and elaboration of defensive structuring practices identified by Siegel (1970).

31. I use the image of negotiation in several ways. In some cases it refers to direct, face-to-face bargaining between Amish representatives and government officials—for example, the development of Amish schools and the use of bulk tanks to refrigerate milk on farms. In other instances, informal negotiations occurred quietly, as sectors of the two cultural systems merged over the decades. Using permanent-press fabrics to make traditional Amish clothing is one of many informally negotiated cultural agreements. Finally, I have also used the metaphor in a symbolic way to capture the dynamic dialogue between Amish life and modern culture.

32. This group has had various names at different stages of its evolution, which is discussed in chapter 7, note 6. For clarity, I have used the term *Peachey* church when referring to this progressive group.

2. The Quilt Work of Amish Culture

1. Known as the Dordrecht Confession of Faith, the creed contains eighteen articles. It was signed by Flemish and Frisian Mennonite pastors in the Dutch city of Dordrecht in 1632. Although many Mennonite groups over the years have adhered to the confession in principle, the Amish have attempted to follow its teachings literally, especially in regard to shunning and foot-

washing. The Swiss Anabaptists never adopted the Dordrecht Confession, which was one of the sources of difference between the Alsatian and Swiss Anabaptists leading to the Amish division in 1693. The Dordrecht Confession is the basis for Amish instruction classes prior to baptism. For a discussion of the Dordrecht Confession, see *Mennonite Encyclopedia* (1956), vol. 2, s.v. "Dordrecht Confession of Faith," and *Mennonite Encyclopedia* (1956), vol. 1, s.v. "Confessions of Faith." Horst (1982, 1988) and Studer (1984) provide updates on the significance of the Dordrecht Confession.

2. Friedmann (1956:448–49; 1957:86–88; 1973:66, 124) surveys the Anabaptist use of the term. Cronk's (1977) analysis of Gelassenheit as a redemptive rite in Old Order Amish and Old Order Mennonite communities has influenced my conceptual framework. I am greatly indebted to her work. In a letter to the author dated 24 September 1987, Amishman David Luthy noted: "Concerning Gelassenheit, I realize the Amish are not familiar with the term . . . but the Amish are familiar very much with the concept. Your use of it is valid and essential."

3. Cronk (1977).

4. *Petition* (1937).

5. Cigars of various sorts and pipes are commonly smoked. Commercial cigarettes in white wrappers are frowned on as "worldly." Hand-rolled cigarettes in brown wrappers are sometimes used. Some observers report a decline in smoking in recent years. Tobacco production is dwindling for a variety of reasons.

6. *Life* (1983:17).

7. *Guidelines* (1981:64).

8. See Bellah et al. (1985:55–84) for a discussion of the modern preoccupation with finding oneself.

9. *Instruction* (n.d.:16).

10. Smucker (1988:226–29).

11. Hostetler (1969:227). For a review of the psychological research on Amish personality types, see Smucker (1988). Hostetler (1969) reports findings on a variety of personality tests administered to Amish schoolchildren in several settlements. An excellent study of the socialization of Amish children is available in Hostetler and Huntington (1971).

12. *Instruction* (n.d.:8–11).

13. *Guidelines* (1981:50). For a collection of source materials used by the Old Order Amish in child rearing and schooling, see Hostetler (1968).

14. *Instruction* (n.d.:9).

15. *Dordrecht* (1976:12, 14).

16. *Guidelines* (1981:47).

17. *Instruction* (n.d.:7–13).

18. *Instruction* (n.d.:26).

19. *Life* (1983:26). In 1988 the Amish reprinted a Mennonite booklet, *Pride and Humility*, by Brenneman (1867). For a good discussion of the role of humility in Amish and Mennonite culture in the nineteenth century, see Schlabach (1988).

20. See, for example, 1 Tim. 2:9 and 1 Pet. 3:3–4.

21. *Life* (1983:7).

22. *Dordrecht* (1976:26).

23. Yoder (1973:38).

24. *Standards* (1981:1, 26).

25. *Papers* (1937).
26. Cronk (1981).
27. *Life* (1983:25).
28. *Guidelines* (1981:46).
29. *Instruction* (n.d.:5).
30. The watercolors and other artwork of Amishman Henry Lapp (1862–1904) are an interesting example of Amish art in the late nineteenth century. Lapp had severe hearing and speech impediments, and thus church leaders may have granted him greater freedom to express his artistic impulses. A discussion of his life and work is recorded in *Diary* (1982:14:329). Barbara Ebersole (1846–1922) made beautiful and colorful Fraktur bookplates. Artistic lettering in a Bible is more acceptable, for example, than artwork that is framed for public display. Amish quilts and flower gardens, of course, have been colorful artistic creations over the generations.
31. *Standards* (1981:7).
32. *Standards* (1981:38–39).
33. *Instruction* (n.d.:22).
34. *Standards* (1981:1).
35. *Guidelines* (1981:5).
36. See Lauer (1981) for a sociological analysis of time as a cultural product.

3. Symbols of Integration and Separation

1. For an earlier discussion of the role of symbols in Amish culture, see Hostetler (1963).
2. Beam (1982) has produced an English/Pennsylvania Dutch dictionary. A grammar of the Pennsylvania Dutch dialect is also available (Frey 1981). See Huffines (1988) for a discussion of the influence of English on the Pennsylvania German dialect.
3. *Diary* (1977:9:30).
4. Although High German is the target language for Amish sacred ritual, in actual practice it is at best only approximated. The *Martyrs Mirror*, the Bible, and other sacred writings used by the Amish are written in an older form of German. The spoken German in worship services is highly diluted with the dialect.
5. Wickersham (1886:168) and Ellis and Evans (1883:343).
6. Klein (1924:368).
7. My description of Amish dress is indebted to Sara E. Fisher, who kindly shared an unpublished paper (1972) on female garb and noted recent changes. For an extended discussion of dress practices among a variety of plain groups, see Scott (1986). Gingerich (1970) traces the history of Amish-Mennonite attire through four centuries. The rise and fall of veil-wearing among Mennonites in the Lancaster area is analyzed by Kraybill (1987b).
8. Fisher (1972).
9. Fisher (1972).
10. Fisher (1972).
11. As the Amish have moved into small towns and boroughs the horse has created some zoning problems. A lengthy dispute between two sisters who wanted to keep their horse in the village of Strasburg and the borough council

continued for several months in 1983. See *Intelligencer* (21 Sept., 28 Sept., 12 Oct.) and *New Era* (13 Sept., 14 Sept., 14 Nov.) for accounts of the dispute.

12. Fisher (1978:233).

13. For a study of energy conservation on Amish farms, see Johnson, Stoltzfus, and Craumer (1977).

14. A thorough description of the various types of horse-drawn transportation in several Amish and Mennonite settlements was written by Scott (1981).

15. Gibbons (1869:16) noted that at the end of the Civil War the Lancaster Amish were driving to their worship services in simple farm wagons covered with a yellowish oil cloth. The Amish did not begin using buggies as quickly as other groups and they were slow to adopt steel springs to cushion the load on their wagons. By 1880 Amish youth were beginning to drive simple buggies, and tarps in a variety of colors were being stretched over Amish wagons. While a few changes were underway, the Amish were nevertheless maintaining austere standards on their vehicles at the end of the nineteenth century. Whip socks (whip holders) and whips themselves were prohibited, likely to protest the speed symbolized by the dashing horse under whip. Whips are still forbidden. The early Amish buggy and wagon did not have an "easy back" (backrest) on the seat, or a dashboard on the front to obstruct flying mud.

16. Although gray is the standard color for the carriage top in the Lancaster area, black, white, and even yellow tops are common in other Amish settlements.

17. The slow moving vehicle signs were required by law and enforced in 30 June 1977; see *Intelligencer* (30 June 1977). An editorial in the *Intelligencer* (22 Aug. 1988) praised the Amish for using the reflective orange triangles on their buggies and concluded: "We doubt that God will look with disfavor on the Amish for using these symbols."

18. *Intelligencer* (7 July 1987).

19. There have been periodic discussions between township supervisors and the Amish regarding the damage horseshoes cause to public roads. Informal agreements have been made to control the type of weld cleats on the bottom of horseshoes to prevent slippage. One township is experimenting with rubber horseshoes to control road damage. For a record of these issues, see *New Era* (25 Oct. 1982, 27 Oct. 1982, 1 Apr. 1983, 30 June 1988) and *Intelligencer* (26 Oct. 1982, 20 Mar. 1987).

4. The Social Architecture of Amish Society

1. Hostetler (1980:173).

2. In the fifties and sixties, many Amish children were born in hospitals. Since 1980 most children are born at home, with the assistance of a certified midwife. Some are delivered in outpatient clinics and doctors' offices. For colorful descriptions of a midwife's and doctor's work among the Amish, see, respectively, Armstrong and Feldman (1986) and Kaiser (1986).

3. The role of the Amish wife is described by the bishop in the wedding ceremony: "The man should know that God has appointed him as head of his woman, that he is to lead, rule and protect her lovingly." The wife "is to honor and respect him and be subject to him . . . she shall be quiet . . . and take good care of the children and housekeeping." Wives are told to conduct themselves

submissively and are asked to pledge to "live in subjection to their husband"; see *Handbuch* (1978:38–39).

4. Huntington (1981) has written an excellent essay on the Amish family. For a description of age roles in the Amish family, see Hostetler and Huntington (1971:12–34).

5. It is possible that some progressive Amish couples use artificial means of birth control. However, church leaders and most of the community would condemn such behavior as morally wrong. For a variety of reasons, older women sometimes undergo sterilization to prevent further births. The acceptance of sterilization represents a modernizing trend—a shift from fate to choice.

6. Orthodontia is considered superfluous and rarely used for aesthetic purposes; if they have serious dental problems, the Amish will undergo orthodontic treatment.

7. One Amish farmer has a homemade putting green hidden in a secluded section of his pasture where he can practice his golfing on the sly. Another Amishman occasionally flies in a private plane with a pilot friend. If such activities became public knowledge, they would likely trigger some form of discipline in the church.

8. Businessmen and their families and well-to-do retired farmers travel occasionally and sometimes take vacations or "trips." They may travel by bus, train, or rented van; air travel is prohibited. Some Amish in the Lancaster area routinely take a winter vacation in Florida. Amish from various parts of the United States congregate in Pinecraft Village, southeast of Sarasota. For a description of this small Amish village, see *Intelligencer* (14 Jan. 1987).

9. A household is defined as a living area having separate eating facilities. Many extended families have two or three households in the same house. This estimate of the size of the Lancaster church districts is based on the research described in Appendix A.

10. Hostetler (1980:111).

11. The leaders are called *Diener* (servant). The *Handbuch* (1978) identifies them as *Volliger Diener* (bishop), *Diener zum Buch* (minister, or servant, of the book), and *Armendiener* (deacon, or servant, to the poor). Their roles are described in *Gemein* (n.d.) and in the *Handbuch* (1978:29–33). Yoder (1987b) provides an excellent review of the ordained offices and notes that the term *bishop* was not used by the Amish until the 1860s.

12. A bishop is not required by church polity to have two districts. Typically a bishop has a "home" district but often oversees a second district for several years until the congregation is ready to ordain its own bishop. In some instances, a bishop may oversee three districts and in other cases only one. A bishop usually is responsible for two districts.

13. Schlabach (1988) and Yoder's (n.d.) recent study of the minutes of the nineteenth-century ministers' meetings provide the best introduction and analysis of these meetings, which played a key role in the formation of Old Order Amish identity. For a discussion of the role of the Ordnung in the ministers' meeting, see Gingerich (1986). An Amish deacon from the Lancaster area, "Tennessee" John Stoltzfus, participated in the series of ministers' meetings. His relationship to the meetings is traced by Yoder (1979a, 1979b). See also Yoder and Bender (1979).

14. The progressives in the lower Pequea district formed what eventually

became the Millwood Mennonite church. Progressives in the Conestoga district were the progenitors of what is today the Conestoga Mennonite church. For primary source materials on these divisions, see Yoder (1979a, 1987a). A discussion of the Conestoga division can be found in Mast and Mast (1982). For the Pequea division, see King (1977).

15. Steering Committee (1983:35–36).

16. *Diary* (1975:7:80).

17. A seventh organization is the Amish Book Committee, which publishes the *Ausbund,* prayerbooks and other religious books. It was founded in 1913. A detailed history of its origins is recorded in *Diary* (1970:2:191–95).

18. Although Fisher (1978:379) gives 1885 as the date of origin, the Amish Historical Library in Aylmer, Ontario, has a professionally printed policy from the Amish Aid Insurance Company dated 1879, suggesting it originated prior to 1879.

19. For historical background on Amish Aid, see Fisher (1978:335, 379) and *Diary* (1973:5:86).

20. *Directory* (1973:19–24).

21. *Diary* (1969:1:4; 1976:8:177).

22. For the minutes of the annual meetings, see Steering Committee (1966–86).

23. Steering Committee (1971:58).

24. *Diary* (1973:5:4).

25. *Rules* (1983).

26. *Articles* (1984).

27. The Pequea Bruderschaft Library primarily collects materials related to the Lancaster settlement. The Amish Historical Library in Aylmer, Ontario, holds a collection of Amish-related materials covering all the settlements.

28. *Ordnung* (1983:37).

29. Wagler (n.d.:7).

30. *Standards* (1981:41).

5. Rites of Redemption and Purification

1. Gingerich (1986:181).

2. Beiler (1982:383).

3. *Ordnung* (1983).

4. Beiler (1982:383).

5. The eighteen articles of the Dordrecht Confession of Faith form the basis of the instruction classes. The classes emphasize the importance of baptism and communion as the principal components of "true Christian faith." At the end of the instruction period, applicants are asked a series of questions to measure their theological knowledge—for example, "Who has called you?" "Who has redeemed you?" The last session of instruction emphasizes the importance of complying with the Ordnung and the ministers make "it very clear to the applicants what kind of a covenant they are making" (*Handbuch* [1978:24–26]). The Lancaster ministers' manual says the candidates are to be asked several times if they are willing to submit to the order of the church (*Gemein* [n.d.:4]).

6. Hostetler (1980:81).

7. *Handbuch* (1978:26), *Gemein* (n.d.:6), and informants.

---

8. *Handbuch* (1978:25) and *Gemein* (n.d.:5–7).

9. The description of the worship service is based on participant observation in worship services in Lancaster County in the spring of 1986.

10. Hostetler (1980:212–13).

11. For background and scholarly sources on the *Ausbund,* consult the *Mennonite Encyclopedia* (1956), vol. 2, s.v. "Ausbund," as well as Bartel (1986), Hostetler (1980:225–30), Luthy (1971b), Ressler (1986), and Schreiber (1962a). The first known European edition, published in 1564, has been followed by many other editions and printings. The American edition used in the Lancaster settlement includes stories of some forty Swiss Anabaptists who suffered severe persecution between 1635 and 1645. These vivid stories of suffering have been translated and published by Kauffman (1975).

12. Ressler's (1978) article details the background of this hymn and its use among the Amish and Mennonites.

13. Gibbons (1869:59–69).

14. *Handbuch* (1978:21–22).

15. Luthy (1975) describes Amish ordination customs across several settlements.

16. *Gemein* (n.d.:10–11).

17. *Handbuch* (1978:33).

18. The use of the lot is based on the account recorded in Acts 1:23–26, where lots were cast to select someone to replace Judas Iscariot.

19. The Lancaster ministers' manual distinguishes between "sins of brotherhood or weakness that can be corrected between brothers . . . and sins of carnality, such as adultery, fornication. . . ." The more serious sins, which also include "inordinate living, idleness in useless words, business conduct, and external appearances," are cause for cutting sinners off like a branch until they are willing to be fruitful again. This six-week exclusion is sometimes referred to as "setting someone back from counsel." They are to take no part in members' meetings or in communion and should not receive the brotherly greeting, or kiss (*Gemein* [n.d.:18–20]).

20. *Handbuch* (1978:26–28) and informants.

21. Technically, the ban or excommunication refers to the exclusion of members from communion and the fellowship of the church. The six-week exclusion from communion is sometimes called the *small ban,* in contrast to the *big ban*—excommunication. *Meidung,* or shunning, refers to the social avoidance of those who are excommunicated or excluded from communion. Because the *Bann,* or excommunication, automatically implies *Meidung,* in everyday discourse *Bann* and *Meidung* are used interchangeably. Such overlap of terminology occurs in the Lancaster County bishop's statement on *Bann und Meidung* in *Bericht* (1943).

22. *Dordrecht* (1976:35).

23. The Moses Hartz controversy at the turn of the century, in Lancaster County (discussed in chapter 7), prompted debate on whether people who left the Amish church for a more progressive group, such as the Mennonites, should be shunned. Those who advocated a strong shunning (*Streng Meidung*) felt that such people should be shunned by the Old Order Amish. More progressive members felt that the shunning should be relaxed in such a case. The debate surrounding the Hartz case was one of the factors leading to the 1910 division. Even after this division, the debate continued to smolder, until the Old Order bishops issued a special statement in 1921, in which they argued

that they were not practicing a new form of shunning but were merely following the traditional Amish custom, as agreed to in a ministers' meeting in 1809
and as taught by Bishop David Beiler in 1861. Discussion of the proper application of shunning continued during the first half of the century, prompting
publication of several statements on it in *Bericht* (1943). The long and heated
debates over the use of shunning from 1693 to the present testify to its potent
power as a social control device and to its cardinal role in Amish identity and
polity.

24. *Dordrecht* (1976:36). Scripture verses that are used to support the practice of shunning, identified in the Dordrecht Confession of Faith, include
1 Cor. 5:9–11; Rom. 16:17; 2 Thess. 3:14, 15; and Titus 3:10, 11.

25. *Bericht* (1943:2).

26. When a major internal division occurs within the Amish church, members are given a grace period—a time to decide whether they want to leave
without the threat of ostracism. The grace period ends if someone excommunicated by the Old Order Amish is later accepted into the more liberal group
without a confession. In other words, when the splinter group no longer respects the *Bann* that the Old Order Amish apply to their wayward members,
the lines are drawn. After that, Old Order members who transfer to the more
liberal group are shunned. This was the case in both the 1910 and 1966 divisions in Lancaster County. Thus, Old Order members who joined the New Order Amish in 1966 at the time of the division are not shunned by the Old Order
Amish. However, today Old Order members who joined the New Order Amish
after the period of grace are shunned.

6. Passing on the Faith

1. For a chronology of Amish court cases involving educational disputes,
as well as the landmark 1972 Supreme Court decision, see Keim (1975). A history of Amish education prior to 1968 is summarized by Cline (1968:73–121).
See also Hostetler and Huntington (1971:97–104).

2. Keim (1975:163).

3. Wickersham (1886:168).

4. *Diary* (1972:4:155).

5. Fisher (1978:312).

6. Fisher (1978:313).

7. Harnish (1925).

8. This series of anonymous articles appeared in *Intelligencer* in four in-
stallments in 1931 (19 Feb., 20 Feb., 21 Feb., and 10 Mar.).

9. The East Lampeter Township dispute of 1937 and 1938 is chronicled in
two local Lancaster papers, *Intelligencer Journal* and *New Era*. It also received national press coverage. See especially the *Intelligencer*. For 1937: 26
Mar., 29 Apr., 13 May, 15 May, 27 May, 28 May, 12 June, 24 June, 3 July, 7 July,
20 Aug., 30 Sept., 2 Oct., 5 Oct., 30 Oct., 6 Nov., 9 Nov., 10 Nov., 11 Nov., 4 Dec.,
6 Dec., 7 Dec., 24 Dec., 30 Dec. For 1938: 4 Feb., 9 Feb., 24 Feb., 28 June.

10. Because lawyers were involved, the Amish community was divided internally over the East Lampeter Township dispute. However, a substantial
portion of Amish residents in the township supported the resistance to the
consolidated school. Approximately twenty Amishmen rode the train to the

Federal Court Building in Philadelphia to attend a hearing on 12 May 1937 (*Intelligencer* [13 May 1937]).

11. Historical documentation of the Amish school movement in Lancaster County is preserved in *The Papers of the Amish School Controversy* (1937–68). This excellent collection of Aaron E. Beiler's papers contains the petitions, correspondence, and minutes of the Old Order Amish School Committee, which first met on 14 September 1937 at the home of Stephen F. Stoltzfus, its first chairman. He moved to Maryland in 1940. Beiler was then appointed chairman and served in that role until his death in 1968 (*Directory* [1973:20–21]). A booklet describing the move to Maryland in 1940 was published twenty-five years later (*Amish Moving to Maryland* [1965]). Unless otherwise indicated, this chapter's citations of Amish positions, attitudes, and actions are based on documents in *Papers* (1937–68). Several documents from this collection were published by Eli M. Shirk (1939) as part of a booklet he prepared on the history of the school controversy. Shirk was an Old Order Mennonite leader who worked closely with the Amish School Committee.

12. *Papers* (27 Mar. 1937).

13. *Papers* (2 Sept. 1937).

14. *Papers* (14 Sept. 1937).

15. *Papers* (28 Sept. 1937).

16. *Papers* (17 Nov. 1937).

17. *Gemeinden* (1937:4).

18. For documentation related to this case, see Keim (1975:94) and *Intelligencer* (17 Nov. 1937, 18 Nov. 1937, 24 Nov. 1937, 2 Dec. 1937, 3 Dec. 1937, 29 Jan. 1938, 1 Feb. 1938).

19. *Papers* (12 Jan. 1938).

20. *Papers* (13 Jan. 1938).

21. *Papers* (27 Jan. 1938).

22. *Papers* (23 Mar. 1938).

23. *Papers* (22 July 1938).

24. The sale of public one-room schools is reported in *Intelligencer* (10 Nov. 1938). *Directory* (1973) provides a chronological listing of the opening of Amish schools from 1938 to 1973.

25. *Papers* (4 Feb. 1941).

26. *Papers* (1 July 1943).

27. Keim (1975:95).

28. For a review of the court cases that were tested during these years, including several in Lancaster County, see Cline (1968:109–15).

29. "Statement" (1950).

30. *Intelligencer* (30 Sept. 1950).

31. *Intelligencer* (21 Sept. 1950).

32. Smith (1961:247) and Keim (1975:96).

33. *Papers* (30 Aug. 1953).

34. *Papers* (30 Sept. 1953).

35. *Papers* (11 Dec. 1953).

36. Guidelines for the Vocational School Program were spelled out in memorandums from the Pennsylvania Department of Public Instruction (22 September 1955 and 16 January 1956) and are included in *Papers* (1937–68). The program conceived by the Amish was first approved in a joint meeting of the bishops and the school committee on 30 September 1953 (*Papers* [30 Sept.

1953]). A printed version of the principles governing the program was later distributed in pamphlet form—*Vocation* (1956). For another discussion of the vocational school program, see Hostetler and Huntington (1971:71–79). Amish views and vocational school policies can be found in *Vocation* (1956) and *Standards* (1981).

37. The first vocational school classes were held at the Aaron F. Stoltzfus home in Upper Leacock Township. The vocational program was supervised by the Old Order Amish School Committee; see *Directory* (1973:21). It marked the end of the legal battles, begun in 1937, and ushered in a new era of peaceful coexistence in Pennsylvania. The vocational school solution became a model for some other localities as well. In some states legal disputes continued until they were silenced by the Supreme Court decision of 1972 which affirmed the right of the Amish to keep their children out of public high schools. For an excellent discussion of the Supreme Court ruling, see Keim (1975). The vocational program continues in the Lancaster settlement out of respect to the agreement negotiated with the Commonwealth of Pennsylvania between 1953 and 1955. In some other localities the program has been discontinued.

38. *Papers* (9 Aug. 1954).

39. This summary of the reasons behind the Amish protest of consolidated high schools was gleaned from numerous source documents in *Papers* (1937–68).

40. This quote is in the summary paragraph of a four-page review of the history of the Amish School Controversy, covering the years 1937–50. It was likely compiled by Aaron E. Beiler sometime after 18 February 1950, and the statement is probably his. The undated historical review "Repeal from 1937 Enactment" is with Beiler's documents in *Papers* (1937–68).

41. For an extended treatment of Amish schools and childhood socialization, see Hostetler and Huntington (1971). Fisher and Stahl (1986) provide an insider's view of the daily routines and organization of the one-room Amish school. See Esh (1977) for an Amishman's account of the development of Amish schools.

42. *Blackboard* (1986:9–23).

43. *Standards* (1981:2).

44. Hostetler and Huntington (1971:92).

45. *Standards* (1981:30).

46. *Guidelines* (1981:12).

47. The Old Order Book Society evolved out of the School Committee, which first met in 1937 to protest the new school-attendance laws.

48. *Standards* (1981:31).

49. Outley (1982:45).

50. Township supervisors wrote to an Amish official and asked him "to do all in your power to correct the drinking and drunkenness that presently prevails among Amish youth . . . according to records the last fatal accidents that occurred in Leacock township were either the direct results of, or involved drinking Amish youth." The Lancaster bishops, in response to this plea, met and agreed upon five points of an Ordnung which in rare fashion was published (*Ordnung* [1983], Steering Committee [1983:35–36]).

7. The Riddles of Technology

1. For extended treatments of the Moses Hartz incident, consult Hostetler (1980:277–80), Yoder (1987:103–6), Hartz and Hartz (1965), and Mast and Mast (1982:83–87). The most detailed analysis of this never-ending affair and a list of source documents are provided by Paton Yoder (n.d.) in chapter 13 of "Amish Church Affairs in the Nineteenth Century." Virtually all of the published accounts were written by Mennonites or Amish-Mennonites. Amos J. Stoltzfus (n.d.), who witnessed the episode as a young church member, wrote from an Old Order Amish perspective.

2. The Hartzes were received into the Conestoga Amish-Mennonite congregation after making a "kneeling" confession of failure—one of several options recommended by an out-of-state committee called in to investigate the matter. Old Order Amish preacher David Beiler is typically cited as spearheading the renewed shunning of the Hartzes. Paton Yoder (n.d.) points out, however, that a single minister could not have brought about the reversal without the support of others, including the bishops.

3. *Bericht* (1943).

4. The text of the "demand" for a more lenient interpretation of shunning, and a threat to secede from the Old Order Amish, dated 29 September 1909, was reprinted in *Bericht* (1943). No names were signed to the "demand," and in their response the bishops curtly noted that "ordinarily one pays little attention to letters without names" (*Bericht* [1943:5]). The bishops also argued that their interpretation of shunning simply followed "what the old bishops and ministers taught concerning separation and shunning, some forty, sixty or up to a hundred years ago. We want nothing else than to stay in what we have been taught" (*Bericht* [1943:5]).

5. The separation began when the dissenting group made its demand on 29 September 1909. The first worship service with ordained ministers present, on 27 February 1910, marks the formal culmination of the division. Thus I have used the year 1910 in the text to mark this schism. For a chronology of the events surrounding the division, see Glick (1986) and Lapp (1963). The most extensive discussion, written from the progressive point of view, is included in Yoder's (1987:103–12) history of the Beachy Amish.

6. Christian J. Beiler (1850–1934) was a spokesman for the dissenting group, but the name Peachey church was used, because Samuel W. Peachey and, in a lesser role, Christian D. Peachey, from Mifflin County, Pennsylvania, were instrumental in providing ministerial leadership to the group in its first two years (Yoder [1987:108–9]). After Christian L. King was ordained bishop on 24 April 1913, the group was sometimes referred to as the King church. With a small following, Christian L. King broke off from the Peachey church in 1925 and formed a separate King church, which eventually became defunct. The Peachey church remained a viable group under the leadership of John A. Stoltzfus, who was ordained bishop in April 1926. After that the Peachey church was sometimes called the "John A. church," but the Peachey label prevailed until the group began worshipping in the Weavertown Church building in 1930. The local historian of the group traces the further evolution of the name: "After the church house at Weavertown was acquired it [the group] became known as the Weavertown Amish-Mennonite Church. When the Church joined the Beachy Affiliation it became known as a Beachy Amish-Mennonite denomination" (Lapp [1963:11]). The group affiliated with the Beachy Amish

in 1950. For a recent history of the congregations in that affiliation, see Yoder (1987). Today three congregations (Weavertown, Pequea, and Mine Road) represent the growth of the original body. Since 1969 several small groups, springing from the Old Order Amish division of 1966, have also affiliated with the Beachy Amish. The membership of all Beachy Amish congregations in Lancaster County today is less than one thousand (Yoder 1987:84, 351–55; Kraybill 1985).

7. Yoder (1987:125–27, 351–55).

8. Lapp (1963), Yoder (1987) and Glick (1986), writing from the progressive perspective, emphasize the strict interpretation of shunning as the cause for the division.

9. The written demand of the withdrawing group and the response of the bishops, recorded in *Bericht* (1943), clearly identifies the strict interpretation of shunning as the ostensible reason for the division.

10. This perception was confirmed by several leaders and oral historians when asked about the reasons for the 1910 division. Regardless of the phone's actual role in the division, its importance in the schism may have increased over time in the Amish mind as a means of diverting attention from the severe enforcement of shunning. Of the Amish use of phones, Amishman John K. Lapp (1986:7) says "some were willing to put them away and others were not, so that is when the Kinig gma [Peachey church] started, the phone was one of the issues but I suppose there were some more." Amish minister Beiler, in the foreword of Gingerich and Kreider (1986:14), says the 1910 schism was "caused by indifferent views in church discipline, most concerning newly invented contraptions that our conservative church leaders could not tolerate." In contrast, oral historians in the progressive group contend that as late as 1916 members of the Peachey church were asked to take out phones when they bought a farm that had them. This suggests that the Peachey church did not accept the phone for at least six years after the division.

11. Fletcher (1955:525).

12. A similar version of Amish phone usage in the early days is provided by John K. Lapp, born in 1897 (Lapp 1986:7).

13. Lapp (1986:7).

14. Fletcher (1955:525).

15. Berger (1979:6–7) briefly discusses the phone as an instrument of modernity which requires a technological mentality.

16. Armstrong and Feldman (1986:65).

17. *Diary* (1976:8:43).

18. Hostetler (1984).

19. Some farmers installed phones in sheds near their barns in order to call the artificial inseminator for their cows. This was particularly irksome to some bishops, who were opposed to artificial insemination of dairy cows.

20. Klein (1941:101).

21. Fletcher (1955:62–65).

22. The use of the Delco and Genco plants by members of the Peachey church was confirmed by several Old Order Amish informants. Surprisingly, an Old Order Amishman remembers taking his batteries to a member of the Peachey church to have them charged.

23. Throughout the text, the distinction between 12-volt and 110-volt current is simplified for the sake of clarity. While the distinction for the most part is correct, there are minor technical variations. As electricity was coming

into use, different types of batteries produced various levels of voltage. The Amish had always accepted the simple dry cell battery, but they opposed the Genco and Delco plants, which used wet cell batteries and produced a variety of voltages for electric light bulbs. As electrical technology changed over the years, the Amish continued to accept the use of direct current stored in batteries, which typically is 12 volts. They opposed the use of alternating current taken from the public utility lines, which normally is 110 volts. Their substantive opposition was to electricity from public power lines or in a form—even though home-generated—that could be used to operate standard electrical motors and appliances, rather than to the specific voltage level per se. For all practical purposes, this amounted to a distinction between 12-volt and 110-volt current.

8. Harnessing the Power of Progress

1. Klein (1941:119).
2. Klein (1941:120).
3. Fletcher (1955:525).
4. Fletcher (1955:328).
5. Amish historians and informants are not able to pinpoint a specific date for the ban on car ownership, because the church never seriously considered such ownership. By 1917, Mennonite bishops in the Lancaster area were buying cars. It is likely that the Amish consensus against cars had crystallized before this time. The date 1915, however, is an estimate based on conversations with Amish people who recall this time. In any event, the car taboo emerged over several years as cars were coming into popular use.
6. Flink (1975:2).
7. Fletcher (1955:330). For a discussion of the social effects of the car, see Allen (1957), who concludes that they are so numerous as to be incalculable.
8. Flink (1975:40).
9. For an Amishman's view of the pros and cons of car ownership, see Wagler (n.d.). A statistical analysis of the use of the car for travel between the Amish settlement in Nappanee, Indiana, and other Amish settlements is provided by Landing (1972).
10. *New Era* (18 Feb. 1977).
11. A record of the controversy surrounding the PUC regulation of Amish taxis can be found in *Intelligencer* and *New Era*. See especially *New Era* (18 Feb. 1977, 22 Feb. 1977, 8 Mar. 1977, 1 Nov. 1977, 21 Apr. 1978) and *Intelligencer* (23 Feb. 1977, 2 Mar. 1977, 9 Mar. 1977, 17 Mar. 1977).
12. *Intelligencer* (1 Mar. 1977).
13. Ivan Glick, in a letter to the author of 26 August 1987, reports that this farmer was Martin Shirk of Churchtown.
14. Tractor use by the Amish in fields was reported by numerous informants and is also documented by Amishman Lapp (1986:9) in his memoirs.
15. All of the informants living during the first two decades of the twentieth century agree that the Amish church had few if any restrictions on the purchase and use of new farm machinery at that time. Rather than lagging behind their neighbors, Amish farmers often were the first ones in the community to buy new implements as they became available on the public market.

For a history of farming practices and equipment use, see Amishman Fisher's (1978) account of social change on the farm.

16. A similar story of the tractor to car scenario was given by three other informants. Wagler (n.d.:20) makes the same argument.

17. The hay baler brought the first widespread use of gasoline engines. However, some Amish farmers had used "open hopper" engines without radiators on potato diggers before balers came into use.

18. The bishops forbade the use of six mechanical items: combine, forage harvester, barn cleaner, power unit, generator for lights and power, and deep freezer. This list was confirmed by several informants and is explicitly documented in Kauffman's (1962) minutes of the special ministers' meeting held 19 December 1962.

19. Hay balers are not self-propelled. This may have contributed to the ease with which they slipped into practice among Amish farmers. The use of any self-propelled equipment would, in the long run, remove the horse from the field.

20. The technology used to farm and harvest tobacco has changed very little since the early twentieth century. Tobacco production is difficult to mechanize and remains labor intensive. Tobacco farming is on the decline largely because of unstable tobacco prices and other sources of farm and nonfarm income.

21. Kauffman (1962).

22. A systematic account of this division has not been written. The best documentary source is the minutes of the special ministers' meeting, 19 December 1962, recorded by Kauffman (1962). Renno (1985:6–9) has written a brief description of the division but many of his details are not correct, according to oral historians. Beiler (n.d.) has written a short description of the different groups that evolved from the division. See also Yoder (1987:354–56) for a description of the offshoot congregations that eventually affiliated with the Beachy Amish. Although six ordained leaders dissented from the bishops' ruling on the six articles, only two ministers actually left the Old Order Amish. The formal separation occurred 5 June 1966 at a special ministers' meeting. One of the ministers eventually rejoined the Old Order Amish. Members of the Old Order Amish were given several months to decide if they wanted to join the New Order group. Members who chose to transfer during this grace period are not shunned. However, members who joined the progressive group after the grace period ended are shunned by the Old Order Amish.

9. The Transformation of Amish Work

1. For example, Ericksen, Ericksen, and Hostetler (1980:49) argue "that the Old Order Amish culture is largely maintained by the ability of individual Amish families to establish their children on farms."

2. *Directory* (1977).

3. Amish farmer and sage Gideon L. Fisher (1978) wrote a book that examines changes in farm life and provides an Amish view of agriculture.

4. *Standards* (1981:49).

5. *Directory* (1977:3).

6. *Directory* (1977:3).

7. Kollmorgen (1942:29).

8. *Directory* (1977:3).

9. Martineau and MacQueen (1977:384).

10. Kollmorgen (1942:27).

11. *Farm* (1987:6). For an excellent discussion of development issues and pressures in Lancaster County, see the six-day series by Ed Klimuska in *New Era* (27 June–2 July 1988).

12. Kollmorgen (1942:23).

13. *Intelligencer* (7 Apr. 1975).

14. Scholarly articles by Martineau and MacQueen (1977) and by Ericksen, Ericksen, and Hostetler (1980) discuss the impact of nonfarm occupations on the Amish of Lancaster County. Two series in local newspapers have also charted the trend toward nonfarm work (*Intelligencer* [7 Apr. 1975, 8 Apr. 1975] and *New Era* [30 July 1987, 31 July 1987]).

15. Schwieder and Schwieder (1975:53).

16. A history of the Amish migrations to Centre and Clinton counties, Pennsylvania, as well as a directory of those settlements, has been compiled (*Directory* 1973). The last major settlement outside Lancaster County was established in Dauphin County in 1978.

17. *Directory* (1980:2).

18. *New Era* (22 May 1986).

19. The recent settlement in Romulus, New York, has Lancaster lineage but originated from the Brush Valley settlement in central Pennsylvania.

20. *Directory* (1977).

21. *Directory* (1977:3).

22. In an informal survey of one Lancaster district, in 1987 a member reported that, among the married men who had not retired, 37 percent were day workers, 19 percent owned their own business, 11 percent farmed and had a shop, and 33 percent were full-time farmers (*Botschaft* [15 Sept. 1987]).

23. Ed Klimuska's excellent five-part series on the dramatic growth of the quilting industry in Lancaster County appeared in *New Era* (9–13 Mar. 1987) and was reprinted in 1987 in a booklet entitled *Lancaster County: Quilt Capital USA.*

24. Meyers (1983b:177) argues that the presence of ethnic support and network systems in occupational settings—more than the type of work per se—is the critical factor in determining whether the shift away from farming will lead to the collapse of Amish society.

25. Meyers (1983b) conducted a study of stress related to nonfarm occupations among the Amish in Indiana settlements. He found few stress-related differences between Amish farmers and Amish factory workers. The proportion of Amishmen working in modern non-Amish factories varies considerably by settlement. He reported that in the Indiana settlements 20 percent of Amishmen were employed in factories. Foster (1984b) reports that in an Ohio settlement 37 percent of Amishmen were employed in nonfarm traditional work and 32 percent were employed in nontraditional (including factory) work.

26. *New Era* (30 July 1987).

27. For coverage of the zoning problems related to the Amish, see *Intelligencer* (15 Aug. 1987, 18 Aug. 1987, 3 Mar. 1988).

28. *Directory* (1977:1).

29. The hay turner is an advancement over the older hay tedders, because the turner breaks fewer leaves and turns the hay completely upside down.

30. On the discrepancy of practices between shops and farms, as well as numerous reader responses, see *Family Life* (April 1987:31–32; June 1987:16–25).

10. Managing Public Relations

1. Amishman Isaac Glick served as postmaster in the village of Smoketown in the second decade of the twentieth century.

2. Steering Committee (1986:76).

3. Steering Committee (1966:1).

4. Kinsinger (1983:596).

5. Cline (1968:145). My discussion of Social Security is heavily indebted to Cline's work and to an Amish informant involved in negotiations with government officials.

6. Cline (1968:164).

7. For a lengthy description of this case and subsequent legal action surrounding it, see Cline (1968:148–55).

8. In recent years some Amish have opened Individual Retirement Accounts (IRAs). In several cases the IRS revoked the Social Security exemption of those Amish holding IRAs. The IRS position on this issue was unclear at first, but in the late eighties the IRS prohibited the Amish from holding IRAs.

9. For an extended discussion of the Amish reaction to this film as well as a chronology of events, see Hostetler and Kraybill (1988).

10. *Intelligencer* (26 Jan. 1985).

11. *Intelligencer* (28 Feb. 1985).

12. For a history of Amish tourism in Lancaster County, see an excellent article by Luthy (1980). The booklet was Steinfeldt's (1937) *The Amish of Lancaster County*. Fisher (1988) describes the rise of tourism from a local Amishman's view.

13. Fisher (1978:365).

14. Beiler (1976b:482).

15. Beiler (1976b:482).

16. *Intelligencer* (28 Jan. 1988).

11. Regulating Social Change

1. For a structural analysis of social change, see Gallagher's (1981) study of the Lancaster Amish settlement. Other discussions of social change among the Amish in a variety of settlements can be found in Foster (1984a), Hostetler (1980:353–62), Huntington (1956:1045–55), Meyers (1983b), Nagata (1968), and Olshan (1980).

2. Kauffman (1962:7).

3. For additional discussions of Amish survival strategies, see Foster (1984a), Hostetler (1980), Stoltzfus (1973), and Thompson (1981).

12. The Dialogue with Modernity

1. Bellah et al. (1985:viii).
2. Berger, Berger, and Kellner (1973) develop this theme in *The Homeless Mind*.
3. Hunter's essay "The Modern Malaise" offers a superb review of the social criticism of modernity since 1930 (Hunter and Ainlay 1986).
4. Olshan (1981:297) notes that many social scientists ritualistically label the Amish a folk society—a small isolated and traditional group—and thus assume that the Amish are not modern. Berger (1977, 1979), Foster (1984b), and Olshan (1981) contend that choice is central to the modern experience. Olshan (1980, 1981) argues that the Amish are not a folk society, but are rather modern because they engage in rational decision making. However, he focuses on their collective decisions and disregards individual choice, which is central to Berger's definition of modernity.
5. The Amish National Steering Committee serves as a quasi-lobby group that intercedes with government officials on behalf of Amish interests. For a record of this group's activities, see Steering Committee (1966–86).
6. This type of rationality corresponds to what Max Weber (1947:115) called *Wertrational*, rational decisions that are made to uphold or promote absolute religious values.
7. Olshan (1979, 1980) points to the Amish as a model for social development. Berry (1977), Foster (1980, 1981, 1982), and Johnson, Stoltzfus and Craumer (1977) have described the energy efficiency of Amish culture.
8. In their comprehensive study of mental illness in the Lancaster settlement, Egeland and Hostetter (1983:59) report that major affective mental disorders among the Amish are about half the rate of such disorders in other groups. A study of Amish suicide in the Lancaster area found the Amish rate was half that of other religious groups and one-third the rate of nonreligious populations (Kraybill, Hostetler, and Shaw 1986:256–57).
9. In severe cases of psychiatric disorder, Amish people are hospitalized. People with mild psychiatric disorders, retardation, and physical disabilities are cared for by the extended family whenever possible.
10. The notions of freedom and meaning in Amish life are addressed by Olshan (1986). For a perceptive analysis of the Amish plight with modernity, see Enninger (1988).

SELECT BIBLIOGRAPHY

Allen, Francis R.
1957   "The Automobile." In *Technology and Social Change*, edited by
        Francis Allen et al. New York: Appleton-Century-Crofts.
Amish Moving to Maryland, The
1965   Gordonville, Pa.: Printed by A. S. Kinsinger.
Armstrong, Penny, and Sheryl Feldman
1986   *A Midwife's Story*. New York: Arbor House.
Articles of Incorporation of the Pequea Bruderschaft Library
1984   Pequea Bruderschaft Library. Intercourse, Pa.
Ausbund, Das ist: Etliche schöne christlicher Lieder
1984   Lancaster, Pa.: Lancaster Press. First ed. in 1564.
Bachman, Calvin G.
1961   *The Old Order Amish of Lancaster County*. Pennsylvania German
        Society, vol. 60. A reprint of vol. 49, first published in 1941.
Bartel, Lee R.
1986   "The Tradition of the Amish in Music." *Hymn* 37(October):20–26.
Beam, C. Richard
1982   *Pennsylvania German Dictionary*. Schaefferstown, Pa.: Historic
        Schaefferstown.
Beiler, Abner
n.d.   "A Brief History of the New Order Amish Church, 1966–1976."
        Lancaster Mennonite Historical Society Library. Lancaster, Pa.
Beiler, David
1888   *Das Wahre Christenthum: Eine Christliche Betrachtung nach den
        Lehren der Heiligen Schrift*. Lancaster, Pa.: Johann Baers and
        Son.
Beiler, Joseph F.
1976a   "Eighteenth-Century Amish in Lancaster Community." *Menno-
        nite Research Journal* 17(October):37, 46.
1976b   "The Tourist Season." *Gospel Herald* 8(June):482.
1977   "Amish History in Lancaster County." *Mennonite Research Jour-
        nal* 17(April):16.
1982   "Ordnung." *Mennonite Quarterly Review* 56(October):382–84.
1983   "A Review of the Founding of the Lancaster County Church Set-
        tlement." *Diary* 15(December):17–22.

Bellah, R. N., R. Madsen, W. M. Sullivan, A. Swidler, and S. M. Tipton
1985 *Habits of the Heart*. Berkeley and Los Angeles: University of California Press.

Bender, Harold S.
1946 "The Minutes of the Conference of 1809 Probably Held in Lancaster County, Pennsylvania." *Mennonite Quarterly Review* 20(July): 241–42.
1957 "The Anabaptist Vision." In *The Recovery of the Anabaptist Vision*, edited by Guy F. Hershberger. Scottdale, Pa.: Herald Press.

Berger, Peter L.
1967 *The Sacred Canopy*. Garden City, N.Y.: Doubleday.
1974 *Pyramids of Sacrifice*. Garden City, N.Y.: Doubleday.
1977 *Facing Up to Modernity*. New York: Basic Books.
1979 *The Heretical Imperative*. Garden City, N.Y.: Doubleday.

Berger, Peter L., Brigitte Berger, and Hansfried Kellner
1973 *The Homeless Mind*. New York: Random House.

Berger, Peter L., and Thomas Luckmann
1966 *The Social Construction of Reality*. Garden City, N.Y.: Doubleday.

Bericht und klare Darstellung von Bann und Meidung wie es angesehen ist bei den Alt Amischen in Lancaster County, PA, Ein (A report and clear statement of the ban and shunning as it is understood by the Old Amish of Lancaster County, PA)
1943 Translated by Noah G. Good.

Berry, Wendell
1977 *The Unsettling of America: Culture and Agriculture*. New York: Avon.

Blackboard Bulletin
1957– Alymer, Ont.: Pathway Publishers. Monthly periodical published for Old Order Amish teachers.

Bontreger, Eli J.
1946 "Further Notes on Ordinations." *Mennonite Historical Bulletin* 7(March):4. Exceptions to regular ordination practices are cited.

Botschaft, Die
1975– Vols. 1–13 (1975–88). Lancaster, Pa.: Brookshire Publications and Printing. Described on its masthead as "a weekly newspaper serving Old Order Amish Communities everywhere."

Braght, Thieleman J. van
1951 Comp. *The Bloody Theatre; or, Martyrs Mirror*. Scottdale, Pa.: Mennonite Publishing House. Originally published in Dutch (Dordrecht, 1660).

Brenneman, John M.
1867 *Pride and Humility*. Elkhart, Ind.: John F. Funk. Reprinted 1988. Gordonville, Pa.: Gordonville Print Shop.

Brode, J.
1969 Ed. *The Process of Modernization: An Annotated Bibliography*. Cambridge, Mass.: Harvard University Press.

Bryer, Kathleen B.
1978 "Attitudes toward Death among Amish Families: Implications for Family Therapy." Master's thesis, Hahnemann Medical College.
1979 "The Amish Way of Death: A Study of Family Support Systems." *American Psychologist* 34(March):255–61.

Buck, Roy
 1978 "Boundary Maintenance Revisited: Tourist Experience in an Old Order Amish Community." *Rural Sociology* 43(Summer):221–34.
 1979 "Bloodless Theatre: Images of the Old Order Amish in Tourism Literature." *Pennsylvania Mennonite Heritage* 2(July):2–11.

Budget, The
 1890– Sugarcreek, Ohio. A weekly newspaper serving the Amish and Mennonite communities.

Christlicher Ordnung or Christian Discipline
 1966 A Collection and Translation of Anabaptist and Amish-Mennonite Church Disciplines (Artikel and Ordnungen) of 1527, 1568, 1607, 1630, 1668, 1688, 1779, 1809, 1837, and 1865, with Historical Explanations and Notes, translated by William R. McGrath. Aylmer, Ont.: Pathway Publishers.

Cline, Paul C.
 1968 "Relations between the 'Plain People' and Government in the United States." Ph.D. diss., American University.

Cronk, Sandra L.
 1977 "Gelassenheit: The Rites of the Redemptive Process in Old Order Amish and Old Order Mennonite Communities." Ph.D. diss., University of Chicago. Excerpts under the same title appear in *Mennonite Quarterly Review* 55(January 1981):5–44.

Cross, Harold E.
 1976 "Population Studies and the Old Order Amish." *Nature* 262(1 July):17–20.

Cross, Harold E., and Victor A. McKusick
 1970 "Amish Demography." *Social Biology* 17(June):83–101.

Crowley, William K.
 1978 "The Old Order Amish: Diffusion and Growth." *Annals of the American Geographers* 63(June):249–64.

Diary, The
 1969– Vols. 1–19 (1969–88). Gordonville, Pa.: Pequea Publishers. A monthly church newsletter serving the Old Order Amish Society.

Directory
 1965 *Amish Farm and Home Directory.* Gordonville, Pa.: A. S. Kinsinger.
 1973 *Pennsylvania Amish Directory of Lancaster and Chester County Districts.* Gordonville, Pa.: Pequea Publishers.
 1977 *Old Order Shop and Service Directory: United States and Canada.* Gordonville, Pa.: Pequea Publishers.
 1979 *History and Directory of the Old Order Amish of Brush, Nittany, and Sugar Valleys in Centre and Clinton Counties, Pennsylvania.* Gordonville, Pa.: Pequea Publishers.
 1980 *Amish Directory of the Lancaster County Family.* Gordonville, Pa.: Pequea Publishers.
 1987 *Address Directory of the Lancaster County Amish.* Soudersburg, Pa.: Eby's Quality Printing.

Dordrecht Confession of Faith
 1976 Aylmer, Ont.: Pathway Publishers. Various printings. Adopted by the Mennonites at a Peace Convention held in Dordrecht, Holland, 21 April 1632.

Dyck, Cornelius J.
1981　　*An Introduction to Mennonite History.* 2nd ed. Scottdale, Pa.: Herald Press.
1985　　"The Suffering Church in Anabaptism." *Mennonite Quarterly Review* 59(January):5–23.

Egeland, J., and A. M. Hostetter
1983　　"Amish Study I: Affective Disorders among the Amish, 1976–1980." *American Journal of Psychiatry* 140(January):56–61.

Egeland, J., A. M. Hostetter, and Jean Endicott
1983　　"Amish Study II: Consensus Diagnoses and Reliability Results." *American Journal of Psychiatry* 140(January):62–66.

Egeland, J., A. M. Hostetter, and S. K. Eshleman
1983　　"Amish Study III: The Impact of Cultural Factors on Diagnosis of Bipolar Illness." *American Journal of Psychiatry* 140(January): 67–71.

Egeland, J., and J. Sussex
1985　　"Suicide and Family Loading for Affective Disorders." *Journal of the American Medical Association* 254:915–18.

Ellis, Franklin, and Samuel Evans
1883　　*History of Lancaster County, Pennsylvania, with Biographical Sketches of Many of Its Pioneers and Prominent Men.* Philadelphia: Everts and Peck.

Enninger, Werner
1984　　Ed. *Internal and External Perspectives on Amish and Mennonite Life.* Vol. 1. Essen: Unipress.
1986　　Ed. *Internal and External Perspectives on Amish and Mennonite Life.* Vol. 2. Essen: Unipress.
1988　　"Coping with Modernity: Instrumentally and Symbolically, with a Glimpse at the Old Order Amish." *Brethren Life and Thought* 33(Summer):154–70.

Ericksen, Eugene P., J. A. Ericksen, and J. A. Hostetler
1980　　"The Cultivation of the Soil as a Moral Directive: Population Growth, Family Ties, and the Maintenance of Community among the Old Order Amish." *Rural Sociology* 45(Spring):49–68.

Ericksen, Eugene P., J. A. Ericksen, J. A. Hostetler, and G. E. Huntington
1979　　"Fertility Patterns and Trends among the Old Order Amish." *Population Studies* 33(July):255–76.

Esh, Levi A.
1977　　"The Amish Parochial School Movement." *Mennonite Quarterly Review* 51(January):69–75. Reprinted from 1973 *Directory.*

Family Life
1968–　　Aylmer, Ont.: Pathway Publishers. A monthly Amish periodical.

Farm Sales Analysis: 1984–1986
1987　　Lancaster, Pa.: Lancaster County Agricultural Preserve Board.

Ferster, Herbert V.
1983　　"The Development of the Amish School System." *Pennsylvania Mennonite Heritage* 6(April):7–14.

Fisher, Amos L.
1984　　"History of the First Amish Communities in America." *Diary* 16(September):35–39.

Fisher, Gideon L.
1978   *Farm Life and Its Changes.* Gordonville, Pa.: Pequea Publishers.
1987   Comp. *Ein Diener Register von Diener Deaconien und Bischof in Lancaster County, 1788 to 1987.* 2nd ed. Gordonville, Pa.: Gordonville Print Shop.
1988   "The Early Days of Intercourse." *Diary* 20(June):31–35.
Fisher, Sara E.
1972   "Female Garb among the Amish." Typescript.
Fisher, Sara E., and Rachel K. Stahl
1986   *The Amish School.* Intercourse, Pa.: Good Books.
Fishman, Andrea R.
1987   "Literary and Cultural Context: A Lesson from the Amish." *Language Arts* 64(December):842–54.
Fletcher, S. W.
1955   *Pennsylvania Agriculture and Country Life, 1840–1940.* Harrisburg, Pa.: Pennsylvania Historical and Museum Commission.
Flink, James J.
1975   *The Car Culture.* Cambridge, Mass.: MIT Press.
Foster, George M.
1973   *Traditional Societies and Technological Change.* New York: Harper and Row.
Foster, Thomas W.
1980   "The Amish and the Ethos of Ecology." *Ecologist* 10(December): 331–35.
1981   "Amish Society." *Futurist* 15(December):33–40.
1982   "Learning from the Amish." *New Roots* 21(Winter):16–21.
1984a   "Separation and Survival in Amish Society." *Sociological Focus* 17(January):1–15.
1984b   "Occupational Differentiation and Change in an Ohio Amish Settlement." *Ohio Journal of Science* 84(3):74–81.
Friedmann, Robert
1956   S.v. "Gelassenheit." In *The Mennonite Encyclopedia* 2:444–49. Scottdale, Pa.: Herald Press.
1957   "The Hutterian Brethren and Community of Goods." In *The Recovery of the Anabaptist Vision,* edited by Guy F. Hershberger. Scottdale, Pa.: Herald Press.
1973   *The Theology of Anabaptism.* Scottdale, Pa.: Herald Press.
Frey, J. William
1981   *A Simple Grammar of Pennsylvania Dutch.* Lancaster, Pa.: John Baers and Son.
Gallagher, Thomas E., Jr.
1981   "Clinging to the Past or Preparing for the Future? The Structure of Selective Modernization among Old Order Amish of Lancaster County, Pennsylvania." Ph.D. diss., Temple University.
Gascho, Milton
1937   "The Amish Division 1693–1697 in Switzerland and Alsace." *Mennonite Quarterly Review* 11(October):235–66.
Gemeinden, Ein Bericht an Die (A notification to the congregations)
1937   Translated by Noah G. Good. N.p.
Gemein Ordnungen von Lancaster Co., PA (Church ordinances of Lancaster County, PA)

n.d.   Translated by Noah G. Good. N.p.
Getz, Jane C.
1946   "The Economic Organization and Practices of the Old Order Amish of Lancaster County, Pennsylvania." *Mennonite Quarterly Review* 20(January):53–80; 20(April):98–127.
Gibbons, Phebe Earle
1869   "Pennsylvania Dutch" was first published in the *Atlantic Monthly* in October 1869. It then appeared in *Pennsylvania Dutch and Other Essays* in 1872 and was reprinted in 1874 and 1882. Philadelphia: Lippincott.
Gillin, John
1948   "Cultural Situations: Social Life and Customs." In *The Ways of Men: An Introduction to Anthropology*. New York: Appleton-Century-Crofts. A description of the Lancaster County Amish based on the Kollmorgen (1942) study.
Gingerich, H. F., and R. W. Kreider
1986   Comp. *Amish and Amish-Mennonite Genealogies*. Gordonville, Pa.: Pequea Publishers.
Gingerich, James Nelson
1986   "Ordinance or Ordering: *Ordnung* and the Amish Ministers Meeting, 1862–1878." *Mennonite Quarterly Review* 60(April):180–99.
Gingerich, Melvin
1970   *Mennonite Attire through Four Centuries*. Breinigsville, Pa.: Pennsylvania German Society.
Glick, Aaron S.
1986   "A Chronicle of Events Relating to the 1910 Peachey Church Division." Handwritten.
1987   "Pequea Amish Mennonite Church Twenty-Fifth Anniversary." Mimeo.
Gougler, Richard C.
1973   "Amish Weddings." *Pennsylvania Folklife* 22(suppl.):12–13.
Guidelines in Regards to the Old Order Amish and Mennonite Parochial Schools
1981   Gordonville, Pa.: Gordonville Print Shop.
Handbuch für Bischof (Handbook for bishops)
1978   Translated by Noah G. Good. Gordonville, Pa.: Gordonville Print Shop. Published in 1935; reprinted in 1978.
Harnish, C. H.
1925   Letter to the Voters of Upper Leacock Township, 19 October 1925, in *Papers*.
Hartz, Amos, and Susan Hartz
1965   Comp. *Moses Hartz Family History, 1819–1965*. Elverson, Pa.
Hershberger, Guy F.
1951   *The Mennonite Church in the Second World War*. Scottdale, Pa.: Herald Press.
Hopple, C. Lee
1971, 1972 "Spatial Development of the Southeastern Pennsylvania Plain Dutch Community to 1970." Parts 1 and 2. *Pennsylvania Folklife* 21(Winter 1971):18–40; 21(Spring 1972):36–45.

Horst, Irvin B.

1982   "Dordrecht Confession of Faith: 350 Years." *Pennsylvania Mennonite Heritage* 5(July):2–8.

1986   "Menno Simons: The Road to a Believer's Church." *Pennsylvania Mennonite Heritage* 9(July):2–12.

1988   Ed. and trans. *Mennonite Confession of Faith* (Dordrecht). Lancaster, Pa.: Lancaster Mennonite Historical Society.

Hostetler, John A.

1951   *Annotated Bibliography on the Old Order Amish.* Scottdale, Pa.: Mennonite Publishing House.

1963   "The Amish Use of Symbols and Their Function in Bounding the Community." *Journal of the Royal Anthropological Institute* 94, pt.1:11–22.

1968   Ed. "Anabaptist Conceptions of Child Nurture and Schooling: A Collection of Source Materials Used by the Old Order Amish." Temple University, Philadelphia, Pa. Typescript.

1969   "Educational Achievement and Lifestyles in a Traditional Society, the Old Order Amish." Temple University, Philadelphia, Pa. Typescript.

1974   *Hutterite Society.* Baltimore: Johns Hopkins University Press.

1977   "Old Order Amish Survival." *Mennonite Quarterly Review* 51(October):352–61.

1979   "The Old Order Amish on the Great Plains: A Study in Cultural Vulnerability." In *Ethnicity on the Great Plains,* edited by Fred Leubke. Lincoln: University of Nebraska Press.

1980   *Amish Society.* 3rd ed. Baltimore: Johns Hopkins University Press.

1984   "Silence and Survival Strategies among the New and Old Order Amish." In *Internal and External Perspectives on Amish and Mennonite Life,* edited by Werner Enninger. Vol. 1. Essen: Unipress.

1988   "Land Use, Ethics, and Agriculture in Lancaster County." Typescript.

Hostetler, John A., and Gertrude E. Huntington

1971   *Children in Amish Society: Socialization and Community Education.* New York: Holt, Rinehart and Winston.

Hostetler, John A., and Donald B. Kraybill

1988   "Hollywood Markets the Amish." In *Image Ethics: The Moral Rights of Subjects in Photography, Film and Television,* edited by John Katz and Jay Ruby. New York: Oxford University Press.

Huffines, Marion Lois

1988   "Pennsylvania German among the Plain Groups: Convergence as a Strategy of Language Maintenance." In *Pennsylvania Mennonite Heritage* 11(July):12–16.

Hunter, James Davison

1983   *American Evangelicalism.* New Brunswick, N.J.: Rutgers University Press.

Hunter, James Davison, and Stephen C. Ainlay

1986   Eds. *Making Sense of Modern Times: Peter L. Berger and the Vision of Interpretive Sociology.* New York: Routledge and Kegan Paul.

Huntington, Gertrude E.
1956   "Dove at the Window: A Study of an Old Order Amish Community in Ohio." Ph.D. diss., Yale University.
1981   "The Amish Family." In *Ethnic Families in America: Patterns and Variations*, edited by Charles H. Mindel and Robert W. Habenstein. 2nd ed. New York: Elsevier Scientific Publishing.

Instruction of Youth, The
n.d.   Gordonville, Pa.: Gordonville Print Shop.

Intelligencer Journal
1930–   Lancaster, Pa.: Lancaster Newspapers.

Johnson, Warren A., Victor Stoltzfus, and Peter Craumer
1977   "Energy Conservation in Amish Agriculture." *Science* 198(October 28):373–79.

Kaiser, Grace H.
1986   *Dr. Frau: A Woman Doctor among the Amish*. Intercourse, Pa.: Good Books.

Kauffman, John E.
1975   Trans. and comp. *Anabaptist Letters from 1635 to 1645. Translated from the Ausbund*. Atglen, Pa.

Kauffman, S. Duane
1979   "Miscellaneous Amish-Mennonite Documents." *Pennsylvania Mennonite Heritage* 2(July):12–16.

Kauffman, Sam
1962   "Begebenheiten von Eine Lancaster County Diener Versammlung Den 19ten December 1962" (Actions taken at a ministers' meeting in Lancaster County on December 19, 1962). Translated by Noah G. Good. Minutes. Typescript.

Keim, Albert N.
1975   Ed. *Compulsory Education and the Amish: The Right Not to Be Modern*. Boston: Beacon Press.

Kephart, William M.
1987   *Extraordinary Groups: The Sociology of Unconventional Life-Styles*. 3rd ed. New York: St. Martin's Press.

Kieffer, Elizabeth Clark
n.d.   "Christmas Customs in Lancaster County." *Lancaster County Historical Review* 43:175–82.

King, Ada Nancy
1977   "The Mennonite Church of the Millwood District." *Mennonite Research Journal* 18(July):30–31.

Kinsinger, A. S.
1983   "Statement to the Subcommittee on Social Security of the Committee on Ways and Means, U.S. House of Representatives." 9 February 1983. In *Financing Problems of the Social Security System*. Serial 98-5, Washington, D.C.: Government Printing Office.

Klaassen, Walter
1973   *Anabaptism: Neither Protestant nor Catholic*. Waterloo, Ont.: Conrad Press.

Klein, Frederic Shriver
1941   *Lancaster County, 1841–1941*. Lancaster, Pa.: Intelligencer Printing.

Klein, H. M. J.
1924   *Lancaster County, Pennsylvania: A History.* 2 vols. New York: Lewis Historical Publishing.
1946   *History and Customs of the Amish People.* York, Pa.: Maple Press.

Klopfenstein, Joseph
1984   "An Amish Sermon." *Mennonite Quarterly Review* 58(July):296–317.

Kollmorgen, Walter M.
1942   *Culture of a Contemporary Rural Community: The Old Order Amish of Lancaster County, Pennsylvania. Rural Life Studies,* no. 4. Washington, D.C.: U.S. Department of Agriculture.
1943   "The Agricultural Stability of the Old Order Amish and Old Order Mennonites of Lancaster County, Pennsylvania." *American Journal of Sociology* 49(November):233–41.

Kraybill, D. B., J. A. Hostetler, and D. G. Shaw
1986   "Suicide Patterns in a Religious Subculture: The Old Order Amish." *International Journal of Moral and Social Studies* 1(Fall): 249–63.

Kraybill, Donald B.
1987a   "At the Crossroads of Modernity: Amish, Mennonites, and Brethren in Lancaster County in 1880." *Pennsylvania Mennonite Heritage* 10(January):2–12.
1987b   "Mennonite Woman's Veiling: The Rise and Fall of a Sacred Symbol." *Mennonite Quarterly Review* 61(July):298–320.
1988   Review of *Extraordinary Groups: An Examination of Unconventional Lifestyles,* by William M. Kephart. *Mennonite Quarterly Review* 62(January):86–87.

Kraybill, Donald B., and Donald R. Fitzkee
1987   "Amish, Mennonites, and Brethren in the Modern Era." *Pennsylvania Mennonite Heritage* 10(April):2–11.

Kraybill, Eugene
1985   *Seven Hundred Churches: A Special Report.* Lancaster, Pa.: Lancaster Newspapers. Tabloid reprint.

Landing, James E.
1972   "The Amish, the Automobile, and Social Interaction." *Journal of Geography* 71(January):52–57.
1975   "The Old Order Amish: Problem Solving through Migration." *Bulletin of the Illinois Geographical Society* 17(December):36–48.

Landis, Ira D.
1945   "Mennonite Agriculture in Colonial Lancaster County, Pennsylvania." *Mennonite Quarterly Review* 19(October):254–72.
1962   "The Social Security Issue." *Mennonite Research Journal* 3(April):16.
1972   "The Supreme Court Decision—A Landmark." *Mennonite Research Journal* 13(July):34–35.

Lapp, Ferne E.
1963   *History of Weavertown Church.* N.p.: Published privately by Anna Mary Yoder.

Lapp, John K.
1986   *Remarks of By-Gone Days, A Few Remarks of Old Times.* Gordonville, Pa.: Gordonville Print Shop.

Lauer, Robert H.
1973   *Perspectives on Social Change*. Boston: Allyn and Bacon.
1981   *Temporal Man: The Meaning and Uses of Social Time*. New York: Praeger.
Lemon, James T.
1972   *The Best Poor Man's Country: A Geographical Study of Early Southeastern Pennsylvania*. Baltimore: Johns Hopkins Press.
Life, Rules of a Godly
1983   Translated by Joseph Stoll from the German, *Geistliches Lustgärtlein Frommer Seelen*. LaGrange, Ind.: Edwin L. Lambright.
Loomis, Charles P.
1960   "The Old Order Amish as a Social System." In *Social Systems: Essays on Their Persistence and Change*. Princeton, N.J.: D. Van Nostrand.
1979   "A Farm Hand's Diary." *Mennonite Quarterly Review* 53(July): 235–57.
Loomis, Charles P., and Everett D. Dyer
1976   "The Old Order Amish as a Social System." In *Social Systems: The Study of Sociology*, edited by Charles P. Loomis and Everett D. Dyer. Cambridge, Mass.: Schenkman.
Loomis, Charles P., and Carl R. Jantzen
1962   "Boundary Maintenance vs. Systemic Linkage in School Integration: The Case of the Amish in the United States." *Journal of the Pakistan Academy for Village Development* 3(July):1–25.
Luthy, David
1971a   "The Amish Division of 1693." *Family Life* (October):18–20.
1971b   "Four Centuries with the Ausbund." *Family Life* (June):21–22.
1975   "A Survey of Amish Ordination Customs." *Family Life* (March): 13–17.
1980   "The Origin of Amish Tourism in Lancaster County, Pennsylvania." *Family Life* (November):31–34.
1984   "Metal Initial and Date Plates on Amish and Mennonite Books." *Pennsylvania Mennonite Heritage* 7(January):2–8.
1985   *Amish Settlements across America*. Aylmer, Ont.: Pathway Publishers.
1986   *The Amish in America: Settlements That Failed, 1840–1960*. Aylmer, Ont.: Pathway Publishers.
MacMaster, Richard K.
1985   *Land, Piety, Peoplehood*. Vol. 1 of *The Mennonite Experience in America*. Scottdale, Pa.: Herald Press.
Madeira, Sheldon
1955   "A Study of the Education of the Old Order Amish of Lancaster County, Pa." Ph.D. diss., University of Pennsylvania.
Markle, Gerald E., and Sharon Pasco
1977   "Family Limitation among the Old Order Amish." *Population Studies* 31:267–80.
Martineau, William H., and Rhonda S. MacQueen
1977   "Occupational Differentiation among the Old Order Amish." *Rural Sociology* 42:383–97.

Mast, J. Lemar, and Lois Ann Mast
    1982   *As Long as Wood Grows and Water Flows.* Morgantown, Pa.: Conestoga Mennonite Historical Committee.

Mast, John B.
    1950   Ed. and trans. *The Letters of the Amish Division of 1693–1711.* Oregon City, Oreg.: Christian J. Schlabach. Printed by Mennonite Publishing House: Scottdale, Pa.

Mennonite Encyclopedia, The
    1956   Four vols. Scottdale, Pa.: Mennonite Publishing House; Hillsboro, Kans.: Mennonite Brethren Publishing House; Newton, Kans.: Mennonite Publication Office.

Meyers, Thomas J.
    1983a   "Amish Origins and Persistence: The Case of Agricultural Innovation." Paper presented to the annual meeting of the Rural Sociological Society, Lexington, Ky.
    1983b   "Stress and the Amish Community in Transition." Ph.D. diss., Boston University.

Miller, Harvey J.
    1959   "Proceedings of Amish Ministers' Conferences, 1826–31." *Mennonite Quarterly Review* 33(April):132–42.

Miller, Levi
    1981   "The Role of a *Braucher*-Chiropractor in an Amish Community." *Mennonite Quarterly Review* 55(April):157–71.

Nagata, Judith
    1968   "Continuity and Change among the Old Order Amish of Illinois." Ph.D. diss., University of Illinois, Urbana.

New Era, Lancaster
    1930–   Lancaster, Pa.: Lancaster Newspapers.

Olshan, Marc Alan
    1979   "The Old Order Amish in New York State." Cornell University, Cornell Rural Sociology Bulletin Series. Bulletin 94. February.
    1980   "The Old Order Amish as a Model for Development." Ph.D. diss., Cornell University.
    1981   "Modernity, the Folk Society, and the Old Order Amish." *Rural Sociology* 46(Summer):297–309.
    1986   "Freedom *vs.* Meaning: Aichinger's 'Bound Man' and the Old Order Amish." In *Internal and External Perspectives on Amish and Mennonite Life,* edited by Werner Enninger. Vol. 2. Essen: Unipress.

Ordnung Fier Zu Shaffen (Arbeiten) und Halten Unter Unsere Alte Amische Gemeinen und Junge Leut. Der Folgen ist Ubereinkommen bei die Lancaster County Bischofen (Working ordinances to be kept among our Old Order Amish churches and young people. The following was agreed on by the Lancaster County bishops)
    1983   In *Minutes of the Old Order Amish Steering Committee from 1981–1986* 3:36–37. Translated by Noah G. Good. Gordonville, Pa.: Gordonville Print Shop.

Ortmayer, Roger
    1946   "The Amish and Tractors." *Social Questions Bulletin* (October):101. Reprinted in *Mennonite Life* 2(January):43.

Outley, Nancy Fisher
1982   "From Amish to Professional and Back Again." In *Perils of Professionalism*, edited by Donald B. Kraybill and Phyllis Pellman Good. Scottdale, Pa.: Herald Press.
Papers of the Amish School Controversy, The
1937–68 Documents concerning the Old Order Amish School Movement in Lancaster County, Pa., collected by Aaron E. Beiler.
Petition to Our Men in Authority
1937   A request for changes in the Public School law presented to state officials 17 November 1937. Signed by representatives of thirty-seven Old Order Amish and Old Order Mennonite congregations.
Raber, Ben J.
1970–   Comp. *The New American Almanac*. Published annually by Ben J. Raber, Baltic, Ohio. Gordonville, Pa.: Gordonville Print Shop. The earlier almanac in German, *Der Neue Amerikanische Kalender*, dates back to 1930.
Redekop, Calvin, and John A. Hostetler
1977   "The Plain People: An Interpretation." *Mennonite Quarterly Review* 51(October):266–77.
Renno, John R.
1985   Comp. *Brief History of the Amish Divisions in Lancaster County.* Danville, Pa.
Ressler, Martin
1978   "A Song of Praise." *Pennsylvania Mennonite Heritage* 1(October): 10–13.
1986   "American Continuance of European Origins in Mennonite, Hutterite and Amish Music Functions." *Pennsylvania Mennonite Heritage* 9(January):6–10.
Ressler, Miller
1935   "An Amish Wedding." *Historical Papers and Addresses of the Lancaster County Historical Society* 39:62–65.
Revised Regulations and Guidelines for Old Order Amish Liability Aid
1977   Gordonville, Pa.: Gordonville Print Shop.
Rice, Charles S., and John B. Shenk
1947   *Meet the Amish: A Pictorial Study of the Amish People.* New Brunswick, N.J.: Rutgers University Press.
Rice, Charles S., and Rollin C. Steinmetz
1956   *The Amish Year.* New Brunswick, N.J.: Rutgers University Press.
Rohrer, David
1974   "The Influence of the Pennsylvania German Dialect on Amish English in Lancaster Co." *Mennonite Research Journal* 15(July):34–35.
Rules and Regulations of Old Order Amish Church Aid
1983   Gordonville, Pa.: Gordonville Print Shop.
Schlabach, Theron F.
1988   *Peace, Faith, Nation.* Vol. 2 of *The Mennonite Experience in America.* Scottdale, Pa.: Herald Press.
Schowalter, Paul
1957   S.v. "Martyr." In *The Mennonite Encyclopedia* 3:521–25. Scottdale, Pa.: Herald Press.

1963   "Pioneer Nicholas Stoltzfus." *Mennonite Research Journal* 4(April):13, 22.

Schreiber, William I.
1962a   "The Hymns of the Amish Ausbund in Philological and Literary Perspective." *Mennonite Quarterly Review* 36(January):37–60.
1962b   *Our Amish Neighbors.* Chicago: University of Chicago Press.

Schwieder, Elmer, and Dorothy Schwieder
1975   *A Peculiar People: Iowa's Old Order Amish.* Ames: Iowa State University Press.
1976   "The Paradox of Change in the Life of Iowa's Old Order Amish." *International Review of Modern Sociology* 6(Spring):65–74.

Scott, Stephen
1981   *Plain Buggies: Amish, Mennonite and Brethren Horse Drawn Transportation.* Intercourse, Pa.: Good Books.
1986   *Why Do They Dress That Way?* Intercourse, Pa.: Good Books.
1988   *The Amish Wedding and Other Special Occasions of the Old Order Communities.* Intercourse, Pa.: Good Books.

Séguy, Jean
1973   "Religion and Agricultural Success: The Vocational Life of the French Anabaptists from the Seventeenth to the Nineteenth Centuries." *Mennonite Quarterly Review* 47(July):179–224.
1980   "The Bernese Anabaptists in Sainte-Marie-aux-Mines." *Pennsylvania Mennonite Heritage* 3(July):2–9. Translated by Mervin Smucker.

Shirk, Eli M.
1939   Comp. *Report of Committee of Plain People Making Pleas for Leniency from Depressive School Laws.* Ephrata, Pa.

Siegel, Bernard J.
1970   "Defensive Structuring and Environmental Stress." *American Journal of Sociology* 76(July):11–32.

Simons, Menno
1956   *The Complete Writings of Menno Simons,* translated by Leonard Verduin, and edited by John C. Wenger. Scottdale, Pa.: Herald Press.

Smith, Elmer L.
1955   "A Study of Acculturation in an Amish Community." D.S.S. diss., Syracuse University.
1958a   *The Amish People.* New York: Exposition Press.
1958b   "Personality Differences between Amish and Non-Amish Children." *Rural Sociology* 23(December):371–76.
1961   *The Amish Today: An Analysis of Their Beliefs, Behavior and Contemporary Problems.* Allentown, Pa.: Schlechters. Pennsylvania German Society, vol. 24.

Smucker, Mervin R.
1978   "Growing Up Amish: A Comparison of the Socialization Process between Amish and Non-Amish Rural School Children." M.S. thesis, Millersville University.
1988   "How Amish Children View Themselves and Their Families: The Effectiveness of Amish Socialization." *Brethren Life and Thought* 33(Summer):218–36.

Standards of the Old Order Amish and Old Order Mennonite Parochial and Vocational Schools of Pennsylvania.
1981   Gordonville, Pa.: Gordonville Print Shop.
"Statement of the Bishops of the Old Order Amish Church of Lancaster County Regarding Attendance in Public Schools."
1950   22 February. Typescript.
Steering Committee
1966–72   *Minutes of Old Order Amish Steering Committee.* Vol. 1. Gordonville, Pa.: Gordonville Print Shop.
1973–80   *Minutes of Old Order Amish Steering Committee.* Vol. 2. Gordonville, Pa.: Gordonville Print Shop.
1981–86   *Minutes of Old Order Amish Steering Committee.* Vol. 3. Gordonville, Pa.: Gordonville Print Shop.
Steinfeldt, Bernice
1937   *The Amish of Lancaster County.* Lancaster, Pa.: Arthur G. Steinfeldt.
Stoltzfus, Amos J.
n.d.   *Ein Bericht wie es sich begeben hat das der bahn zwichen die Hausgemein und die Kirchgemein gekommen ist in der Conestoga valley, Lancaster County, Pennsylvania* (A report on how the ban between the house church and the church group came about in the Conestoga Valley, Lancaster County, Pennsylvania), translated by Noah G. Good.
1984   *Golden Memories.* Gordonville, Pa.: Pequea Publishers.
Stoltzfus, Grant M.
1954   "History of the First Amish Mennonite Communities in America." *Mennonite Quarterly Review* 28(October):235–62.
Stoltzfus, Victor
1973   "Amish Agriculture: Adaptive Strategies for Economic Survival of Community Life." *Rural Sociology* 38(Summer):196–206.
1977   "Reward and Sanction: The Adaptive Continuity of Amish Life." *Mennonite Quarterly Review* 51(October):308–18.
Studer, Gerald C.
1948   "A History of the Martyrs Mirror." *Mennonite Quarterly Review* 22(July):163–79.
1984   "The Dordrecht Confession of Faith, 1632–1982." *Mennonite Quarterly Review* 58(October):503–19.
Thompson, William E.
1981   "The Oklahoma Amish: Survival of an Ethnic Subculture." *Ethnicity* 8:476–87.
Tortora, Vincent R.
1957   "The Amish at Play." *Pennsylvania Dutchman* 8(Summer–Fall): 14–34.
1958   "The Courtship and Wedding Practices of the Old Order Amish." *Pennsylvania Folklife* 9(Spring):12–21.
1960   "The Get-Togethers of the Young Amish Folk." *Pennsylvania Folklife* 11(Spring):17–21.
1961   "Amish Funerals." *Pennsylvania Folklife* 12(Spring):8–13.
Umble, John S.
1939   "Amish Ordination Charges." *Mennonite Quarterly Review* 13(Oc-

tober):233–50. Contains translated documents on church organization and government.

1941a   "An Amish Minister's Manual." *Mennonite Quarterly Review* 15(April):95–117.

1941b   "Amish Service Manuals." *Mennonite Quarterly Review* 15(January):26–32.

1948   "Memoirs of an Amish Bishop." *Mennonite Quarterly Review* 22(April):94–115.

Vocation on the Farm

1956   A Statement of Principles of a Church Vocation in Agricultural Practice by the Old Order Amish Church of Pennsylvania. Strasburg, Pa.: Homsher Printing.

Wagler, David

n.d.   *Are All Things Lawful?* Aylmer, Ont.: Pathway Publishers. An Amishman's view of the car and its impact on the Amish church.

Weaver, J. Denny

1987   *Becoming Anabaptist: The Origin and Significance of Sixteenth-Century Anabaptism.* Scottdale, Pa.: Herald Press.

Weber, Max

1947   *The Theory of Social and Economic Organization.* New York: Free Press.

Wenger, Samuel S.

1981   "Nicholas Stoltzfus in Europe and America." *Pennsylvania Mennonite Heritage* 4(April):15–17.

Wickersham, James P.

1886   *A History of Education in Pennsylvania.* Lancaster, Pa.: Inquirer Publishing.

Wilson, Bryan

1970   *Religious Sects.* New York: McGraw-Hill.

Wuthnow, R., J. D. Hunter, A. Bergesen, and E. Kurzweil

1984   *Cultural Analysis: The Work of Peter L. Berger, Mary Douglas, Michel Foucault, and Jürgen Habermas.* Boston: Routledge and Kegan Paul.

Yinger, J. Milton

1970   *The Scientific Study of Religion.* New York: Macmillan.

Yoder, Elmer S.

1987   *The Beachey Amish Mennonite Fellowship Churches.* Hartville, Ohio: Diakonia Ministries.

Yoder, John Howard

1973   Ed. and trans. *The Legacy of Michael Sattler.* Scottdale, Pa.: Herald Press.

Yoder, Paton

n.d.   "Amish Church Affairs in the Nineteenth Century." Typescript.

1979a   *Eine Wurzel: Tennessee John Stoltzfus.* Lititz, Pa.: Sutter House.

1979b   "'Tennessee' John Stoltzfus and the Great Schism in the Amish Church, 1850–1877." *Pennsylvania Mennonite Heritage* 2(July): 17–23.

1985   "The Preaching Deacon Controversy among the Nineteenth-Century American Amish." *Pennsylvania Mennonite Heritage* 7(January):2–9.

1987a   *Tennessee John Stoltzfus: Amish Church-Related Documents and Family Letters.* Lancaster, Pa.: Lancaster Mennonite Historical Society.

1987b   "The Structure of the Amish Ministry in the Nineteenth Century." *Mennonite Quarterly Review* 61(July):280–97.

Yoder, Paton, and Elizabeth Bender

1979   "Baptism as an Issue in the Amish Division of the Nineteenth Century: 'Tennessee' John Stoltzfus." *Mennonite Quarterly Review* 53(October):306–23.

INDEX

Affiliation, 11–12; definition of, 11
Age roles, 71, 103
Agriculture. *See* Farming
Air power, 159–60, 202, 235, 239
Alcohol, use of, 138
Alienation, 250, 259
Alsace, 6, 7
Amish: beliefs of, 24, 31–32, 100, 107, 216, 217; history of, 6
Amish Aid Society, 86
Amish-Mennonites, 141
Amish National Steering Committee, 59, 87–89, 217, 218
Ammann, Jacob (founder), 6
Anabaptists, 6–7; beliefs of, 3, 5; persecution of, 3–5, 7, 16, 25, 37
Appliances: electrical, 150, 154, 159, 160, 162, 163, 183, 185, 243; gas, 186, 235; household, 72
Art, 40
Artificial insemination of dairy cows, 213, 238
Attrition rate, 14
Ausbund (hymn book), 5, 103
Automobiles. *See* Cars

Ban. *See* Excommunication
Baptism, 57, 99–100, 117; adult, 3, 5, 59, 252; age for, 100, 138; instruction for, 100; and ordination, 110; procedure for, 100
Beachy Amish church, 12, 142
Beards, 55, 57, 142
Bible, view of, 32, 252
Bicycles, 240
Birth control, 74, 194, 247
Birth rate, 74, 190
Bishops: attitudes of, toward modernization, 126, 173, 179, 183, 190; and control of social change, 236, 237, 240, 243; number of, 84; ordination of, 79; role of, 79, 83, 100, 107–8, 112

Bishops' meetings, 83–84, 85, 107
Blackboard Bulletin (magazine), 136
Botschaft, Die (newspaper), 48
Boundaries: cultural, 239; ethnic, 63
Bruderschaft Library, 89
Buggy: changes in, 66; construction of, 67–68, 241; cost of, 68; symbolic functions of, 63, 64–66, 67, 68; and traffic laws, 67; types of, 63; and youth, 65
Businessmen, 91, 92, 190, 199, 208, 209; dilemma of, 210; use of law by, 222; use of technology by, 114, 148, 162, 169

Cars: as "Amish taxis," 168, 170; ban of ownership of, 166, 168; business use of, 169; compromise with, 168, 169–71; fear of, 166–67; functions of, 167; history of, 165; reasons for use of, 169; use of, 165, 166, 168, 170, 239; use of, by Amish youth, 138, 168; use of, by Mennonite youth, 165–66
Central heating, 235
Child rearing, 119
Children, role of, 29, 39
Church, concept of, 5
Church Aid, 89
Church of the Brethren, 13
Church services, 80, 101; description of, 102–3; functions of, 81–82; order of, 102–3; size of, 82; stability of, 106
Communion services, 6, 57, 107–9, 117
Community involvement, 215–16
Computers, 159, 160, 162, 237
Confession: functions of, 111, 117; stability of, 114; stages of, 111, 112, 113
Conscientious objection, 87, 217. *See also* Nonresistance
Cottage industries, 11, 159, 203, 207. *See also* Occupations
Council meetings, 103, 107
Cultural lag, 243

Cultural resistance, 247
Cultural survival, reasons for, 247–48
Cultural values, 44–45

Deacons, role of, 80, 100
Deviance, 111, 112, 114, 237
Diary, The (newspaper), 48
Diesel engines, 156, 159, 160, 183, 202
District: definition of, 11; functions of,
    78, 101; growth of, 84; size of, 76
Divisions, 21, 236; of 1877, 21, 81, 144; of
    1910, 21, 141, 142, 144, 146, 152, 166,
    182, 243; of 1966, 21–22, 144, 155, 174,
    177, 182, 183, 238, 243; social functions
    of, 22
Divorce, 74
Doctors, use of, 75–76, 213
Dordtrecht Confession of Faith, 24, 100,
    115, 116
Dress: changes in, 7, 56, 59; color of, 52,
    56, 57; material, 58, 240; of men, 55;
    modern view of, 49; reasons for, 56; in
    services, 106, 108; social functions of,
    49–50, 59, 108; of women, 51–55
Dutch Anabaptists, 6. *See also*
    Anabaptists

East Lampeter Township school contro-
    versy, 122, 227
Education: attitude toward, 120, 121,
    130; bishops' statement on, 128; conse-
    quences of, 131, 133; role of parents in,
    130. *See also* Schools
Electricity, 142–43, 150, 183, 185, 202,
    235; ban on, 72, 152, 163, 205, 209, 214,
    239; from batteries, 151, 153, 160, 184,
    205; compromises, 163; from genera-
    tors, 152–54, 157–58, 183, 184, 185,
    202; history of, 151; inverters of, 160–
    62; social functions of, 153; types of,
    153, 159, 160, 163, 235; use of, 67, 151,
    152, 158, 162, 183; welders, 163, 184
Employers, non-Amish, 200–201
Employment of women, 72
Excommunication, 137–38, 142, 192, 217;
    in Amish division, 6; for car owner-
    ship, 165; functions of, 115; procedure
    of, 112, 114

Family: composition of, 70; functions of,
    29, 74; integration, 242; size of, 14, 69,
    74, 76, 208; stability of, 76
Farming: dairy, 155, 157, 177, 179, 184;
    importance of, 188–90; practices of,
    15; types of, 11
Farm machinery: ban on, 183, 184; self-
    propelled, 175, 179, 180; types of, 154,
    171, 173, 176, 178–83, 184, 185, 187,
    235

Fasting, 108
Foot-washing, 6, 37, 108–9, 117
Freedom, personal, 251, 258
Funerals, 76

Gelassenheit, 25–26, 30, 49; and attitude
    toward force, 26, 217, 223; definition
    of, 25; importance of, 247; in ministe-
    rial selection, 110; organizational
    forms of, 91, 93; in services, 105; social
    functions of, 25, 27–28; in social inter-
    action, 30; structural expression of, 82;
    symbols of, 68; traits of, 29, 43, 44,
    113
Government programs: agricultural
    subsidy, 222; attitude toward, 88, 256;
    concessions of, to Amish, 233; involve-
    ment in, 216; unemployment insur-
    ance, 222; workmen's compensation,
    222. *See also* Social Security

Hartz, Moses (minister), 141
Hats, 55, 57, 58; hard, 58
"Holy kiss," 109
Horses: compared to tractors, 62; cost
    of, 60; lore of, 62, 176; social functions
    of, 60–63, 84, 177, 239; use of, 60, 171,
    173, 174
Hospitalization, 89
Humility, 34, 36, 105, 106, 109, 113
Hutterites, 10
Hydraulic power, 159–60, 202, 214, 235,
    239

Immigration, 7–8. *See also* Migration
Imprisonment, 126
Individualism: consequences of, 259; in
    modern life, 250, 253; rejection of, 29,
    30, 34, 41, 106, 110, 254, 257; and
    social change, 242; symbolized by car,
    167; threat of, 18, 37, 133
Insecticides, 236
Insurance, objections to, 87, 89, 193–94,
    219
Interaction with non-Amish, 19, 214, 215,
    242
Internal Revenue Service (IRS), 220, 222
Inventions, 205

Jewelry, rejection of, 36

Lancaster, Pa., Amish settlement, 7–8;
    division of, 85; population of, 10, 12,
    14; size of, 12, 13, 14, 84, 236
Lancaster County, Pa.: agriculture in, 8,
    10; location of, 9; Mennonite settle-
    ment in, 7; population of, 9; religious
    groups in, 12–14; tourism in, 10
Land: cost of, 93, 191–92, 194, 196; scar-

city of, 197, 231; subdivision of, 195;
use of, 189
Language. *See* Pennsylvania German
dialect
Law, use of, 223, 225
Lawyers, use of, 122, 210
Leadership, 18; roles, 79–80, 83, 103;
structure, 84; women's roles in, 72
Leaders' meetings, 84, 85–86, 107, 154,
183, 236
Lebanon County, Pa., 15, 168, 194
Liability Aid, 87
Luther, Martin, 3

Marriage, 74, 80, 99
Martyrs Mirror (book), 5, 48, 115, 130; use
of, in sermons, 102
Medicine, use of, 75–76, 213
Meeting house, rejection of, 80–81
"Meeting House Amish," 21
Meidung. *See* Shunning
Members' meetings, 103, 107
Mennonites, 6–8, 13, 14, 21, 81, 91, 116,
200; origin of name, 5
Migration, 14–15, 168, 194, 225, 232, 234
Military service. *See* Nonresistance
Milk tank (bulk), 155–57, 162, 163, 184,
235
Ministers: role of, 79, 103, 105, 113;
selection of, 110
Ministers' meetings, nationwide, 81. *See
also* Leaders' meetings
Modernization, 15–17; definition of, 252;
examples of, 213; pressures of, 244;
resistance to, 17
Mutual aid, 10–11, 28, 86, 103, 207, 255;
threat to, 193, 216, 219

Names, popular surnames, 77–78
Negotiation with modernization, 17, 20–
21, 247
New Order Amish, 12, 14; origins of, 10,
174, 183
Nonresistance, 5, 26, 210, 217, 218, 256

Obedience: to Christ, 5, 6; to the church,
18, 99, 100; to leaders, 25, 33; to
Ordnung, 140; to parents, 29, 33; role
of, 32; to Scripture, 102; to spouses,
33
Occupations: changes in, 192; compromise in, 211; control of, 197, 201;
cottage industries, 11, 197; crafts, 198;
ethnic setting of, 199; factory work,
192–93, 200–201; farming, 11, 197;
mobile crews, 202; nonfarm, 11, 190,
192, 197, 199, 201, 202–3, 206, 208, 211
Old Order Amish: definition of, 10, 80;
origin of name, 21

Old Order Book Society, 136. *See also*
School Committee
Old Order Mennonites, 13, 80; and
tractors, 177
Ordination: functions of, 110–11; procedure for, 109–10, 117
Ordnung: and changes, 96, 237–38, 241;
definition of, 95; and electricity, 158,
162; functions of, 95, 98, 107; and
machinery, 187; in services, 106, 108;
violations of, 111–12
Organizational structure. *See* Social
structure
Organizations of laymen, 86–89

Peachey church: origin of, 142, 144, 146,
150; and technology, 152, 153, 166, 172
Pennsylvania Dutch Visitors' Bureau,
226, 227, 228
Pennsylvania German dialect, 11, 47, 80;
role of, 47–49
Pennsylvania Public Utilities Commision,
169
Photography, rejection of, 34, 231
Political involvement, 215, 217
Population: growth, 190, 213, 236; size,
12. *See also* Lancaster, Pa., Amish
settlement
Prayer, 105, 110, 117
Prayer veilings, 51, 57
Pride: examples of, 36; rejection of, 34
Professionals, use of, 213, 214, 223. *See
also* Doctors, use of; Lawyers, use of
Protestant Reformation, 3
Public transportation, 240

Radio, 157, 160, 163, 186
Rebellion. *See* Youth
Recreation: examples of, 74–75; prior to
baptism, 216
Reist, Hans (Anabaptist bishop), 6
Retirement, 11, 206, 219
Rituals: functions of, 94; and social
changes, 241

St. Mary's County, Md., 15, 194
School Committee, 86
Schools, 92–93; compulsory attendance
of, 122; consolidation of, 120, 123, 124,
214; control of, 135; curriculum of,
134; first Amish, 125, 214, 236; history
of, 119–20, 134, 214; number of, 134;
parents' relation to, 136; public, 120,
137; social functions of, 131, 133; state
regulations of, 137; values taught by,
136; vocational program of, 128–29
Schoolteachers, 72, 134, 222; selection of,
136; training of, 136
Scooters, 240

Selective Service, 87, 217
Separation from the world, 5, 16, 18, 96, 153, 160, 212, 213, 217, 243; Anabaptist, 37; biblical basis of, 37–38
Sermons, 102, 106, 107
Settlement, definition of, 11. *See also* Lancaster, Pa., Amish settlement
Sex roles, 71–73, 103, 252
Sexual relations, 27
Shops: characteristics of, 211; development of, 190; equipment in, 160; examples of, 201, 204; as legal partnerships, 222; modernization of, 239; number of, 197; role of, 214; size of, 203; for tourists, 201; types of, 66, 201–2; wages in, 206
Shunning, 33, 112, 115, 116, 142, 143; function of, 116–17; origin of, 6; of unbaptized, 140
Simons, Menno (Mennonite leader), 5
Singing, 103, 105
Small-scale size, 82, 91, 242, 248
Smoking, 27
Social changes, 142, 212–13, 214, 235, 250; as compromise, 240, 244, 245; definition of, 236; management of, 248; morality of, 239; and political considerations, 242; rate of, 243; regulators of, 236, 240–42; source of, 243, 244; stages of, 240; types of, 244
Social class, 93, 209–11
Social control, 80, 94, 113, 114–15, 117, 133, 248; and defensive tactics, 18–19
Social integration, 92
Social interaction, 93, 214–15
Socialization, 18–19, 252
Social sanctions, 18
Social Security, 219, 256; enforcement of, 220; exemption from, 206, 220–21; exemption number, 221; hearings on, 219; payment of, 221–22; rejection of, 88, 219, 221; for self-employed, 220
Social separation, 16
Social structure, 69, 82, 84, 89, 93
"Sowing wild oats," 138. *See also* Youth
Steam engines, 175
Stoltzfus, Gideon (preacher), 81
Supreme Court: decision on schools, 120, 129, 137, 138, 233, 245; decision on Social Security, 222

Swiss Anabaptists, 3, 6, 115. *See also* Anabaptists
Symbols: of identity, 46; importance of, for survival, 248; negative, 141; role of, 46; and social changes, 241

Taxes, 217, 219; school, 136, 217, 219, 256; Social Security, 206
Technological changes, 238
Telephones, 142–43, 235; ban on, 240; and businessmen, 148; "community phones," 146; functions of, 144, 145, 148; history of, 143; in shops, 148; use of, 144, 146, 150, 237, 239
Thrift, importance of, 41
Time, cultural use of, 43–44
Tourism: Amish involvement in, 228; consequences of, 231–34; coping methods with, 232; economic benefits of, 10, 228, 229–30; history of, 227; promoted by *Witness*, 227; size of, 191, 228
Tourist sites, role of, 228–30
Tractors, 142; ban on, 172, 237; cost of, 62; history of use of, 171–72; power unit of, 173–74; rejection of, 175, 239; and steam engines, 171; use of, 171, 172, 173, 176, 183, 239
Tradition, role of, 41, 255

Urbanization, 191

Values, 18
Voting, 217

Weddings. *See* Marriage
Witness (film), 223–27; and compromise, 226; protest of, 224
Work: nature of, 39; social functions of, 38–39. *See also* Occupations
Worldliness, examples of, 23, 38, 239
Worship. *See* Church services

Youth: rebellion of, 82, 96, 99, 138, 139; recreation of, 138

Zoning regulations, 203, 215
Zwingli, Ulrich (reformer), 3